QUEEN VICTORIA'S
PALADINS

QUEEN VICTORIA'S PALADINS

Garnet Wolseley and Frederick Roberts

[signature: John Philip Jones]

JOHN PHILIP JONES

Xlibris, Random House
Bloomington, Indiana
2018

Library of Congress Control Number: 2018903193
ISBN: Hardcover   978-1-9845-1454-7
               Softcover   978-1-9845-1455-4
               eBook   978-1-9845-1456-1

Print information available on the last page.

Rev. date: 05/23/2018

To order additional copies of this book, contact:
Xlibris
1-888-795-4274
www.Xlibris.com
Orders@Xlibris.com
772698

CONTENTS

This book is dedicated to the British army.

Winston Churchill, who was a regular soldier before he became a politician, understood the ethos of the British army and described it well:

In war, resolution; in defeat, defiance; in victory, magnanimity; in peace, goodwill.

MAPS

PLATES

1. Garnet Wolseley
2. Frederick Roberts
3. Duke of Cambridge
4. Charles Gordon
5. British trenches at Sebastopol, 1854–1855
6. The Martinière, Lucknow, 1857
7. Peiwar Kotal, Afghanistan, 1878
8. Kandahar Gate, 1880
9. British camp in Ashanti, 1873–1874
10. Gordon Relief Expedition (1884–1885), unloading whalers
11. Gordon Relief Expedition (1884–1885), guards Camel Corps
12. Battle of Abu Klea, January 1885
13. Redvers Buller
14. Herbert Horatio Kitchener
15. South Africa, 1900—Roberts with staff

THE GENESIS OF
QUEEN VICTORIA'S PALADINS

I have been thinking about this book since 2012, when I published *Johnny: The Legend and Tragedy of General Sir Ian Hamilton*. Hamilton was a protégé of Frederick Roberts, whom he regarded with great respect and affection. I was naturally drawn to write about Roberts, but I found it increasingly inadequate to regard Roberts in isolation. Roberts and Wolseley were direct contemporaries, and they both climbed to the top of the military pyramid in step with each other. When they reached high rank, they had no serious competitors. This also led me to study the wide-ranging military career of Garnet Wolseley. What is surprising about my idea of a dual biography is that no one had attempted to do this before.

As in all my books, the first person I wish to thank is my wife, Wendy, who is my most rigorous critic. She also has the skill to work on my numerous drafts to produce an immaculate final manuscript.

Many of my friends have a more than amateur interest in military history, and they include members of the Military History Group at the Oxford and Cambridge Club, London, which is run by my friend Robert Bartlett. The club holds regular meetings to discuss papers written by members of the group. One of these members has been a very valuable consultant. He is Richard Mead, the author of a number of notable military biographies. He has discussed parts of *Queen Victoria's Paladins* with me, and I am very grateful for his contributions.

Two other people provided perceptive insights. They are my son Philip, who is an experienced editor, and Brigadier John Smales, who had a long and successful career as an officer in the British Army.

I also wish to thank Scott Bunting of Fresher Graphics, Syracuse, New York, for generating, by computer, the excellent maps that appear in my book; also Dawn Watkins of the National Army Museum, London, for providing access to all the plates, which are images of historical importance.

MAPS

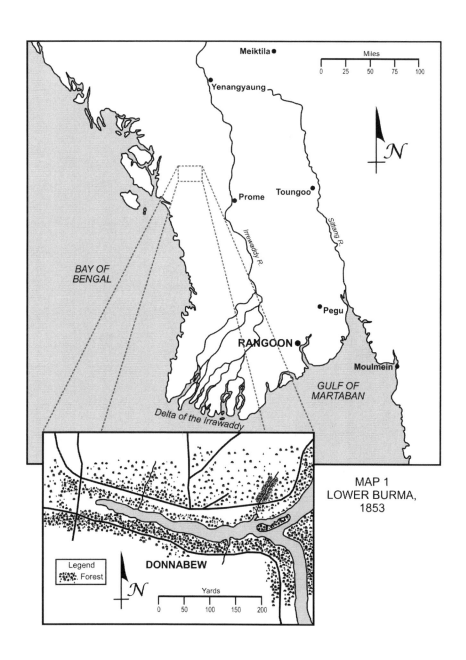

Meiktila

Yenangyaung

Miles

0 25 50 75 100

N

Prome Toungoo

Irrewaddy R. *Sittang R.*

BAY OF
BENGAL

Pegu

RANGOON

Moulmein

GULF OF
MARTABAN

Delta of the Irrawaddy

MAP 1
LOWER BURMA,
1853

Legend
Forest

DONNABEW

N

Yards

0 50 100 150 200

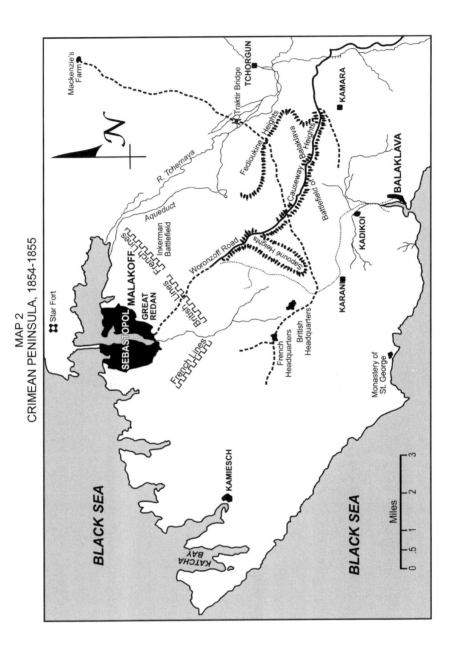

MAP 2
CRIMEAN PENINSULA, 1854-1855

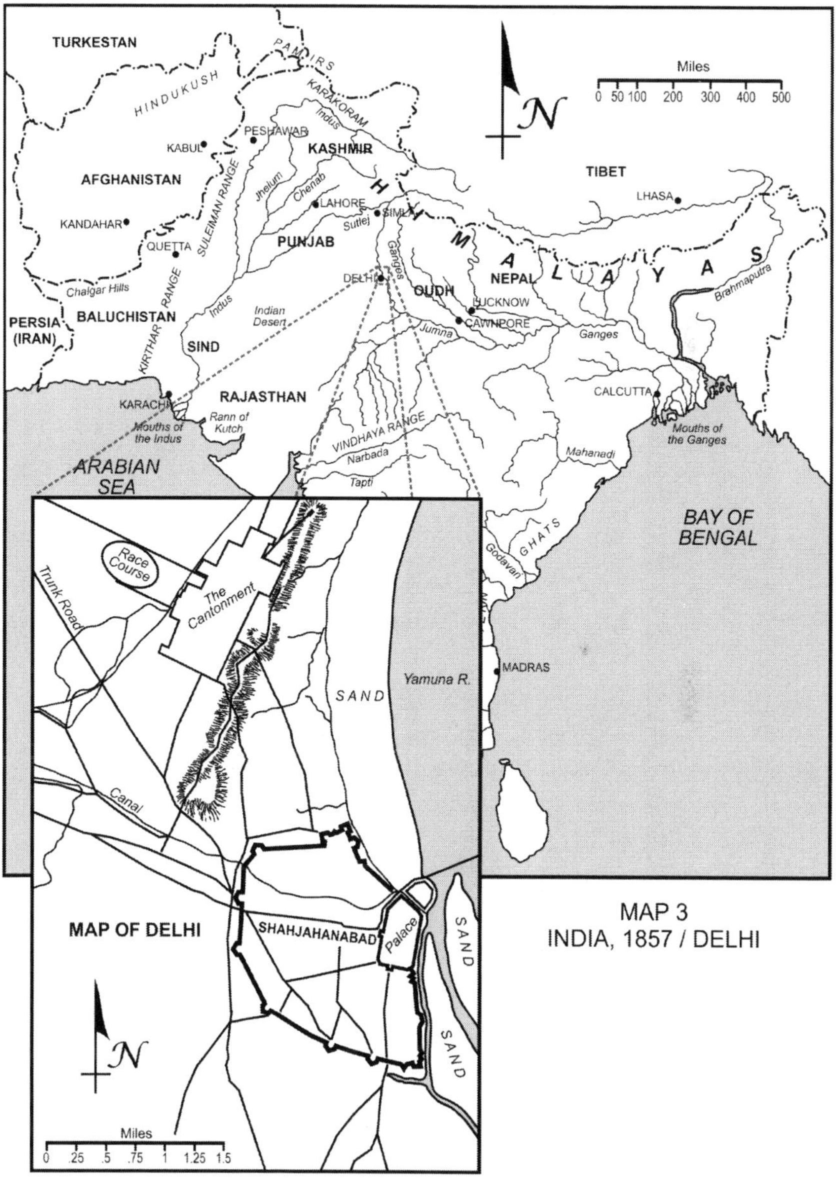

TURKESTAN

HINDUKUSH

PAMIRS

KARAKORAM

KABUL

PESHAWAR

KASHMIR

SULEIMAN RANGE

AFGHANISTAN

KANDAHAR

QUETTA

Indus

Jhelum

Chenab

LAHORE

Sutlej

SIMLA

PUNJAB

TIBET

LHASA

H I M A L A Y A S

Chalgar Hills

KIRTHAR RANGE

PERSIA (IRAN)

BALUCHISTAN

SIND

Indus

Indian Desert

DELHI

OUDH

LUCKNOW

CAWNPORE

Jumna

Ganges

NEPAL

Brahmaputra

Ganges

Miles
0 50 100 200 300 400 500

KARACHI

Mouths of the Indus

Rann of Kutch

RAJASTHAN

CALCUTTA

Mouths of the Ganges

ARABIAN SEA

VINDHAYA RANGE

Narbada

Tapti

Mahanadi

Godavari

GHATS

BAY OF BENGAL

MADRAS

Yamuna R.

SAND

Race Course

The Cantonment

Trunk Road

Canal

SAND

MAP OF DELHI

SHAHJAHANABAD

Palace

SAND

SAND

Miles
0 .25 .5 .75 1 1.25 1.5

MAP 3
INDIA, 1857 / DELHI

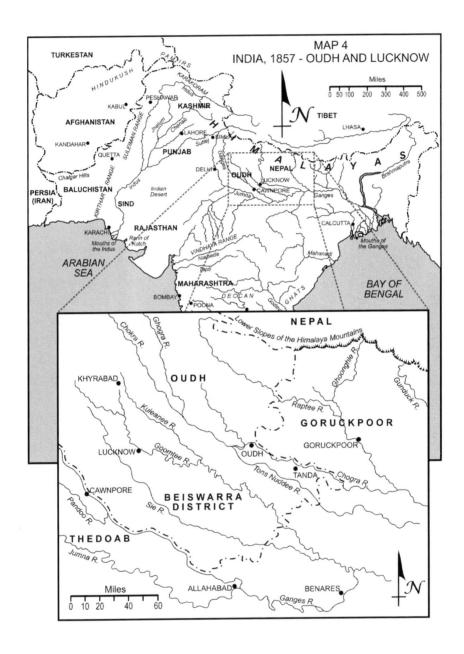

MAP 4
INDIA, 1857 - OUDH AND LUCKNOW

MAP 5
NORTH CHINA, 1860

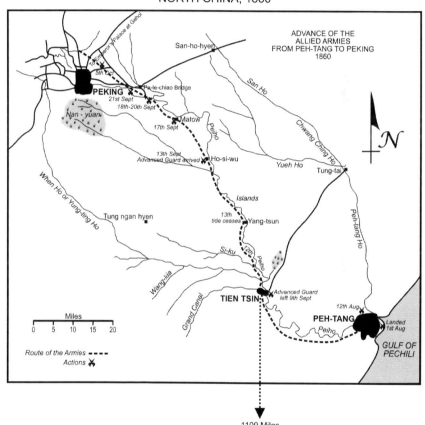

ADVANCE OF THE
ALLIED ARMIES
FROM PEH-TANG TO PEKING
1860

San-ho-hyen

To Emperor's Palace at Gehol

5th Oct

PEKING ✗
21st Sept
18th-20th Sept

Nan - yuan

Pa-le-chiao Bridge

San Ho

Matow
17th Sept

Peiho

Chwang Ching Ho

13th Sept
Advanced Guard arrived ✗ Ho-si-wu

Yueh Ho

Tung-tai

When Ho or Yung-ting Ho

Tung ngan hyen

Islands

13th
tide ceases Yang-tsun

Si-ku

12th

Peiho

Peh-tang Ho

Wang-kia

Grand Canal

TIEN TSIN
Advanced Guard
left 9th Sept

12th Aug

PEH-TANG
Landed
1st Aug

Peiho

Peiho

GULF OF
PECHILI

Miles

| 0 | 5 | 10 | 15 | 20 |

Route of the Armies - - - -
Actions ✗

1100 Miles
Due South to Hong Kong

MAP 6
INDIA / NORTH-WEST FRONTIER PROVINCE

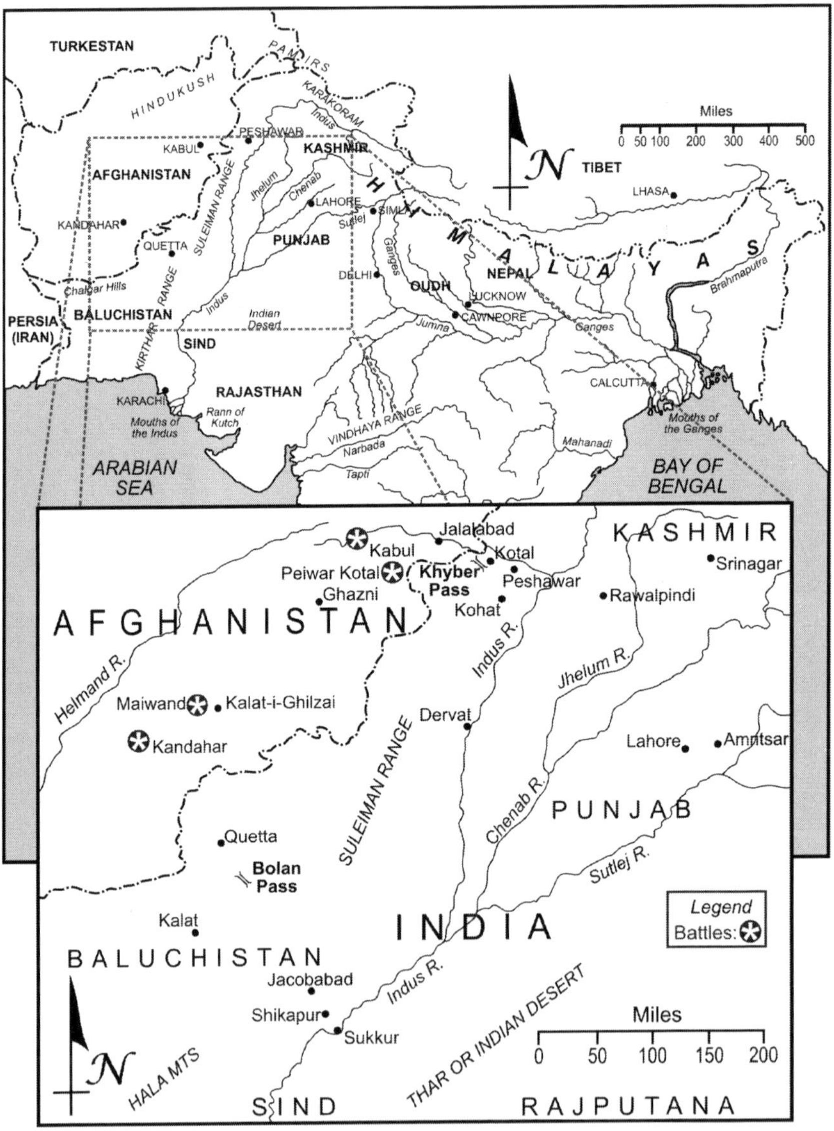

TURKESTAN

PAMIRS

HINDUKUSH

KARAKORAM

Indus

PESHAWAR

KABUL

KASHMIR

AFGHANISTAN

SULEIMAN RANGE

Jhelum

Chenab

LAHORE

Sutlej

SIMLA

TIBET

LHASA

Miles

0 50 100   200   300   400   500

N

KANDAHAR

QUETTA

PUNJAB

Ganges

H I M A L A Y A S

KIRTHAR RANGE

Chagar Hills

Indus

DELHI

OUDH

NEPAL

Brahmaputra

PERSIA
(IRAN)

BALUCHISTAN

Indian
Desert

LUCKNOW

CAWNPORE

Jumna

Ganges

SIND

KARACHI

RAJASTHAN

Rann of
Kutch

Mouths of
the Indus

VINDHAYA RANGE

Narbada

Tapti

CALCUTTA

Mouths of
the Ganges

ARABIAN
SEA

Mahanadi

BAY OF
BENGAL

Kabul

Jalalabad

KASHMIR

Peiwar Kotal

Kotal

Khyber
Pass

Srinagar

Ghazni

Peshawar

Rawalpindi

A F G H A N I S T A N

Kohat

Helmand R.

Indus R.

Jhelum R.

Maiwand

Kalat-i-Ghilzai

Dervat

Kandahar

SULEIMAN RANGE

Lahore

Amritsar

Chenab R.

P U N J A B

Quetta

Bolan
Pass

Sutlej R.

Kalat

I N D I A

Legend
Battles: ✪

BALUCHISTAN

Jacobabad

Indus R.

THAR OR INDIAN DESERT

Miles

0   50   100   150   200

Shikapur

Sukkur

N

HALA MTS

S I N D

R A J P U T A N A

XX

MAP 7
CANADA - RED RIVER EXPEDITION, 1870

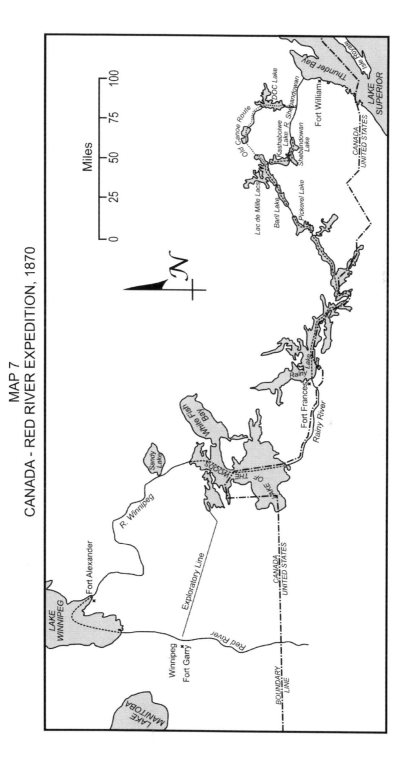

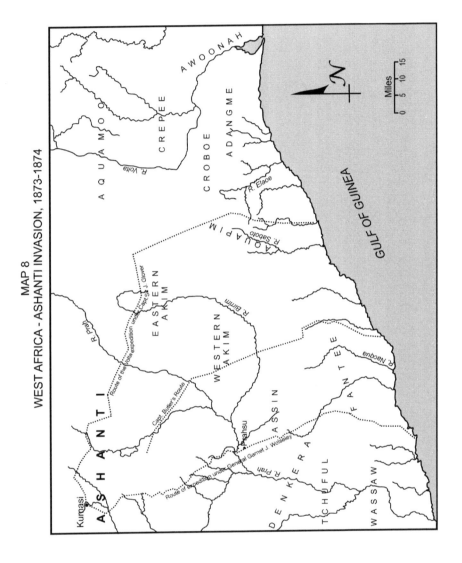

MAP 8
WEST AFRICA - ASHANTI INVASION, 1873-1874

MAP 9
AFGHANISTAN, 1878-1880

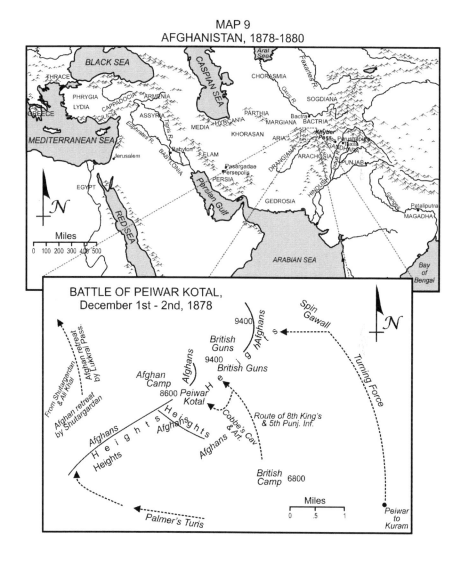

BLACK SEA

THRACE

PHRYGIA
LYDIA
CAPPADOCIA   ARMENIA
CILICIA
ASSYRIA
GREECE

MEDITERRANEAN SEA

CASPIAN SEA

CHORASMIA

Oxus R.   SOGDIANA

PARTHIA   Bactra
HYRCANIA   MARGIANA   BACTRIA
MEDIA   ARIA   Khyber
KHORASAN   Pass   Purushapura
Jerusalem   ELAM   Taxila
BABYLONIA   DRANGIANA   GANDHARA
Babylon   ARACHOSIA   PUNJAB
Pasargadae
Persepolis
PERSIA

EGYPT

RED SEA

Persian Gulf

Aral Sea

Jaxartes R.

Indus R.

HINDUSH

Ganges

GEDROSIA

Pataliputra
MAGADHA

Miles
0 100 200 300 400 500

ARABIAN SEA

Bay
of
Bengal

BATTLE OF PEIWAR KOTAL,
December 1st - 2nd, 1878

Spin
Gawall

9400
British
Guns

Afghans

9400
British Guns

Afghan
Camp
8600 Peiwar
Kotal

Afghans

Heights

Route of 8th King's
& 5th Punj. Inf.

Cobbe's Cav
& Art.

Afghan retreat
by Lukkrai Pass.

From Shuturgardan
& Ali Khal

Afghan retreat
by Shuturgardan

Afghans
Heights
Heights

Afghans
Heights

Afghans

Turning Force

British
Camp 6800

Miles
0   .5   1

Palmer's Turis

Peiwar
to
Kuram

xxiii

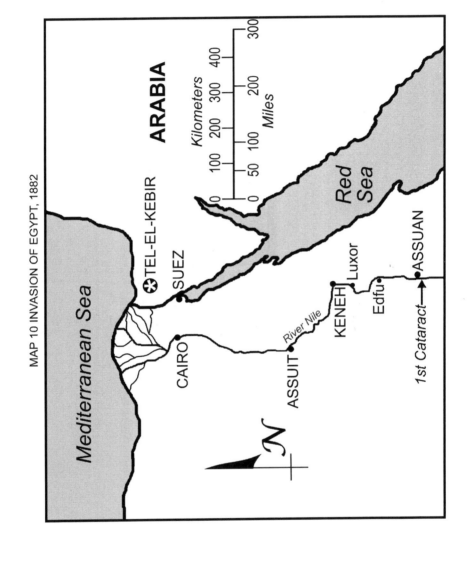

MAP 10 INVASION OF EGYPT, 1882

Mediterranean Sea

Red Sea

ARABIA

⊗ TEL-EL-KEBIR

SUEZ

CAIRO

ASSUIT

River Nile

KENEH

Luxor

Edfu

ASSUAN

1st Cataract

Kilometers
0   100   200   300   400
0   50   100   150   200   300
Miles

N

MAP 11 GORDON RELIEF EXPEDITION, 1884-1885

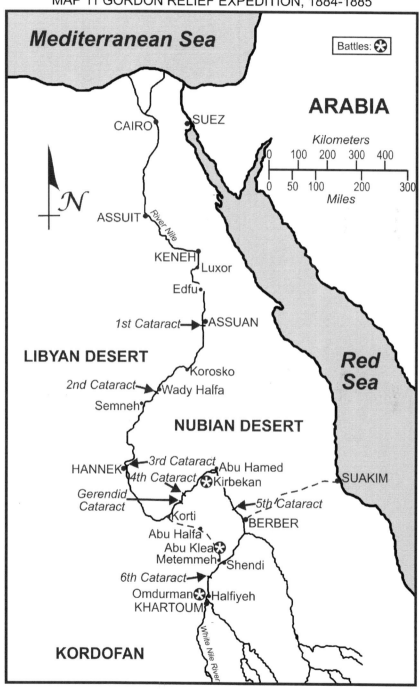

Mediterranean Sea

Battles: ✵

ARABIA

CAIRO   SUEZ

Kilometers
0   100   200   300   400

0   50   100   200   300
Miles

ASSUIT

River Nile

KENEH
Luxor

Edfu

1st Cataract → ASSUAN

LIBYAN DESERT

Korosko

2nd Cataract → Wady Halfa

Semneh

NUBIAN DESERT

Red Sea

HANNEK   3rd Cataract   Abu Hamed
4th Cataract ✵ Kirbekan

Gerendid
Cataract

5th Cataract

SUAKIM

Korti

BERBER

Abu Halfa

Abu Klea ✵
Metemmeh   Shendi

6th Cataract →

Omdurman ✵ Halfiyeh
KHARTOUM

White Nile River

KORDOFAN

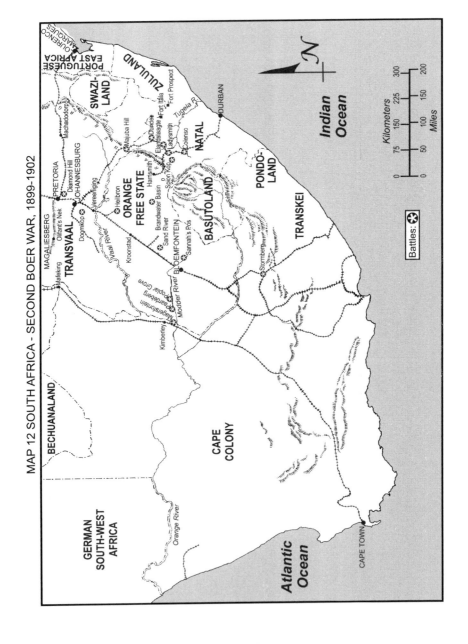

MAP 12 SOUTH AFRICA - SECOND BOER WAR, 1899-1902

Battles: ✪

GERMAN
SOUTH-WEST
AFRICA

BECHUANALAND

Orange River

CAPE
COLONY

Atlantic
Ocean

CAPE TOWN

Kimberley
Magersfontein
Paardeberg
Poplar Grove
Modder River
BLOEMFONTEIN
Sand River
Brandwater Basin
Sannah's Pós

Mafeking
MAGALIESBERG
TRANSVAAL
Olifant's Nek
Dornkop
Vaal River
Kroonstad
Vereeniging
Heilbron

ORANGE
FREE STATE

BASUTOLAND

PONDO-
LAND

TRANSKEI

Stormberg

PRETORIA
Diamond Hill
JOHANNESBURG

Machadodorp

SWAZI-
LAND

ZULULAND

PORTUGUESE
EAST AFRICA
LOURENÇO
MARQUES

Majuba Hill
Dundee
Elandslaagte
Sand Spruit
Ladysmith
Colenso
Harrismith
Fort Itala
Fort Prospect
Tugela R.

NATAL

DURBAN

Indian
Ocean

N

Kilometers
0   75   150   225   300
0   50   100   150   200
Miles

PREFACE

In my library, there are a couple of porcelain bowls that contain military artifacts that I have collected during my visits to battlefields around the world. One contains some lead bullets that had been fired at Gettysburg in July 1863, the greatest battle of the American Civil War and the limit of the Confederate army's advance into Union territory. The bullets are oxidized, which gives the lead slugs a coating of white. Some are round balls; others, known as Minié bullets, are pointed. They were fired at Gettysburg from muzzle-loaded rifles. Rifles were more accurate than their predecessors, smooth-bore muskets, but the rate of fire was still extremely low: no more than two rounds a minute. This is because the charge and then, separately, the bullet had to be forced down the barrel with a ramrod before the weapon was lifted to the soldier's shoulder and fired.

The second bowl contains some brass bullet cases I picked up at Paardeberg in South Africa, where a major battle was fought in February 1900. These bullet cases are still strewn over the ground more than a hundred years after the rounds were fired, giving some idea of the intensity of the small-arms fire where the fighting was taking place. Some of the bullet cases have rims, which identify them as from British Lee-Enfields; others are rimless, fired by the German Mauser rifles used by the Boers. A one-piece round, with a brass case containing propellant and a bullet fitted into the end, was designed for breech-loaded rifles. During the Second Boer War, these rifles all had magazines, and the rounds were fed into the chamber with a hand-operated bolt. By this means, the infantry could fire fifteen aimed rounds a minute. Infantry became the queen of the battlefield because massed small-arms fire from the infantry could stop a cavalry charge in its tracks.

This revolution in firepower in all major armies dated from the introduction of single-shot breech-loading in the 1860s, which boosted the rate of fire to *five times* what it had been with muzzle loading. A further improvement came in the 1880s, with rounds in magazines and fed by bolt action. These were the decades when Wolseley and Roberts established their reputations as successful commanders of overseas campaigns, when the British Empire was being consolidated and expanded following the suppression of the 1857 Indian mutiny, which had rocked the foundations of the Empire.

Garnet Wolseley (1833–1913) and Frederick Roberts (1832–1914), contemporaries who were born a few years before Queen Victoria ascended the throne, were universally regarded as Britain's most important soldiers during the last quarter of the nineteenth century. They both became field marshals and were raised to the peerage, Wolseley as a viscount and Roberts as an earl. They had no equals and deserved the title of Queen Victoria's paladins. Since they were direct contemporaries, they learned their business as young officers during the 1850s. This was the era of primitive firepower. Small-arms and artillery fire were inaccurate, could not reach distant targets, and had a rate of fire that was painfully slow. The two young officers learned their tactics on the ground and soon demonstrated their bravery in action. Roberts won the Victoria Cross, and both he and Wolseley were promoted because of their gallant service.

During the 1860s and 1870s—when increased firepower transformed the battlefield—both Wolseley and Roberts had the opportunity of commanding military expeditions: Wolseley in North America and in various parts of Africa, and Roberts in Afghanistan and, at the end of his fighting career, in South Africa. In addition to their tactical skills, they both demonstrated a 'grip' of battlefield strategy and logistics. These factors led to their successes. During this time, steamships and railroads began to influence grand strategy. Steamships transported the troops for the British overseas expeditions, and the American Civil War was profoundly influenced by railroads, which enabled the Confederate army to switch positions in response to enemy threats, by moving on interior lines.

Wolseley and Roberts had much staff experience and also spent many years holding peacetime commands. They showed themselves to be important army reformers and became well known to the public. Wolseley published a great deal. He wrote clearly and in a nontechnical way: a writing style that reflected the clarity of his thinking. Roberts, meanwhile, spent his career in India; and he only left the subcontinent when he retired from his position as commander-in-chief. Shortly afterwards, he published his memoirs, *Forty-One Years in India*, which struck a chord with the public and became a bestseller.

Queen Victoria's paladins had reached the top of their profession. Their contributions were recognized by the Queen and politicians who awarded them many honours. However, there is an open question about whether they were 'big' men with dominating personalities who got things done that other people considered impossible. A. J. P. Taylor, the controversial but persuasive historian, argued that Britain produced only two generals of international importance since the Napoleonic War: Wellington, who won that war by commanding a national army, which he led to victory at Waterloo in 1815, and Montgomery, who changed the fortunes of the country with his victory at El Alamein in 1942. Taylor did not recognize any first-rate British generals during the 127 years between 1815 and 1942.

Wolseley and Roberts won battles in small colonial wars; but during that whole time, Britain was free of any major conflict, which meant that there were no big battles for them to fight. Wolseley's largest command was two divisions, and Roberts's was four. During the First World War, Haig commanded more than forty divisions, although without conspicuous success. It did not occur to Taylor that during the 127 years between Waterloo and El Alamein, there were two unquestionably 'big' men whose contributions were not on the battlefield but were the result of their vision and mastery of grand strategy. They were Field Marshal Lord Kitchener and Marshal of the Royal Air Force Lord Trenchard.

Kitchener, who was a generation behind Roberts, followed him as commander-in-chief in South Africa and was destined to be the leading military decision-maker at the beginning of the First World War. He alone realized that the war would be a long one and therefore created, from scratch, the largest army that Britain had ever sent to war. He dominated British military thinking from his position as Secretary of State for War, although this job was interpreted by Kitchener as a military rather than civilian one. He hardly recognized that he was not a commander-in-chief.

Trenchard, whose dominant personality was underscored by his booming voice (which gave him his nickname), realized more vividly than anyone else that air power—for both tactical and strategic reasons— added a new dimension to war. Equally importantly, he managed to persuade the politicians to create a new armed service to fight alongside, but separate from, the army and navy. The Battle of Britain in 1940 was the ultimate demonstration of Trenchard's vision.

Roberts's greatest success came at the end of his career, when he was sixty-eight. However, Wolseley had no field command after the age of fifty-one, with the failure of the Gordon Relief Expedition. When the paladins were at the peak of their careers, Britain's only wars were small affairs, which meant that it is virtually impossible to rank Wolseley and Roberts in the hierarchy of great generals, or to guess how they would have fared if they had fought in the great wars of the twentieth century. The First World War did not show British generalship at its best, mainly because the generals' experience—like that of Wolseley and Roberts—had been in small colonial wars. Things were different during the Second World War. In this, the generals had fought as junior officers in the First World War and were determined not to repeat the mistakes of their predecessors. As a consequence, they demonstrated an impressive 'grip' on the complexities of modern command.

CHAPTER 1

RED ON THE MAP:
THE BRITISH EMPIRE, THE
ARMY AND ITS LEADERS

'War is a continuation of politics by other means.'[1] This aphorism by Clausewitz is familiar enough, but it does not make the point that war can bring to a head political tensions and release them, at great human cost. To Winston Churchill, what he called 'jaw-jaw' was greatly preferable to 'war-war'. But he admitted that it had to come to 'war-war' on rare occasions. When this happened, the army was the engine of victory, and the army's driving force was its commander.

Great generals are high-profile figures and are often remembered much more lastingly than the political leaders who were their masters. France was led by undistinguished politicians when Napoleon was cutting a swath through enemy armies. Before the end of the eighteenth century, he had entered the pantheon of the great captains, respected and feared in all parts of the civilized world. The French guillotined their king in 1793, but a mere eleven years later, they crowned their greatest general as emperor, because he was by now rampaging over the European continent and creating a Greater France. Napoleon made a permanent impact on French law, geography, society, and self-esteem. But this was not as profound as his influence on the art of war. He was eventually defeated by Wellington, a highly skilled battlefield general, but few people will remember the names of the British prime ministers during the years before 1815, when the man later known as the Iron Duke was building his reputation, particularly in Spain. Great generals march across the pages of history.

Britain did not fight a major war against a militarily sophisticated European power for almost a century after 1815. With no obvious demand for military talent, what opportunity was there for great generals to emerge? The prominent Oxford historian A. J. P. Taylor—someone not known for circumlocution—thought that Montgomery was the only British general since Wellington who had any talent at all.[2] By saying this, Taylor clearly saw nothing to admire about the top British commanders of the First World War, who were all rewarded with peerages and tax-free grants to buy country estates. A century after that war, their reputations are still being questioned.

In fact, the nineteenth century was a period during which Britain was involved in much warfare, although nothing on a large scale. The conflict in the Crimea in 1853–1856 involved four countries, including Britain. However, it was really a relic of the eighteenth century, with its sieges and cavalry charges and flamboyant uniforms. The first wars of the industrial age—with their developing military technology, vast scale, and horrendous casualty lists—were fought only a few years after the Crimea. The first industrial wars were the American Civil War and Prussia's defeat of Austria and France. These were precursors of even worse clashes in the twentieth century. During the nineteenth century, the other conflicts in which the British army fought were a procession of relatively minor wars of colonial conquest. It was in these that the two heroes of this book, Garnet Wolseley and Frederick Roberts distinguished themselves and became Queen Victoria's paladins. They were both Irish, and both were sons of army officers. They were neither aristocratic nor rich; but they made their reputations early, and this gave them a flying start.

During the second half of the nineteenth century, at the Horse Guards Headquarters in London (not at the War Office in Whitehall), the British army had an officer with the archaic title of commander-in-chief. He was Queen Victoria's cousin, the Duke of Cambridge, an extreme reactionary even by the standards of Victorian England. Surprisingly, his conservative values did not impede the rise of two men of outstanding talent, Wolseley and Roberts. Wolseley, whose reputation was built in Africa and in the War Office, eventually succeeded the Duke of Cambridge. Roberts, who made his reputation in India, succeeded Wolseley at the beginning of the twentieth century and was the last commander-in-chief before the appointment was abolished. Both Wolseley and Roberts had charisma, and each gathered around him a group of like-minded officers who became known as the Wolseley 'Ring' and the Roberts 'Ring'—officers who operated like the commander's military staff. (Military staffs were not formally organized at the time.) Regrettably, when these younger followers eventually became senior generals, they did not always fulfill their promise, which raises inevitable doubts about the ability of Wolseley and Roberts to judge the talents of their subordinates.

Empire-building—the national policy of Britain, Spain, Portugal, Holland, France, and later, Belgium and Germany—was driven by a number of motives. The strongest was conquest in search for booty like the silver in Latin America, but trade also soon became important, with the conquering nations importing cheap goods and exporting expensive ones. But countries often fought wars of conquest to elbow out European rivals, e.g. the eighteenth century wars between Britain and France to gain territory in North America and India. Finally, some conflicts were fought in the name of Christianity (e.g. the Spanish invasions of Latin America) and to suppress slavery (e.g. British expeditions to West Africa and the Sudan).

At the very end of the nineteenth century, the British Empire covered a quarter of the area of the globe: patches of territory of different sizes in all parts of the world that were printed in red in the atlases used by schoolchildren. The earlier colonies occupied by immigrants from the British Isles had by now become self-governing dominions. However, India—the largest dependency of all—was firmly under British rule. In India and in all the other colonies that were not self-governing, the British army played an important role, and half its manpower was in overseas garrisons, where most soldiers served for seven years. Wolseley and Roberts and most other generals had the job of building and consolidating the British Empire, commanding districts during peacetime and conducting small but tough campaigns when troublesome enemies appeared on the borders.

Empires are an anachronism in the twenty-first century. Yet the British Empire, which grew inexorably by acquiring territory over a period of almost five hundred years, did not fade away and vanish like those in the ancient world. It was transformed into the British Commonwealth, and important countries like Australia, Canada, and New Zealand became fully independent within the Commonwealth family. The many other former colonies that are now unconnected with the Commonwealth, notably the United States, retained their British legacy—in particular the English language, common law, and democratic government. The importance of Wolseley and Roberts is that they were the best fighting generals when the British Empire was at its apogee, the last quarter of the nineteenth century. This preceded the Second Boer War, the largest and most complex of the colonial conflicts, which revealed defects in the British army that demanded reforms that had to be implemented at the highest political level. The result was the creation of the British Expeditionary Force (BEF), which went to France in 1914 and was qualitatively the finest army that Britain had ever put in the field.

The First World War, despite Britain's decisive contribution to victory after four terrible years, saw the beginning of the decline of the British Empire. The twenties and thirties brought great economic problems. Then the Second World War, with its late flowering of British influence on world events, was followed by a further crumbling of the Empire—stimulated by a massive jolt from the premature end of the Raj in 1947. At the end of the twentieth century, Britain remained a relatively successful country. It is true that the Empire was no more, and many immigrants from the old Empire were now living in the British Isles. But Britain's international position was only in the second rank. Britain in 2000 was totally different from Great Britain in 1900.

This book is about the historical importance of Wolseley and Roberts, the two last military heroes of the British Empire. We know a great deal about them, not least because they wrote a surprising number of books, and these were not ghostwritten. The last authoritative biography of Roberts was published in 1954, but after this was completed, the author destroyed the Roberts papers![3] We can nevertheless get a real picture of the man from Roberts's autobiography and other published documents relating to his years of command.

The Five Phases of War

This book attempts to compare the two heroes and measure them against other generals who came before and after. However, comparing military figures across periods is surprisingly difficult. This is because military technology has evolved. Chapter 13 describes the most serious failure of Wolseley's career, the abortive attempt in 1884–1885 to rescue General Gordon in Khartoum. This meant a long and exhausting advance for a thousand miles up the Nile, negotiating cataracts in the river that made for maddeningly slow progress. Wolseley was defeated by the problems of transport and supplies: what are now called logistics. The political leadership in London took far too long to provide the funds needed for the expedition, and Wolseley became bitterly antagonistic towards the prime minister, William Ewart Gladstone. By the time Wolseley began to launch his expedition, the clock was ticking; and in his frustration, he had to race to relieve Gordon before Khartoum fell. Alas, Wolseley ran out of time.[4]

Wolseley's difficulty was time and distance—not the forces of the Mahdi, the religious leader of the Muslim hordes who were besieging Khartoum. Wolseley was, of course, operating with the military technology of the 1880s. But if he had been fighting in the 1920s, the situation would have been totally different. Motorized transport and air power would have made Wolseley's job relatively easy. And as Kitchener was to discover at Omdurman in 1898, the Sudanese army was no match for British firepower. Wolseley's experience demonstrated that new technology could make a general's job easier, although this was almost certainly the exception rather than the rule. New technology influences the forces of attack and the forces of defence, and they tend to cancel out. This is why the United States, which has fought six wars since 1945, has ended up with an approximate *status quo*: one victory, one defeat, and four conflicts that have been neither.

Military technology has gone through four clear phases (with danger of a fifth). The **first**—and also, by far, the longest—was the period without firepower. Battles were fought with weapons wielded by men or projected by simple devices like the longbow. It was warfare that was portrayed in the Bayeux Tapestry. The speed at which armies moved was determined by marching men and animal power (horses, mules, oxen, camels, and Hannibal's elephants). Ships were propelled by sail or by prisoners behind banks of oars.

The **second** phase saw the introduction of firepower: handguns and primitive cannon. The ranges were short, the targeting inaccurate, and the rate of fire low because the weapons had a smooth bore and were muzzle-loaded. This phase covered half a millennium, from the fourteenth to the mid-nineteenth century. The American Civil War (1861–1865) witnessed the transition to the third phase. The change was a big one. Wolseley and Roberts learned their business 'on the job' when warfare was in its second phase. However, when they had both reached senior rank, warfare was moving fast into its third phase, stimulated by the introduction of breech-loaded rifles fed by bolt action, and then by machine guns.

In the **third** phase, warfare was transformed into a manifestation of industrial mass production. It saw the first use of railways to deploy troops according to a strategic plan, and also, there was the introduction of small arms and artillery with improved accuracy and increased rate of fire because of greatly improved rifles and the first machine guns. Wolseley's and Roberts's successes in small colonial wars were substantially the result of increased infantry firepower: something not shared by their brave but less well-armed opponents. One change of enormous tactical importance was that infantry virtually took over the battlefield. Mass cavalry charges could no longer sweep forward because they were stopped by the rapid aimed fire of the infantry. At about the same time, navies were also revolutionized by mechanical propulsion and armour plate.

The First World War revealed the full panoply of war: troop trains crossing Europe; infantry with large numbers of machine guns and improved skill in the use of rifles, with marksmanship replacing volley firing; artillery, with shells of various calibres with different ranges, producing an unprecedented volume of accurate fire; engineering work demanded by the siege conditions of trench warfare; armour with caterpillar traction, which was the greatest single innovation in land warfare during the twentieth century; submarines; and—not least—air power, which grew rapidly from an arm of intelligence to a fighting force. The Second World War saw an extremely important new weapon in the aircraft carrier and the more controversial innovations of airborne forces and combined operations. The most striking feature of this new type of conflict was the size of the casualty lists, although these would be nothing compared with the result of the fifth phase (if this were ever reached).

The **fourth** phase dates from the 1960s and is likely to be the norm unless a major world power emerges to challenge the United States. The twentieth-century world wars were fought between large armies roughly equal in size. They can therefore be called *bipolar*. In contrast, Vietnam, Iraq, and Afghanistan are *asymmetrical*, since the two opposing sides of the conflict are unequal in size. This does not mean that the large army finds it easy to defeat the small one. The large army is strong but rigidly organized and not well equipped to search for and crush small bodies of elusive opponents: skilled, dangerous, and self-immolating fanatics. The American army has been unsuccessful in winning asymmetrical wars because, at heart, all generals are conventional thinkers. They have not grasped the reality that most of their effort must be political rather than military. There are clues as to how this can be done successfully from the British suppression of the communist insurgency in Malaya in the mid-1950s.

The **fifth** phase would see the use of tactical nuclear weapons. This has, of course, not arrived. But if it did, it would surely be the end of military conflict—and even civilization—as we know them.

The Emergence of the General Staff

As warfare grew to such a large scale during the early twentieth century, the work of a general became technically complicated, and this contributed to the growth of military staffs. The army staff was a relatively new function in the British army. The first British officer who had employed a staff was the Duke of Wellington, who had commanded an army composed of a number of divisions during the Peninsular War in the early nineteenth century (and before he became a duke). Wellington's staff was made up of three parts: first, a Staff Corps of Engineers, who looked after the technical functions of the army; second, a group of twenty officers and clerks under a quartermaster general as chief of staff, who accompanied the commander to help him plan military operations; and third, a group of a dozen aristocratic ADCs, 'gallopers' who charged around the battlefield, passing on the commander's orders and acting as his eyes and ears. These young men were precursors of the liaison officers in Montgomery's tactical headquarters in North-West Europe in 1944–1945, who used jeeps and two-way radios. The tactical headquarters, which was a remarkable innovation, was made possible by the way in which Montgomery's chief of staff, Francis de Guingand, ran the fully staffed main headquarters. It operated so smoothly that Montgomery needed to visit it on only rare occasions.[5]

After the defeat of Napoleon in 1815, the British army was reduced in size. Some men in the ranks served for decades, with seven-year tours in foreign garrisons. It was the army that kept the British Empire in being. Since the army no longer contained large formations, Wellington's staff system fell into decay. It was only revived in a modified form in the middle of the nineteenth century.

At that time, the army that developed the most sophisticated and powerful general staff was that of Prussia (which was later transformed into the army of the German Empire). As a result of careful personal recommendation, staff officers were selected from the most promising officers in the army: a handful of brainy and aggressive men who spent two years at the War Academy in Potsdam, followed by a probationary period on the job. Their education concentrated on the staff function normally abbreviated as 'G' (operations and intelligence) because the War Academy was set up to identify and force-feed future generals. It did not take long for a graduate to become chief of staff of a division. If a chief of staff found himself disagreeing with the general he was serving, he had the right to appeal over the general's head. Officers in the general staff 'owed a caste loyalty to their leader, the Chief of the General Staff; a loyalty parallel with, and sometimes transcending, that which was claimed by their own unit commander. From this double loyalty grew up that peculiar institution characteristic of the Prusso-German direction of operations, the dual command.'[6] The numbers were small, but the ethos was powerful. The crimson stripes on the staff officers' breeches were recognized, and the symbolism was respected.

In Britain during the late nineteenth century, the Staff College in Camberley (formerly known as the Senior Division of the Royal Military College) became increasingly important, despite the fact that it was sometimes resented by officers who devoted their lives to regimental service. British staff training emphasized 'the principles of administration'[7] because many of the officers would be engaged in 'A' (personnel and discipline) and 'Q' (supplies and logistics). Entry into the British Staff College was competitive, based on a difficult examination and a personal recommendation from a senior officer. About a hundred officers were accepted every year for the two-year course. The number of graduates—who carried the prestigious initials *psc* (*passed staff college*) alongside their names in the Army List—was a good deal higher than their German opposite numbers, and the German army was also much larger. This meant that the German General Staff was proportionately smaller than the British one. But the Potsdam War Academy was a hothouse for exceptional intellectual gifts; the graduates were taught to 'think big' and were not much concerned with administration. (The Germans had a separate system of training 'A' and 'Q' officers for their more routine jobs.)

A graduate from the British Staff College would probably get a major's appointment as a general staff officer, second grade (GSO2), e.g. brigade major, deputy assistant adjutant general (DAAG), or deputy assistant quartermaster general (DAQMG). These were a good deal short of chief of staff of a division, which went to a lieutenant colonel GSO1. The job of the latter was to write out his general's orders and make sure that they were carried out. The situation was different in Germany, where the chief of staff had to accept a virtually equal share in life-and-death decisions. There are many cases of German staff officers, on their own initiative, issuing orders directing advances and retreats. The way this was done was that the chief of staff of a large formation would issue orders to the chief of staff of a smaller one, and the commanders of the two formations would receive a copy of the orders, for their information.

The British army staff was a relatively large body, and it was not short of critics. During the First World War, there was much antagonism between the staff and the regimental officers and men, mainly because the staff lived in some comfort behind the lines. Attitudes became more accommodating during the Second World War, when the staff—like the commanders—lived in caravans.

This book concentrates mainly on the third phase of warfare. This is when the last patches of British Empire red were appearing on the map. Towards the end of the period, the largest of the colonial wars ended with a tenuous British victory: the Second Boer War of 1899–1902. At the other side of the world, the Russo-Japanese War of 1904–1905 demonstrated lessons of great importance. These were not noticed in Western Europe but were confirmed by the Balkan War of 1912.

During all the conflicts of the third phase, the increase in firepower led to an unexpected phenomenon. This was the dramatic reinforcement of defences, which made direct attacks costly and difficult. Although a small voice was heard that predicted the eventual stalemate that was to come—that of an unknown Polish banker called Ivan Stanislavovich Bloch[8]—he was laughed out of court by the generals in every country who believed that bravery, discipline, and a will to win would overcome the effects of the fire of enfilading machine guns. Military leaders had not noticed the beginning of trench warfare at Petersburg, Virginia, as early as 1864. The experience of 1914 demonstrated, with great brutality, that Bloch had been right and the generals had been wrong.

The careers of Wolseley and Roberts came to fruition during the third phase of warfare. They died in 1913 and 1914 respectively. They both left a reputation as being great generals.

Great Generals

What distinguishes a great general from his lesser contemporaries?[9] I believe there are four qualities: (1) a command of battlefield tactics, (2) an imaginative ability to think strategically, (3) a 'grip' on logistics, and (4) a powerful personality.

These are four substantial demands on any individual. However, when officers are being chosen for the highest ranks, they must be judged by the most rigorous standards. Commissioned ranks in any army progress upward in a pyramid. At the bottom, there are large numbers of junior officers; then as individuals ascend the pyramid, the numbers progressively decline. At all stages (in particular the move up from major), the number of men chosen will be far fewer than the number who will be disappointed. In what ways were the unsuccessful soldiers deficient? These points will help to explain.

Of these qualities, tactics, strategy, and logistics can be studied and taught. Officer cadets and young officers spend much time on tactics. And at the Staff College, students devote a good deal of attention to studying past campaigns and participating in tactical exercises without troops (TEWTs) and other types of exercise evaluating strategic alternatives. These three skills are a necessary condition for any officer to be promoted to higher rank. However, the fourth point—a powerful personality—describes the psyche of the individual, and it is generally the reason that explains why one man is selected from a group who are all well versed in tactics, strategy, and logistics. His personality is the essential discriminator.

The Three Necessary Skills

These can be simply described as follows:

1. **An understanding of battlefield tactics**, i.e. military operations when friendly and opposing forces are actually in contact. This includes having the flexibility to adapt plans according to the nature of the ground and the dispositions of the enemy. Effective tactics stress the importance of misleading and surprising the enemy.

2. **The imaginative ability to think strategically**, with a full appreciation of ways and means. A decision has to be made about whether a planned operation is feasible in logistical terms. This was not done before Wolseley embarked on the Gordon Relief Expedition. Wolseley and his soldiers paid the price: Gordon's death was inevitable because the relief was not a practical operation of war. There are two types of strategy: *grand strategy* and *battlefield strategy*. Grand strategy is at the higher level. It is mainly the concern of politicians, who should consult their military advisers. Battlefield strategy is determined by the general commanding the proposed operation, in consultation with the politicians. Towards the end of the Second World War, Hitler combined both functions. As a result, he emasculated his generals, which hastened the defeat of the German army. An effective battlefield strategy concentrates the strength of the friendly forces against the place where the enemy is weakest. By this means, good strategy lightens the burden on the soldiers in the front line.

3. **Logistics** are like plumbing. They are unglamorous but indispensable. Amateurs—armchair generals—have a reputation for discussing war in terms of tactics and strategy. Professionals—battlefield generals—discuss war in terms of tactics and logistics.

To illustrate the difference between grand strategy and battlefield strategy, the story of the Gallipoli expedition of 1915 makes the point clearly. It was set in train by the British cabinet, under the pressure of the two service ministers: the First Lord of the Admiralty (Winston Churchill) and the Secretary of State for War (Field Marshal Lord Kitchener, who was serving in a civilian capacity). The grand strategy was to drive the navy, against opposition, through the Dardanelles Straits and the Sea of Marmara to reach Constantinople, which they would then shell with all their guns. This would almost certainly have caused the Turkish government to sue for peace. To implement this grand strategy, the army commander devised his battlefield strategy. He was Sir Ian Hamilton, a protégé of Roberts: he will appear on a number of occasions in this book. Hamilton's strategy was to clear the territory north of the Straits by landing two attacking forces: the first at the southern tip of the Gallipoli peninsula (where the enemy was expecting it), and the second on the west coast, where the landing was dominated by formidable hills that were soon strongly defended. The two landings had no common objectives and were not mutually supporting. The battlefield strategy led to a tragically unsuccessful campaign as the invading troops were quickly and permanently blocked by the enemy. The tactical skills and heroism of the British and ANZAC soldiers were just not enough to break the deadlock.

Churchill's experience as a war leader demonstrates the increasing importance of logistics. Despite his personal (although unhappy) experience of grand strategy in 1914–1915, and his brief experience of commanding a battalion in the static warfare of the trenches in 1916, Churchill found it very difficult during the Second World War to understand why an army needed a long 'administrative tail'. These men had to be fed but were not participating directly in combat. With his experience of a static battlefield, he found it difficult to appreciate the difficulties in a mobile war of transporting, *inter alia*, gasoline, spare parts for tanks and trucks, and artillery and tank ammunition.

The Discriminator—A General's Personality

While tactics, strategy, and logistics can be studied and taught, the fourth and last quality possessed by successful generals is embedded in the individual's psyche. It cannot be modified by him, nor can it be passed on to other people, no matter how close the comradeship between the seniors and the juniors. This last factor is the most important of all. It is often connected with tactics, strategy, and logistics; and it acts in such a way that it amplifies their effects.

It includes a range of qualities that vary between individuals. They include mental clarity, the ability to pick good subordinates, obsessive determination, a feel for the psychology of the enemy, and a subtle understanding of the men he commands. Above all, a successful general is a powerful figure whose decisions make an impact and will lead to action. Here is a brief description of eight notable military leaders— one French, three British, two German, and two American. Exemplary figures are not plentiful, but the eight generals I have listed were not alone. I could have included Grant, the older von Moltke, Atatürk, von Manstein, Eisenhower (who defeated the incomparable German army in Western Europe in eleven months), Zhukov, Brooke, Montgomery, Slim, and a few others. But my eight figures illustrate well enough the power of their personalities and their position in the first rank. (Kitchener and Trenchard have already been mentioned in the preface.)

Napoleon. He was an immensely ambitious master of grand strategy, and this made him—at least temporarily—the master of the European mainland. The intellectual contribution to his victories came from Napoleon, but the engine to achieve them was the *Grande Armée*. There was an unbreakable link between the small figure in a plain uniform with the single decoration of the Legion of Honour on his breast and the common soldiers who followed him. Each soldier believed that he had a marshal's baton in his knapsack. Many of the troops had followed Napoleon for twenty years, and on the field of Waterloo, he summoned the Old Guard to come to his defence at the climax of the battle.

Wellington. His astonishing feat was to conquer Napoleon in battle. Wellington was, above all, a cool strategist who had the mysterious ability of sensing what was happening 'on the other side of the hill'. At Waterloo, he was in the thick of the battle and demonstrated in practical terms that he had not forgotten his skills as a tactician. His soldiers followed him everywhere, despite his low opinion of them: 'the scum of the earth, enlisted for drink,' although he later admitted what 'splendid fellows' they became. It was the British regimental system that generated *esprit de corps* and turned unpromising men into battle-winning soldiers.

Lee. The American Civil War lasted for four years, but in view of the industrial superiority of the North, it should have been much shorter. The leadership of Lee was the main reason why the Southern army was able to maintain its fighting ability. He was a particularly able strategist who used 'internal lines' to shift his troops across the battlefield to meet the threat of enemy attacks. He worked closely with his heroic subordinate Stonewall Jackson, who tragically died of wounds in 1863. Lee is still remembered with affection and respect in both the North and the South, although when he accepted his command in Virginia, he disregarded the oath he had sworn at West Point to support the Constitution of the United States. Wolseley regarded Lee as the greatest man he had ever known.

Kitchener. He had been a proconsul as well as a general, and he had an astonishing grasp of grand strategy. In 1914, he was the only leading figure to forecast that the First World War would last for at least three years, and through the power of his personality, he persuaded the British government to allow him to create a new army that would eventually become larger than any British force up to that time. Kitchener had an arresting presence, and his vast moustache was thought to be the virility symbol of the British Empire (although no one spoke about his ambiguous sexuality). Tactics did not interest him. In the Second Boer War, when he temporarily commanded the British troops at the Battle of Paardeberg, he became confused and lost his 'grip', which prompted Roberts to reassume personal command.

Ludendorff. He was the soldier who revolutionized the tactics of the First World War. He had the imagination to locate and support subordinates with novel ideas, and these included the use of highly trained storm troops and the revival of the classic tactical principle of surprise. This system worked astonishingly well and, almost overnight, broke the trench deadlock. His first main attack in March 1918 led to the destruction of the British Fifth Army. Ludendorff's later and separate attacks on various parts of the front lacked strategic direction, and this is the factor that prevented him from winning the war.

Trenchard. He was the first military leader who realized that air power created a spectacular new dimension to warfare. He created the power of long-range strategic interdiction, which led to a massive campaign to assault enemy industry, raw materials, and transportation (and also, tragically, the German civilian population) during the Second World War. Trenchard was the only person strong enough to force the British government to create, in 1918, the first independent air force in the world. (It took the Americans almost thirty years before they followed suit.)

Guderian. At the beginning of the Second World War, Guderian (who came from an Armenian family), commanded an armoured corps and led the thrust through Northern France in May 1940. Guderian had a dramatic influence on battlefield tactics during the Second World War. Building on the British innovation of the all-arms offensive that achieved a notable—although not decisive—victory in August 1918, Guderian engineered tight cooperation between all attacking forces: closely coordinated operations by armour, infantry, artillery, and air power, to which he added the force of his personal presence and drive. He gave a new name to the lexicon of warfare, *Blitzkrieg*.

MacArthur. He was another proconsul, sometimes called an American Caesar. In his thirties, he commanded a division in France in 1918. In the 1930s, he became chief of staff of the American army. He then went to the Philippines to command their own army, which he trained on American lines. He was in the Philippines when the Japanese attacked in December 1941. Roosevelt ordered him to leave the islands and go to Australia, from where he built up American military strength and commanded one of the two main axes of assault on Japan. (Admiral Nimitz commanded the other.) There followed three years of island-hopping across the Pacific, from east to west. MacArthur accepted the surrender of the Japanese Empire and became a successful proconsul based in Tokyo, virtually ruling the country. But his fighting days had not finished. When the Korean War broke out in 1950, MacArthur was given command of the United Nations forces. After some initial success, he began to dominate the grand strategy, which meant that he sidelined the president of the United States. This cost MacArthur his job.

The main reason for the fame of these eight generals was their ability as soldiers, in particular their powerful personalities: they were 'big' men who got things done. This was the first reason why they became so famous. A second reason was that they fought and usually won big battles in major wars. This does not mean that military leaders in small wars are condemned to second-rate status. Major military leaders have emerged from small unorthodox conflicts, but such conflicts tend to be rare. In the Second Boer War, de la Rey and de Wet emerged as guerrilla leaders who caused immense trouble to the British during the last two years of the war. In the First World War, von Lettow-Vorbeck tied up large British forces in East Africa from the first day of war to the last; and in Arabia, Lawrence gained a worldwide reputation and created Arab kingdoms. In Burma in the Second World War, Wingate became as famous as his distant kinsman Lawrence. Churchill considered Wingate to be a man of destiny. These leaders of small forces, like the eight commanders in large wars, all reinforce Napoleon's conclusion: 'What matters in war is not the men. It is the *man*.'

I have not discussed yet how Wolseley and Roberts can be compared with the great generals of history. This will be taken up in chapter 16. However, there is no dispute that they were both outstanding leaders of men: effective in battle and also popular in the ranks (two qualities that do not always go together). Wolseley told officers to 'make themselves loved as well as respected'.[10] The officer must make the soldiers 'realize that all our interests are identical, causing the newest-joined recruit to feel that success is of as much real moment to him as it can be to the general'.[11] But Wolseley and Roberts did not command big armies by modern standards. As armies became larger and generals more remote, personal leadership became more difficult. In the First World War, Haig was famously distant. But Plumer, who commanded an army, was surprisingly close to his men, as were Montgomery and

Slim during the Second World War. Montgomery made a conscious effort to meet all his troops face-to-face. They were rather amused by his theatrics, but they nevertheless knew that he was not callous about loss of life, and he took planning seriously. To Wolseley and Roberts, their relationship with their soldiers was extremely important. Roberts, with increasing responsibility, managed to maintain his *rapport* with his British and Indian troops. However, Wolseley did not do this quite so well. During his years in London, before his retirement, he became rather introspective and lost some of his popularity. This probably influenced the Secretary of State for War when he selected Roberts rather than Wolseley for the command in South Africa at the end of 1899.

Endnotes

1. Clausewitz, Karl von, *Vom Kriege* (Oxford: *The Oxford Dictionary of Quotations*, Third Edition, 1980), 152.
2. Horne, A. and Montgomery, D, *The Lonely Leader. Monty, 1944–1945* (London: Macmillan, 1994), 1.
3. James, Robert, *Lord Roberts* (London: Hollis & Carter, 1954).
4. Preston, Adrian (ed.), *In Relief of Gordon. Lord Wolseley's Campaign Journal of the Khartoum Relief Expedition, 1884–1885* (London: Hutchinson, 1967).
5. Mead, Richard, *The Men Behind Monty* (Barnsley, South Yorkshire: Pen & Sword, 2015), 245–252.
6. Wheeler-Bennett, John, *The Nemesis of Power. The German Army in Politics, 1918–1945* (London: Macmillan, 1956), 6.
7. Beckett, Ian F. W., *Johnnie Gough, VC* (London: Tom Donovan, 1989), 114.
8. Jones, John Philip, *Johnny. The Legend and Tragedy of General Sir Ian Hamilton* (Barnsley, South Yorkshire: Pen & Sword, 2012), 171–172.
9. Ibid., 3.
10. Wolseley, Garnet, *The Soldier's Pocket-Book for Field Service* (London: Macmillan, 1882), 3.
11. Ibid., 4.

CHAPTER 2

'GAY THE FILES OF
SCARLET FOLLOW'[1]

The Army That Wolseley And Roberts Joined

British soldiers were Redcoats until the 1890s. Red was worn by the infantry, the largest branch of the service. The Rifles wore green, and some cavalry regiments wore blue, as did the artillery, the engineers, and the various services. The conversion to khaki before the end of the nineteenth century was a signal that warfare was being transformed into a more businesslike activity. It was less splendid than red, green, and blue; but it was important that fighting soldiers would benefit from, and appreciate, the camouflage of khaki.

During the eighteenth and nineteenth centuries, British sea power was unrivalled. Britain ruled the waves because she was a trading nation and the trade routes had to be protected. Just as importantly, the British army garrisons throughout the world had to be supplied and reinforced. Britain has never had the biggest army in the world. Unlike the major European countries—Germany, France, Austria-Hungary, and Russia—the British army has traditionally emphasized quality rather than numbers. During the nineteenth century, the British army was an all-regular force (supplemented by part-time volunteer soldiers recruited for home defence). In the early part of the nineteenth century, soldiers in the ranks enlisted for very long periods, and many had served for ten or even twenty years. This changed during the 1870s, when short service was introduced, a change that was substantially engineered by Wolseley. This meant seven years on the active list followed by five years in the Regular Reserve. The average age of soldiers was reduced, although most were still experienced men. And this reorganization, which was inexpensive, provided a substantial reserve that could be called out at a time of general mobilization (as happened in 1914, when many battalions went to war with half their strength coming from reservists).

'A Regiment Which Is Infinitely Superior to the Others'[2]

Since the British regular army was organized to garrison a widespread empire, the regiments—formed into brigades and divisions—often fought small but bloody wars. These experiences did a good deal to boost the practical training and therefore the preparedness of British officers and men. This is the army in which Wolseley and Roberts served, Wolseley in the British infantry and Roberts in the Indian artillery. In contrast to the British army, the leading European countries had large numbers of conscripts who served for two or three years in peacetime, and the regular forces of these countries devoted themselves to training the conscripts. These large continental armies—made up of a few regulars but many conscripts—could not compare with the British army with its overseas experience and high standard of military skill. But Britain's problem was that her army was so small.

There were good reasons why British soldiers were probably superior, man for man, to those in any other army. They had more years of service and—most importantly—many officers and other ranks had heard shots fired in anger. They were better marksmen because their pay depended partly on their skill at arms. The standard of discipline was robust because there was a high degree of mutual respect between officers and men. Most important of all, each man was a member of a regimental family that created, nurtured, and strengthened that most important contribution to military efficiency: *esprit de corps*. The regimental system was so strong that it was able to provide a firm foundation for the army's expansion during the First World War to many times the peacetime regular strength of 240,000 men. At the beginning of the war, there were 161 regular battalions; at the wartime peak, the number of regular, territorial, and new army battalions was 1,750.[3]

The details that follow describe Britain's pre-1914 army. Wolseley and Roberts had both been commissioned in the early 1850s. During the years leading up to the First World War, they had passed from the scene, although Roberts continued to make his voice heard after he had retired. He remained a figure of great renown and was much concerned about an issue of growing importance—the desirability of compulsory service.

The early 1900s saw an army reorganization carried out because of the problems that arose during the Second Boer War. The post of commander-in-chief was abolished, and he was replaced by a general staff based in the War Office: an innovation so radical that it took some years to become effective. The key appointment was Chief of the Imperial General Staff (CIGS), but the first incumbents also had much to learn. When Field Marshal Kitchener became Secretary of State for War in August 1914, even he did not understand that his own job was a civilian appointment. He acted like a field marshal and issued orders to commanders in the field without consulting the CIGS. However, in December 1915, the job of CIGS went to General Sir William Robertson, who at last became an effective military adviser to Kitchener's successor. Robertson reported to the new Secretary of State for War, who was a civilian with a political appointment and membership of the cabinet. Robertson was a powerful personality and was, unfortunately, in constant conflict with the prime minister, David Lloyd George, who finally sacked him in 1918.

The fighting elements of the British army were the infantry, the cavalry, the artillery, and the engineers. (The First World War also saw the dramatic introduction of air power.) The army was supported by a range of non-combatant services: *inter alia* medical, veterinary, ordnance, transport, and supplies. (Every military unit needs substantial regular supplies of food and ammunition. In 1914, the largest individual item was fodder because armies were horse-drawn.)

Britain's main contribution to the art of war is the regimental system, and this applied to all four fighting arms, whose basic units were the infantry battalion, the cavalry regiment, the artillery battery, and the engineer field company. In almost all circumstances, the four arms cooperated on the battlefield, and the commanders of brigades and divisions had to exploit the advantages of this. This is an important tactical skill (i.e. the first point among the attributes of a great general).

In the infantry and cavalry, most officers and men spent their careers in their individual units: one thousand men in a battalion and rather more than half that number in a cavalry regiment. The regiment was more than just a body of men; it was a soldier's professional family. Most regiments had a royal connection, and this made the regiment a source of tradition and pride. In the eyes of its members, their own regiment was unique and superior to all the others. (The heading of this section quotes Wolseley's own words.) The word *regiment* had one meaning in the infantry but another in the cavalry. In the infantry, the basic tactical unit was the battalion, and a regiment was made up of a number of different battalions. Each was separate. It trained in peacetime and went to war accompanied by battalions from other regiments. Battalions were fitted into larger formations, with four from different regiments in a brigade, and three brigades (plus supporting arms) in a division. The one thousand men in an infantry battalion was a nominal figure that varied a good deal according to casualties and reinforcements.

There were seventy-four infantry regiments, in the Foot Guards and the infantry of the Line. Each was composed of at least two regular battalions; one of militia, later entitled Special Reserve (part-time soldiers who agreed to serve abroad if mobilized); and two or more battalions of volunteers, later known as Territorials, part-time soldiers who were recruited for home defence.[4] (The Foot Guards were an exception because they were all-regular.) An important innovation of the 1870s by the war minister, Edward Cardwell, was that the number of regiments was reduced, and all were reorganized into two regular battalions which were linked, with one serving in Britain and the other in an overseas garrison. The latter was kept at full strength by drafts from the battalion at home. In contrast to the infantry, each of the thirty-one cavalry regiments was a tactical unit since there were none with multiple battalions. A cavalry regiment had fewer soldiers than an infantry battalion, but it had as many horses as men. Three cavalry regiments made up a brigade, and three brigades (with supporting arms) composed a cavalry division.

There were 279 batteries in the Royal Artillery: twenty-five of Royal Horse Artillery (RHA), supporting the cavalry; and 147 of Royal Field Artillery (RFA), supporting the infantry. The normal arrangement was for a single RHA battery to support a cavalry regiment, and an RFA battery an infantry battalion. The Royal Engineers contained fifty-nine field companies, and these were attached to brigades and divisions.

British regiments all had a long history and a formidable fighting record. This was emblazoned on the colours of the infantry and the guidons of the cavalry. Colours and guidons were handled and displayed with great reverence. (The Royal Artillery had no colours, because to the regiment, the guns themselves were the source of pride.) Each regiment had a march, many had a motto, and some had an animal who went on parade. The goat of the Royal Welch Fusiliers (note the unique spelling) was the best-known example. All regiments had nicknames, and these were generally a reminder of some historical feat of arms: *The Bird-Catchers* (the Royal Scots Greys, raised in 1681); *The Bloody Eleventh* (the Devonshire Regiment, 1685); *The Right-Abouts* (the Gloucestershire Regiment, 1694); *The Emperor's Chambermaids* (the Fourteenth Hussars, 1715); *The Die-Hards* (the Middlesex Regiment, 1755); and *The Death or Glory Boys* (the Seventeenth Lancers, 1759).

As can be seen from some of these names, infantry regiments were recruited from different regions of the country; but this was less true of the cavalry, in which only five regiments had recruiting areas: one in Scotland and four in Ireland. Infantry regiments had traditionally been numbered chronologically, following the date when they were raised. But in the 1870s, the regional connections, which had been rare, were applied to all infantry regiments. This was another Cardwell innovation, and it had the positive effect of adding a regional loyalty to the one established by the regiment itself.

The most visible difference between regiments was in their uniforms. Within the limits imposed by standardization, there was no shortage of variations. Full dress was worn until the end of the nineteenth century. In the infantry, this meant scarlet tunics, but regiments had their own facings: differently coloured collars and cuffs. Even with the introduction of the durable and practical khaki uniform before the Second Boer War, regiments found ways to differentiate. Each had its own cap badge, a version of which was also often on the epaulettes and collars. Every regiment had its own button design, which was stamped on the rounded surface of the metal. Most buttons were polished brass, but some regiments had polished silver ones, and others had black ones made of horn. Some regiments wore lanyards, mostly with a historical meaning, and others had their own badges of rank. There were variations in headdress, especially in the Scottish regiments. In fact, the Scots had greater differences than anyone else. Each Highland regiment had its own tartan for its kilt, and every Lowland regiment had its own for its trews. Kilts were worn in battle up to the end of the First World War, although they were camouflaged by drab aprons.

Variations in uniform were symbols of regimental pride. Since senior officers recognized the contribution of this to discipline and morale and soldiers' ability to withstand hardship and losses, it is not surprising to read what Wolseley himself said on the subject: 'No man who knew soldiers or their peculiar way of thinking, or who was acquainted with the many little trifles that go to make up *esprit de corps*, and that form as it were a lien between it and discipline, would ever deprive a soldier of any peculiarity that he prided himself on . . . In their endeavours to foster this spirit, colonels are greatly aided by being able to point to some peculiarity in dress or title.'[5]

Commissioned Rank, Regiment, and Social Class

The British regular army in 1914 numbered 240,000 men (excluding regular reserves) in all regiments, corps, and services: 13,000 were officers, or 5 percent of the total. In the infantry, the number of officers in a battalion was thirty, or 3 percent of total strength. Although officers, warrant officers, and non-commissioned officers (NCOs) had clearly defined authority and issued orders that had to be obeyed, the most rigid division was between officers and everybody else. The highest other rank was held by the regimental sergeant major (RSM). 'The gulf between the RSM and the youngest officer in the battalion was equally great, if not greater, than the gulf between the RSM and the youngest recruit.'[6] NCOs and warrant officers were promoted from the ranks. Officers came directly to a battalion from the outside, except for the quartermaster (one per battalion), who was a promoted warrant officer, often the RSM.

The gulf between officers and other ranks was the result of an officer's family background and education, both of which were influenced by his family wealth. Officers came from the top 5 percent of British society. These included the small number of families in the aristocracy and landed gentry, plus a much larger number of educated *bourgeoisie*: from the families of serving and retired officers of the army and navy; members of the learned professions: the church, law, and medicine; politicians and senior government servants; well-established businessmen, particularly in the City of London; and a surprising number of 'gentlemen with independent means'.[7] Traditionally, all these families educated their children in public schools (i.e. fee-paying and private).

Although most potential officers went to a public school, very few went to a university. If they were intended for the infantry or cavalry, they spent eighteen months at the Royal Military College, Sandhurst; if intended for the artillery or engineers, they spent two years at the Royal Military Academy, Woolwich. Unlike the United States Military Academy at West Point, which awarded a four-year university degree, Sandhurst and Woolwich had curricula based on military discipline and leadership, with little study of liberal arts and sciences. Sport played an important part. Woolwich had an orientation towards mathematics and science, appropriate to an officer's service in the technical arms. Sandhurst and Woolwich did not spell the end of an officer's training. When he joined his regiment, he continued to learn, not least from his platoon sergeant. He also had to devote a good deal of time to personal study during his late twenties if he chose to compete for a place in the Staff College.

Sandhurst and Woolwich charged fees, although there were some scholarships, particularly for the sons of officers who had lost their lives during their service. A young officer needed at least a small private income to cover his mess bill. All ranks received basic rations based on meat, bread, and limited extras. But life in an officers' mess offered a more attractive cuisine as well as relatively comfortable living conditions, although many army barracks were crumbling with age. While other ranks had their main meal at the middle of the day, officers dined in the evening, often formally when they entertained generals, officers from other regiments, and landowners from the counties where the regiment was stationed. Much champagne, claret, and port was drunk. A young officer's pay was too low to cover all his expenses and leave anything over, hence the need for his family to supplement his income. Things became easier when he was posted to India, where his pay was higher and his expenses, particularly the wages of his servants, were much lower. (This was the case with Robertson, one of the very few officers who was commissioned from the ranks and had no private income.) Officers knew the importance of comradeship in the officers' mess. Therefore, if a cadet planned to join a particular regiment, he had to be accepted. This meant that the seniors—and, in particular, the colonel-in-chief—had to give him the once-over.

Officers' uniforms were similar to those worn by other ranks, but they were well tailored and cut from superior cloth. During the nineteenth century, there were a number of separate uniforms worn on different occasions, and they were all expensive. On active service, officers' uniforms were different enough from those worn by other ranks to make officers special targets for sniper fire. During the First World

War, platoon and company attacks were led by officers wearing private soldiers' uniforms. During the nineteenth century, tropical uniform was worn, and this was lighter than that worn in Europe. Wolseley designed comfortable tropical uniforms, including the ubiquitous Wolseley Helmet. However, the army's insistence on flannel spine pads under the shirt to ward off the effects of the sun was a curious manifestation of Victorian medical practice.

Officers and other ranks never mixed socially. However, they played sports together; and in field training and on active service, officers lived with their platoons, although company officers' messes were set up if possible. With every regiment, the strongest bond between all ranks was the regiment itself. This was a matter of pride and family loyalty, and it was reinforced by their local patriotism to their home county. As mentioned, all regiments had splendid fighting records, and some made much of their service in India, Egypt, the Peninsula, Waterloo, and other places where soldiers fought and died. Recruits were invariably indoctrinated. Cap badges also showed symbols of regimental history.

There were also subtle—although widely understood—differences between regiments. A number attracted aristocratic and wealthy officers, especially those who had family connections with it. These regiments were the three of Foot Guards (four from the beginning of the twentieth century); the two regiments of Rifles, known as Green Jackets; the six Highland infantry regiments; and the thirty-one of Cavalry. Added together, they accounted for less than 20 percent of the total strength of the army. There was snobbery because of the *cachet* possessed by each regiment, but this provided an extra dose of regimental pride. And although these fashionable regiments were in their special position because of their attraction to officers, all men in the ranks felt the same way. They were often known as crack regiments. One problem was that they produced an unusually—and perhaps unfairly—high number of generals (e.g. the number of army commanders in the First World War who came from the cavalry). However, Wolseley, from the infantry, and Roberts, from the artillery, were not handicapped.

The regimental system had another extraordinary feature. This was abolished by Cardwell in 1871, but it should be described briefly because of its importance at the time when Wolseley and Roberts first joined the army. This feature was the purchase of commissions.

The purchase of commissions for cash is a system with its roots in the Middle Ages, the era of feudalism, although the British army, as we know it, dated only from the seventeenth century. It was only partly true that the system existed because the money that came from purchase reduced the cost of national defence. The more important reason was that it ensured that the army was led by people of the highest social position and who had a stake in the country. Many leading figures like Wellington and Palmerston, who both became prime ministers, supported this view. Palmerston emphasized the importance of 'those whose property gave them an interest in the welfare of the country', and the danger of 'unprincipled military adventurers'.[8]

Despite these supremely upper-class English judgments, the purchase system had a devastating downside. Officers were not appointed because of their ability, and they were not even expected to have graduated from a military college. The system did nothing to encourage officers to develop military skills, the result of which brought another serious problem. Many senior officers were younger and therefore less experienced than many junior but older officers, and the latter had to spend long periods in their present positions, thus stultifying their ambition and energy.

In 1855, each rank had an official price, and this varied by regiment, e.g. a higher price reflecting the superior *cachet* of the Foot Guards. The purchase price for the rank of lieutenant colonel in these was £9,000; in the Cavalry, £7,250; and in the infantry of the Line, £4,500.[9] In the most fashionable regiments, the price was often bid up and could reach double the official amount. (There is no precise measure of the difference in the value of money between the mid-nineteenth century and the early twenty-first, but a reasonable approximation is to multiply the earlier figure by 100. This means that the highest rank in the Foot Guards would have a price of £900,000 in today's money, and it might even have been twice as much.) Officers climbed the ladder by buying a higher rank and, at the same time, selling their existing one. In 1855, an ensign's commission in the infantry of the Line cost £450. When he became a lieutenant, he paid £700, which meant an additional payment of £250. When a senior officer eventually retired, the value of the commission he sold would give him enough money to live on.

Purchase was only needed in the infantry and cavalry, and even then, there were limited exceptions. Officers who had replaced others who had died during their service were exempted. This is how Wolseley slipped into the army; there was no way in which he could have had the funds to purchase a commission. And purchase was not needed for the artillery and engineers, and this opened the door for Roberts.

During the half century following Waterloo, the army gradually lost its leanness and efficiency: the qualities that had enabled it to win the battles of the Peninsula and, finally, Waterloo. There was a slow increase in sloth and arthritic conservatism. The purchase system had its effect on this, and no one regretted its eventual abolition. The price of cavalry commissions was high: a reflection of the esteem in which the cavalry was held.

However, during the 1870s, the cavalry suddenly became an anachronism. For centuries, the shock effect of a cavalry charge with lances and sabres had been regarded as the most powerful force on the battlefield. But the great improvement in infantry firepower that came from magazine rifles fed by bolt action, and the first machine guns, meant that the infantry rapidly became the dominant fighting force. The cavalry charge held no fear for infantry, who could throw up a thick curtain of defensive fire. In the Second Boer War, the cavalry began to give way to mounted infantry. In the Russo-Japanese War of 1904–1905, a conflict of infantry and artillery, cavalry played no part. And shortly after the outbreak of the First World War in 1914, the two British regular cavalry divisions fought as infantry in the Ypres salient. After the Second Boer War, British cavalry regiments received new firearms: infantry rifles, the excellent Short Magazine Lee-Enfield (SMLE), in place of the lighter cavalry carbine. This change of weapons made it easier for the cavalry to fight as infantry in 1914. But this was temporary, because cavalry divisions were withdrawn and re-formed behind the lines. Their purpose was to exploit any breakthrough led by the infantry, the anticipated 'big push'. This was planned on many occasions, but no breakthrough took place, at least until August 1918.

Despite such disappointments, the innate conservatism of the British army ensured that the cavalry regiments retained their traditional *cachet*: their attraction to rich and aristocratic officers and the regimental pride felt by the NCOs and troopers. The cavalry retained this rather anomalous position until the 1930s, by which time most of the regiments had converted to tanks and armoured cars. During the Second World War, cavalry regiments fought in many heroic engagements despite the technical inferiority of most of their fighting vehicles. The prestige of these historic regiments was re-created in the North African desert and across the cultivated countryside of North-West Europe.

By the middle of the nineteenth century, the French army, with its Napoleonic heritage, was universally regarded as without equal. But it lost its pre-eminence with its defeat in 1871, when the Prussian army—which soon became the army of the German Empire—rapidly replaced it as the best in the world (incidentally becoming a model for the Japanese army at the time when the Japanese navy was modeled on the Royal Navy). The British army was always small, but after the reforms that transformed it during the early years of the twentieth century, it proved itself to be qualitatively better than any other. One long-range influence on this was that, after the abolition of purchase, all regular officers in the infantry and cavalry had to graduate from the Royal Military College, Sandhurst.

Garnet Wolseley, a newly commissioned ensign who had not been to Sandhurst, joined his regiment in 1852. It was the Eightieth of Foot, which later became a battalion of the South Staffordshire Regiment. He was later to show a sensitive understanding of how a regiment builds and reinforces self-esteem. In Wolseley's own words quoted earlier: 'No man who knew soldiers or their peculiar way of thinking, or who was acquainted with the many little trifles that go to make up *esprit de corps*, would ever deprive a soldier of any peculiarity that he prided himself on.'[10] Wolseley did not have to purchase his commission because he was the son of an officer who had died in the service. In fact, he had no private income, and it was fortunate that his regiment was in India, where he could live on his pay. With his instinctive understanding of soldiers and the bravery he was soon to demonstrate in battle, Wolseley showed himself to be a natural leader of men.

The Army of the Raj

All British soldiers—including native Indian troops, called sepoys—swore allegiance to authority, indicated by the ranks of officers and NCOs. But Britain is the only country that had two separate armies that operated independently in their own parts of the world. These were the British army and the Indian army. Neither was as large as the major European armies, but they were both high-quality regular forces. There were large numbers of British soldiers in the Indian army, but not vice versa.

The Indian subcontinent, with an area fourteen times as large as the British Isles, covered the countries that are today India, Pakistan, and Bangladesh. (Ceylon, now Sri Lanka, was a separate Crown Colony.) The subcontinent is a hot tropical country cooled by the annual monsoon. The temperature is much more comfortable in the hills to the north, and it became normal for British regiments to march to the hills before summer arrived. The population was eight times that of Britain, with more than three hundred million people before the First World War. India has more than thirty different languages, although Urdu/Hindi is a *lingua franca*, and so is English to a more limited degree. The two main religions were (and still are) Hinduism and Islam. Islam came with the powerful Mughal Empire in the north that ruled most of India in the sixteenth century, after which it retreated north again. (Pakistan was a splinter from the Muslim territory in the north-west.) India provided a classic example of Malthusian poverty: with a growing population absorbing any increase in income, e.g. from better farming. This was sometimes called the "Iron Law" and remained a chronic condition until the mid-twentieth century, although it encouraged fit young men to enlist in the Indian army which, during the Second World War, became the largest volunteer army in the world.

British merchants started trading in India during the sixteenth century. They found tea, rice, spices, and various raw materials to export to England. And after a time, they also brought English goods to import into India. In 1600, a commercial organization that had grown rapidly was given a royal charter to operate as a monopoly in trade in the east. This was the Honourable East India Company. The French and Portuguese also traded in India, but over time, the East India Company fought local wars and took over territory that had formerly been in the hands of other European countries. The company made allies of local rulers, and before long, it was itself ruling much of the country, with the support of Indian soldiers commanded by British officers. The early years of the East India Company were a reversal of the normal process of trade following the flag. It was a case of the flag following trade.

Before the end of the eighteenth century, the British government began to realize that it would have to take over much of the control of the company's affairs. This was necessary because of its engagement in diplomacy and even warfare. An important step was that the British government began to take over by weakening the Court of Directors, who represented the shareholders and who nominally ran all the business of the company. A Board of Control, appointed by the British government, eventually took over most of the running, which included appointments in the Indian Civil Service and the Indian army (which did not have the purchase system).

By 1822, the East India Company controlled most of western and central India. More territory came as a result of wars, notably the two Sikh wars of 1845 and 1848, and a number of wars in Burma. However, no progress was made on the barren North-West Frontier, from where an invasion of Afghanistan in 1839 turned into a costly and futile enterprise. An important change took place in 1833, when the East India Company relinquished its commercial activity and devoted itself totally to government. In 1853, the Board of Control took over complete responsibility for Indian appointments.

Also in 1853, a governor general was appointed, located in Calcutta. (The move to New Delhi only took place during the 1920s.) The Indian army commander-in-chief, who reported to the governor general, exercised command over three districts, based in Calcutta in the northeast, Madras in the south, and Bombay on the west coast. The Indian army had two elements. The first was the East India Company army: mainly native regiments, but some recruited from British men who were not British regular soldiers. (The native regiments had, in the senior ranks, British officers who had knowledge of Urdu and sometimes other native languages.) The second part was made up of units of the British regular army on garrison duty in India. The normal system was for one British infantry battalion to serve in the same brigade as three Indian battalions, and one British cavalry regiment with two Indian regiments. British officers in native regiments normally spent their whole careers in India. But British officers in each garrison battalion returned to Britain when the battalion's tour of duty had finished.

The Indian army was popular with British officers, and because of the higher pay and lower cost of living, it attracted many of the best cadets from Sandhurst and Woolwich. In addition, the Indian army had its own college in Addiscombe (which closed in 1861). Roberts graduated from both Woolwich and Addiscombe and was commissioned in the Royal Artillery and went to India in 1851. During the 1850s, the Indian army was made up of 352,000 men: 314,000 (89 percent) in the East India Company army, and 38,000 (11 percent) British regular soldiers.[11] The Artillery had a preponderance of British over Indian troops: 10,600 men of whom two-thirds were British.

Short in height, with sprouting whiskers and a very businesslike manner, Roberts was only nineteen when he was commissioned in 1851. Note the parallel with Wolseley, who was an almost direct contemporary. They were both teenagers, both relatively impecunious, and both ambitious to build a career in India. About five years after their arrival, grumbling resentment of British rule led to a catastrophic breakdown of discipline. The specific cause was the new Enfield rifle, which had a cartridge that contained the gunpowder propellant to fire it. The cartridge, which a sepoy had to tear apart with his teeth, was greased with animal fat. Using grease from oxen is deeply offensive to Hindus because the animal is sacred to them. And pork fat is repulsive to Muslims because their religion treats pigs as unclean animals. Many native regiments mutinied in 1857, and the insurrection was suppressed with great brutality by British troops led by officers who ruled with an iron fist.

After the mutiny, the British garrison was made much larger. And although the British government eventually made efforts to invite educated Indians to take part in running the country, the attitude of most British people living there was antagonistic. The British rank and file, in particular, were contemptuous of the native population.[12] Roberts's part in fighting mutinous troops made his name. However, he afterwards became increasingly disturbed by the hostility between the British and the Indians. During his long career in the subcontinent, he aimed for friendship, and eventually his native soldiers gave him the affectionate title of *Bobs Bahadur*. Establishing a rapport with his Indian-born troops became an important theme throughout his military life.

Endnotes

1. Housman, A. E., *A Shropshire Lad*, Poem xxv (London: Penguin Random House, 2010).

2. Wolseley, Garnet, *The Soldier's Pocket-Book for Field Service* (London: Macmillan, 1882), 4.

3. Broad, Roger, *The Radical General. Sir Ronald Adam and Britain's New Model Army, 1941–1946.* (Stroud, Gloucestershire: Spellmount, 2013), 26.

4. Money Barnes, R., *The British Army in 1914* (London: Seeley Service, 1968). Contains many accurate and interesting details of the British army.

5. Wolseley, *The Soldier's Pocket-Book*, 3–4.

6. Richards, Frank, *Old Soldier Sahib* (London: Faber & Faber, 1936), 156.

7. Heathcote, T. A., *The Indian Army* (Newton Abbot, UK, 1974), 142. Succinct history of the Indian army, 1822–1922.

8. Maurice, F., *The Life of Lord Wolseley* (New York: Doubleday, Page, 1924), 8.

9. Heathcote, *The Indian Army*, 118.

10. Wolseley, *The Soldier's Pocket-Book*, 3.

11. Mollo, Boris, *The Indian Army* (Poole, Dorset: New Orchard 1981), 87. Heathcote, *The Indian Army*, 201. Heathcote gives lower figures than Mollo. I have chosen the Mollo alternatives because his book was published later.

12. Richards, *Old Soldier Sahib*. Full of shocking comments by British soldiers in the ranks expressing contempt for the Indian population.

CHAPTER 3

BURMA AND THE CRIMEA: WOLSELEY'S 'GOOD AND GALLANT CONDUCT'[1]

Military memoirs are written by senior officers whose careers have provided much to talk about. They reach high rank because they win battles, or at least command armies and navies and effectively prepare them for war. They do this by instilling discipline and pride, selecting and promoting talent, and ferocious training in the field. Most memoirs tell the stories of the later stages of the author's career and explain why he became celebrated. This approach seems, to me, to be inadequate. The early years are equally—if not more—important.

Ranks in the armed services are like a pyramid, with large numbers of officers at the bottom and progressively fewer as a man moves up. Competition therefore becomes increasingly heated at each upward step in the pyramid.[2] An officer's early career is particularly important, because if he manages to leap ahead of his contemporaries during his first few years, seniority will keep him ahead, and his personality may produce some further jumps. But if an officer makes a slow start, it becomes progressively difficult for him to catch up.

Promotion is the result of five factors: an officer's seniority in his rank, the money to purchase the next step up (until the system was abolished in the 1870s), his proven ability, the patronage from which he has benefited (a more important factor in the nineteenth century than it is today), and—surprisingly—luck. Garnet Wolseley forged ahead at the beginning of his career, and the only factor that drove him forward was his ability. He had no other advantage. He left his own modest account of his early service years, with their hardships, valour, and glory. He was a prolific writer, with a style that was clear and accurate, fast-paced and vivid. If his writing lacked the flash of originality that would make it great literature, this is also true of the vast majority of military writing. Wolseley's ability to write is a tribute to his good but rather unusual early education.

Wolseley was born on 4 June 1833, the oldest of seven children. His family had its roots in the English Midlands, with origins traceable to before the Norman Conquest. The name *Wolseley* is a contraction of the words *Ousley* and *Wislia*, tracts of land in Staffordshire possessed by the family in the tenth century. The Wolseley family provided many army officers in both the cavalry and the infantry. During the eighteenth century, they spent much time fighting and on garrison duty in Ireland and settled there as members of the English Protestant establishment. However, the family fortunes gradually declined. Wolseley's father and uncle served in an English infantry regiment in the West Indies, a quiet and unglamorous station. Wolseley *père* sold his commission when he was a major and died not long afterwards, when his eldest son was seven.

Wolseley's mother, to whom he was deeply attached, was twenty-five years younger than her husband. As a widow, she did not have the money to send her children to fee-paying boarding schools; but at Garnet Wolseley's day-school in Dublin, he was given an excellent basic education. He was encouraged to read widely, especially English history and the classics. He left school when he was fourteen and got a job in a land surveyor's office in Dublin. He continued his education in the evening; and during the day, at his office, he learned draughtsmanship and freehand drawing, which were later useful to him when, as a young officer, he was asked to make maps and topographical sketches. Surprisingly, in March 1852, he was able to receive an ensign's commission without purchase. This was because of a regulation that a commission could be provided *pro bono* to the son of an officer who had died after long service. Without any military training at all—and before his nineteenth birthday—Wolseley was commissioned into the Eightieth Regiment of Foot, first raised in 1793. It had been formerly known as the South Staffordshire Regiment (a name that it readopted after the Cardwell Reforms in the 1870s).

By 1815, the British army, commanded by Wellington, had become a superb instrument of war. But it was to be almost forty years before the army was next ranged against a major European enemy. The long years of peace meant that the British government lost interest in its army. The force that served in many parts of the world was in the hands of seven different bodies in London that managed small parts, with no coordination between them. Another problem was that the purchase of commissions did not encourage ambition and the development of professional skills in peacetime. The Indian army fought a number of local wars, but there was a wall between it and the home army. Despite the defeat of the French in 1815, Napoleon's legendary reputation lingered, and the French army was generally considered the best in the world.

The Psychology of Leadership

When Wolseley began to write his memoirs, he only managed to complete two volumes, which took his life up to the age of forty.[3] He then had to put the job on hold because his career was, at that time, reaching its apex. His description of his early years as an officer, written in the memoirs and based on the diary he kept at the time, provides a remarkable insight into aspects of the character and personality of the young Wolseley.

At the end of June 1852, Wolseley embarked on a troop ship bound for India. It was a sailing vessel with 150 soldiers and some family members on board, and the voyage took a slow and interrupted fifty days. This was tedious but uneventful. Wolseley, active as ever, determined to use his time for his own benefit. He took his first lessons in Hindustani. He made sketches of the places where the ship made brief landings. He read as widely as he could. And he kept physically fit by scrambling constantly over the rigging and helping to unfurl the sails in the company of the ordinary seamen. Wolseley's lifetime habit was to study life around him.

He kept a diary. In private, he did not withhold criticism of senior officers. And his youthful opinions about colonial conquest were clear and direct, although not at all appealing to twenty-first-century readers. Wolseley was ambitious, and his attitude to colonialism was a driving force behind his military career:

> 'Conquering races may be inferior as poets, artists, and writers to those they subdue, but the latter would not have been subdued had they retained the manly virtues that made their forebears great. National greatness can only continue to thrive whilst it has fighting strength for its foundation.'[4]

Wolseley did not have long to wait before he experienced colonialism in practice; he was impressed by what he saw. But even before that, he received a reminder of its heritage. When his ship landed at Calcutta, those on board heard salutes fired by the artillery of the garrison, following the news that the Duke of Wellington had just died. Before Wellington's triumphant campaign in the Peninsula and his defeat of Napoleon at Waterloo, he had been a 'sepoy general' who had won his spurs in battles on the Indian subcontinent. Wolseley thought Wellington a rather cold figure and admired Napoleon more. When the youthful Wolseley was sailing back to Britain after being wounded in Burma, his ship stopped at St. Helena, and he made a sketch of the house in which Napoleon had lived during his exile.

India during the mid-nineteenth century was known, all too accurately, as the 'sloth-belt'. Newly arrived troops were assembled in camps and carried out desultory training until they were dispatched to their various units in different parts of the country. The junior officers had few duties and spent their time shooting snipe, taking pot-shots at buildings (particularly the clock on the church tower), and holding parties as lavish as they could afford on their meagre pay.

Wolseley was soon sent to join the Eightieth Regiment in Rangoon in southern Burma. Burma was an independent kingdom plagued by banditry from lawless tribes called dacoits. The country is mountainous and jungle-covered and has a border with India's eastern flank. It is split by two large rivers, the Chindwin and the Irrawaddy, that run from north to south. War had broken out in 1852 when the Royal Navy had sent a frigate to Rangoon to make sure that British merchants could conduct their business in peace. This frigate was fired on, and British troops entered the city, and plans were made to move north. The British encampment in Rangoon was a large, strong timber stockade. One perennial problem was that the army was being weakened by cholera, a then-mortal disease that spread rapidly through the ranks and made for constant difficulties with military plans.

It was here that Wolseley learned enough parade ground drill to carry out efficiently the duties of a subaltern. Even more importantly, he learned some of the secrets of personal command. He learned from his sergeant the way in which the commissioned and non-commissioned ranks worked together, with the junior officers absorbing the secrets of man-management from the senior NCOs. He also began to understand the subtle psychology of the rank and file and how to get the most from the soldiers: simple but occasionally bloody-minded former farm boys. A young officer had to make sure that his orders registered with the troops so that they would not make the same mistakes twice.

Wolseley reported to Colonel Grattan of the Royal Irish, an eccentric but highly experienced officer. Wolseley was on picket duty and gave three privates a routine order. However, they would not cooperate. Quite correctly, they were charged with a serious offence and had to appear the next morning in Colonel Grattan's orderly room. They were marched in with rigid formality, and Wolseley gave his evidence, after which everyone waited for the colonel's response:

> 'I looked at the sergeant-major; his face was wooden and devoid of all expression as he stolidly looked straight before him into nothing. In a moment, a volley of oaths from the colonel relieved the atmospheric pressure. He called the

prisoners "limbs of Satan," and choking, partly at least, I should say, from an assumed fury, and partly because his vituperative vocabulary had come to an end, he jumped to his feet, upsetting the table, with its ink bottle, papers etc., and rushed upon the prisoners, kicking hard at the nearest, and crying aloud: "Get out, ye blackguards; never let me see you again.""[5]

During his time in Rangoon, Wolseley studied the Burmese people and found them more attractive than the Bengalis he had met in India. He was also impressed by Buddhism and thought it had much to teach Christianity. He went alone on long rides, sketching the countryside. However, he became anxious that the fighting would leave him behind, and he could not wait to go to Prome, the forward English base one hundred miles north of Rangoon.

In early 1853, trouble broke out when dacoits seized a strong position north of the river crossing at Donnabew, twenty-five miles beyond Prome. A hastily mounted expeditionary force was sent up the Irrawaddy under the command of a captain in the Royal Navy. This was a disaster, and the captain was killed. Wolseley was still at Rangoon, but he was soon ordered north. His voyage up the river was on a crowded, uncomfortable boat. The river was muddy and flowed south with a strong current, and this delayed matters. (See **Map 1**.)

In the second week in March, two days after Wolseley had landed, the new and larger relieving force began to move forward through an unpleasant countryside of jungle, tracks, and creeks. The British force totaled one thousand men, put together from a number of subunits of British and Indian regiments. The officers and men wore thick European uniforms, including buckskin gloves: a costume that Wolseley thought absurd. (Later in his career, Wolseley introduced more suitable tropical uniforms.) He soon got to know some of the senior officers and developed a high opinion of them. The dacoits they would be facing were primitive but tough, and armed with the dah, the Burmese sword that doubled as a woodcutting tool. They also had many ancient smooth-bore muskets that fired a heavy shot. The British soldiers had the ancient and reliable Brown Bess smooth-bore musket with a bore of three-quarters of an inch. The force included two light artillery pieces.

Because of the dense terrain, the British force was broken down into independent detachments, one of which was commanded by Wolseley. He spread his men out in a skirmishing line, and they soon came under desultory fire, which attracted more curiosity than terror. At the end of the day, they lit fires and made a bivouac. Wolseley wandered over to a nearby stream, where engineers were building barrel rafts that would be fastened together to make a bridge. He lent a useful hand because he had read a military manual on the work. The scene of the bridge-building was very busy, with many bullocks which became restive because of the continuing enemy fire.

Cholera was still rife, and Wolseley lost some men to it. They were buried before the bodies were reached by the vultures flying overhead. Wolseley was nevertheless confident that his first command was in good shape, although he was often exhausted through marching over rough ground after sleepless nights on picket duty. Every day that passed brought them closer to the enemy position, and they could soon hear the noise of the enemy cutting wood to reinforce their stockade. Fog was usually on the ground, but it lifted with the heat of the day.

Wolseley, for a time, took the point position—the furthest position in the advance—accompanied by four young soldiers who would all be hit by musketry fire before the battle came to an end. It was now 19 March, and the enemy stockade was at last visible, only a hundred yards away. The enemy was not alert, and Wolseley and his men had not yet been seen. A senior major of the British force joined him and was told the situation. This led to the British force forming a rough line to assault the enemy position, which would eventually lead to victory.

The enemy woke up at last to what was happening, and they began a rapid but inaccurate fire. Inexperienced troops fire high, and this is what the Burmese did. Nevertheless, there were a number of casualties among the British officers and men. As Wolseley and his party advanced, he came across a number of Bengali troops who were cowering in terror, but there were also a number of Sikhs who showed exemplary bravery. (British officers serving in India usually had a higher opinion of the

Muslim and Sikh 'martial races' from the north-west than the more easy-going Hindu races from the north-east.)

In the meantime, Wolseley took his men very quietly along a nullah—a stream bed—that led to the left. His intention was to reach a position from which his men would be in an excellent place to assault the enemy. The general now arrived and immediately saw the value of Wolseley's concealed route. He then called for a volunteer to form and lead a storming party to charge the enemy position. This is exactly what Wolseley had been hoping for, and he and another young officer volunteered for the job. The effort was mounted in a rush, and the enemy fully expected it and encouraged the charging troops with ironic shouting. Unfortunately, this first assault went off at half-cock. Wolseley fell into a concealed mantrap, and by the time he had got out of it, his men had melted away. He ran to the rear for his life.

The general now called for a fresh storming party, and Wolseley and another young officer, Lieutenant Taylor, assembled as many men as possible and dashed forward, carefully avoiding the mantrap that had caught Wolseley. There was also a good deal of help from the two small artillery pieces that moved up to fire at the enemy over open sights. The adrenaline was now flowing:

> 'In a long and varied military life, I have never experienced the same unalloyed and elevating satisfaction, or known again the joy I then felt as I ran for the enemy's stockades at the head of a small mob of soldiers, most of them boys like myself.'[6]

But before the triumphant soldiers reached the enemy positions, both Wolseley and Taylor had been hit—Wolseley with a large wound from a musket ball at the top of his left thigh. He barely made it: a regimental doctor arrived and applied a tourniquet that staunched the flow of blood. Taylor had an even more serious wound and, alas, bled to death. The Victoria Cross was introduced during the Crimean War, only three years after Wolseley's gallant action. It has always been more often a reward for heroic success than for heroic failure. There is little doubt that if Wolseley and Taylor had fought in Burma three years later, they would have received that incomparable decoration.

Wolseley had a painful and uncomfortable journey by boat along creeks and down the Irrawaddy back to Rangoon, where he spent some weeks of recovery. He was still unfit when he boarded a large ship that travelled to Calcutta, then to various islands in the Indian Ocean and around Africa, eventually reaching England. For his service in Burma, he received an official commendation. When he got to England, he was promoted lieutenant without purchase and transferred to the Ninetieth Light Infantry, which had been raised in 1794, and was stationed in Dublin. He was still under twenty. The Ninetieth became a battalion of the Cameronians at the time of the Cardwell Reforms.

The Ninetieth, being Light Infantry, was regarded, professionally and socially, as a step above the infantry of the Line. Light Infantry drill originated in the Peninsular War, and even today, works at a fast, urgent pace. In 1854, the regiment received the new Minié rifle, which fired pointed bullets and was more accurate than the old Brown Bess. But it was still only suitable for volley firing. It was not until the end of the nineteenth century that greatly superior rifles made it possible for many infantry soldiers to fire rapidly and become marksmen (and receive extra pay for it.)

Winter in the Crimea

By the middle of the nineteenth century, the Ottoman Empire, 'the sick man of Europe,' had become feeble and vulnerable. It was ruled by a sultan, a hereditary figure of high prestige. But he was a weak ruler, although his court in Constantinople, to which foreign ambassadors were accredited, was known as the Sublime Porte. The territory of the empire was geographically huge, comprising Turkey, the Arab countries of the Middle East, and North Africa and the Balkans. The Balkans are Slav peoples in Eastern Europe who came under Russia's influence because the Russians are also Slavs, and the Russian czars were always ambitious to find groups of people whom they could dominate. Russia had a population of eighty million, in a highly polarized society: vast numbers of illiterate peasants; a small but immensely rich aristocracy; and the czar an autocrat who deployed an army of a million men who were ill-armed but brave and hardy.

Russia, always anxious to protect the fifteen million Orthodox Christians in the Balkans, was constantly at loggerheads with the Ottoman Empire. There was also a dispute in Jerusalem, where the Turks entrusted the protection of the Christian holy places to the Roman Catholics, not the Orthodox. Russian demands on the Ottoman Empire came to a head, and this led to a breakdown in diplomacy. Turkey declared war in October 1853, and this was followed by a number of Turkish defeats in the Balkans.

Meanwhile, Britain and France came on the scene. Britain had long been suspicious of Russian designs on India, and the difficult relationship between the two countries over Asia was known as 'The Great Game.' France was closely concerned with the position of the Roman Catholics in Jerusalem. The French emperor Napoleon III, with the ambition but not the ability of his uncle Napoleon I, was anxious to make his presence felt on the international scene; and he was joined by a small ally, Sardinia, which was independent before Italy was united. British and French warships exchanged fire with some Russians in November 1853, and this significantly increased the temperature. The English and French declared war on Russia in March 1854, followed by preparations for military and naval invasions of Russia in the Black Sea and the eastern Baltic.[7] Operations in the Baltic were to be much less important than those in the Crimea, where the British army dispatched an expeditionary force. The two Western nations had blundered into the war. During the following months, they were to fight with spectacular ineptitude, the British suffering 30 percent casualties.

The Crimea is a peninsula shaped like a lozenge on its side, and it measures 150 miles from north to south and 200 miles from west to east. It has different types of terrain: open plains and, to the west, extensive high ground and inlets in the coast. The naval base of Sebastopol and the port used by the British at Balaklava were in the west. Across the

Black Sea, Constantinople is 350 miles to the south-west from the southern tip of the Crimea. (See **Map 2**.)

Invading the heartland of Russia was not a serious operation of war, as Napoleon found and Hitler was later to discover. But assaulting the isolated peninsula of the Crimea was a way to focus on the Russian navy and the country's main sea route across the Black Sea. Anglo-French success in the Crimea and continued Turkish control of the straits between Asia and Europe would mean that Russia would be cut off from its most important link to the West. The first British units were sent to the Crimea in February 1854. The British commander-in-chief was Field Marshal Lord Raglan, a famous soldier who lost his right arm in the Battle of Waterloo. However, he had led an inactive life since then and was not physically fit. During his first two years in the Crimea, he found his load too heavy. He died in June 1855, many soldiers believing that he died of a broken heart.

After the first few months of the war, which had seen two major battles, British military strength at home was being run down: both the number of troops and important military equipment (in particular, artillery). The troops who left for the Crimea were given the Minié rifles that had been in the hands of the Ninetieth Regiment. When, in turn, the Ninetieth went to war, they were armed with the old Brown Bess muskets. The British fought in their normal flamboyant uniforms, the Foot Guards wearing bearskins. One feature of the Crimean War made it fascinating. It was the first major conflict that was recorded by photography. The British strength in the Crimea was much less than the French, to which a number of Turkish units were attached. At the Battle of the Alma in September 1854, there were only 20,000 British troops, with many battalions with far too few men in the ranks.[8]

The Ninetieth Light Infantry departed by steamship and, in unpleasant winter weather, arrived in Balaklava harbour in early December 1854. In October, the British had fought the Battle of Balaklava, which included the disastrous Charge of the Light Brigade. The Ninetieth was at full strength, with 840 officers and men. They were badly needed because the British had suffered severe losses at the Battle of Inkerman in early November. Young Wolseley was highly critical of

British logistics—food and supplies—mishandled by everybody from the War Office down, and in his diary, he was full of unfavourable comments about senior British officers and, in particular, the British military staff. The shocking British inefficiency in their care of the wounded and the supply of hot food was to lead to major changes during and after the war. Before the arrival of the Ninetieth, a good deal of fighting had already taken place, and Sebastopol had by now been besieged by the French and British armies.

The Ninetieth were soon on picket duty in the ravines running east in the mountains near Sebastopol. Each company of one hundred men was on duty for twenty-four hours in dangerous outposts in cold wintry weather. Wolseley was the only one of the three officers in his company who had campaigning experience, which meant that he had the job of arranging the routine duties of the NCOs and men. After this experience of picket duty, the British troops occupied trenches in the rear. Their supplies of ammunition were severely limited because it all had to be manhandled forward from Balaklava. At the end of his long career, Wolseley wrote a letter for publication about the appalling sloppiness of these transport arrangements. The Russians, in their fixed positions, had no such problem.

Siege warfare demands engineers, and Wolseley made a sideways move at the beginning of 1855. He became an assistant engineer because the Royal Engineers did not have enough officers and were forced to borrow some junior officers from the infantry regiments. Initially, Wolseley was given simple jobs in the trenches, e.g. draining ditches. The engineers' positions were dangerous because they were both at the forward edge of the infantry positions and with the artillery batteries, whose positions were known to the enemy. Some of the staunchest gunners were sailors from the Royal Navy. The newcomers like Wolseley were not welcomed at first, but before long, he started making friends among the sappers. The worst problem was the weather: rain, snow and mud, and the total lack of wood to make fires to cook food. The life of the engineers could be described as tense watchfulness, and Wolseley made occasional efforts to add some excitement by night-time patrolling to within a short distance of the enemy lines.

Among the sapper officers whom Wolseley met in the trenches was a subaltern who made a great impression on him. His name was Charles Gordon, a man who would influence Wolseley's life.

> 'He was a good-looking, curly-haired young man of my own age. His full, clear and bright blue eyes seemed to court scrutiny, whilst at the same time they searched into your inner soul. His absolute single-mindedness of purpose startled me at times, for it made me feel how inferior I was to him in all the higher qualities of character.'[9]

After an adventurous career in China, Gordon later became the governor of the Sudan, where he was besieged in Khartoum in 1884. And it was Wolseley who mounted a relief expedition that made a desperate but vain effort to rescue him.

At last, in clear summer weather, the Anglo-French forces prepared a major assault on the Russian positions, in the ring of fortifications two miles east of Sebastopol. Photographs and sketches dating from the war show each military fort containing a glacis, and walls constructed of stones, bricks, timber, sandbags, and gabions (large baskets of thick tree branches filled with stones).[10] There were also heavy guns and mortars in strong positions. After being fought over, each fort was badly mauled but were still good defensive positions.

On 6 June 1854, 600 guns started bombarding the Russian positions, which had been dug in with great skill. However, with 30,000 heavy shells landing on the Russian guns, these were finally silenced on 7 June. The British assault on a fortification in a group of quarries was led by Colonel Campbell of the Ninetieth Light Infantry. The French carried out separate assaults on the British right. Wolseley initially led a party of officers and men in the engineers, but he soon had to take over an infantry company whose commander had been killed. In the infantry assault, Wolseley was hit in the right thigh and suffered a bloody flesh wound, although this did not put him out of action. The British took the position in the quarry but soon lost it in a Russian counter-attack. For his bravery during this fighting, Wolseley was recommended for the Victoria Cross.[11] The fact that he did not receive it may have been due to a superior officer's view that the operation had not been a complete success. (As mentioned earlier, VCs for heroism in unsuccessful operations are even more rare that those in successful ones.) Close-quarter fighting in all the Russian defensive positions continued intermittently until 9 August 1855, when Sebastopol was evacuated. All this time, Wolseley was carrying out his engineering work, but he had the ill luck to be badly wounded on 30 August. This time he was hit in the head, his left cheek and jaw were badly damaged, and he lost the sight in his right eye.

He was now out of action. However, on 8 October, an unusual official report was written about him.[12] This came from the Horse Guards in London and was sent to the Royal Engineers. It made extremely favourable remarks about the young Wolseley (the title of this chapter contains an extract from it). This report proposed that Wolseley should be promoted to the rank of major. However, this was not immediately possible because of a regulation that demanded six years' service to qualify for a majority. Nevertheless, he was soon offered a major's job. He became a staff officer, a deputy assistant quartermaster general, which needed skill but was not a dangerous job. He was given the task of surveying the battlegrounds.

Wolseley spent his second winter in the Crimea and continued there until the autumn of 1856. After the evacuation of Sebastopol in August 1855, the war seemed to be running down. The Russian army dug in on the heights above the port, and the result was a stalemate. The armies opposing the Russians had achieved little, despite the loss of many lives. (The British army had nineteen thousand men killed, and the French even more.) The war can best be judged as a defensive victory for the Russians, and it had no long-term consequences. Peace negotiations began in Vienna in February 1856, and a peace treaty was signed at the end of March.

Wolseley, having completed his staff assignment and taken some leave, returned to the Ninetieth Light Infantry and joined the regiment in Aldershot in 1856. He was now twenty-three and had served for four years. In that time, he had fought in two wars. He had been severely wounded twice. His work had been favourably noted in official reports, and his name had been put forward for the Victoria Cross. He had been promoted on merit from ensign to lieutenant and then to captain. And although he had been recommended for a majority he had not served long enough to receive it. However he did a major's job as a staff officer for a number of months. He became a brevet major in the spring of 1858, when he was in India. A brevet rank was recognition of ability and drive. As a reward for outstanding service, an officer could receive a higher, or brevet, rank which did not mean extra pay but counted towards seniority. This meant accelerated promotion on merit.

The beginning of this chapter argues that if a young officer begins his career with a flying start, he has a good chance of maintaining the impetus. This proposition will be used to evaluate Wolseley's subsequent career.

Endnotes

1. The reference to 'good and gallant conduct' comes from an official report on Wolseley's performance in the Crimea. See endnote 12.
2. Since this book is about the British army during the nineteenth century, it is not necessary to refer to soldiers as men and women. And since the book describes Wolseley's career, it is appropriate to confine the discussion of ranks to commissioned officers.
3. Wolseley, Field Marshal Viscount, *The Story of a Soldier's Life, Volume I, Volume II* (London: Archibald Constable, 1903).
4. Ibid., *Volume I,* 20.
5. Ibid., *Volume I,* 34.
6. Ibid., *Volume I,* 70.
7. Chesney, Kellow, *A Crimean War Reader* (London: Severn House, 1975). Judd, Denis, *The Crimean War* (London: Book Club Associates, 1976). Palmer, Alan, *The Crimean War* (New York: Dorset Press, 1987).
8. Judd, *The Crimean War,* 185–186.
9. Wolseley, *The Story of a Soldier's Life, Volume I,* 148.
10. Chesney, *A Crimean War Reader,* Plates 7, 8, 22, 23.
11. Maurice, F., and Arthur, G., *The Life of Lord Wolseley* (New York: Doubleday, Page, 1924), 19.
12. On 8 October 1855, a letter of recommendation was sent by the Horse Guards in London, and this included the following words:

> 'Having laid before the Field Marshal Commanding in Chief the letter which you forwarded from Lieutenant General Sir H. Jones, reporting the zealous and meritorious manner in which Captain Wolseley, of the Ninetieth Regiment, assistant engineer, had performed his duty in the trenches, and stating the high opinion which you entertain of that officer, whose uniform zeal and good and gallant conduct you consider to render him deserving of promotion . . .'

CHAPTER 4

LIEUTENANT ROBERTS IN INDIA: 'THE WONDERFUL LAND OF MY ADOPTION'

When Frederick Roberts arrived in Calcutta to begin his service in India, he was following a well-trodden path. For more than two centuries, there had been a connection at many levels between Britain and India. The East India Company stimulated continuous trade between the two countries. Great fortunes were often made—a process that someone with a humorous imagination called 'shaking the Pagoda tree'—and these fortunes were, in many cases, large enough to buy country estates in the Shires (and in one case, to found an American university, Yale, in New Haven, Connecticut). For centuries, tea has been, by far, the most popular British beverage. Most came from plantations in Assam and Ceylon, all owned or managed by British planters.

The connections between the two countries in government and administration were even more important than the commercial ones, because India was a colony until the end of the Raj in 1947. Ultimate control was in the hands of the Secretary of State for India, who was in the cabinet in London. In India, the viceroy ruled in great state in Calcutta and, during the 1920s, in Delhi. British control was absolute, although the Indians were gradually invited to participate as they gained experience.

Young British men of the 'officer class' were attracted to careers in India because they were better paid than in similar positions in Britain, and the cost of living was lower. Servants were plentiful and cheap. Applicants for the jobs in India had to be suitably qualified by background and education, and most came from the top 5 percent of families: those who also provided officers for the British army and the Royal Navy. The young men who went to India entered government administration—later known as the Indian Civil Service (ICS)—and ruled substantial districts as commissioners and also acted as political advisers to the quasi-independent princely states, held commissions in the Indian army, received cadetships in the Indian police, and followed many other callings, *inter alia*, as lawyers, medical practitioners, educators, engineers, agriculturalists, and foresters.

At the higher levels of government, senior army officers held some of the most important administrative posts normally the province of the Civil Service. Abraham Roberts, father of Frederick Roberts, held senior civil appointments.

These government jobs developed during the long years of East India Company control. However, everything became more rigid and formalized after the mutiny, when the East India Company was wound up. In particular, entrance into the ICS was carefully controlled. The total number of positions was one thousand, and the members were sometimes referred to as the 'white nabobs'. Entry was now restricted to university graduates (mainly confined to Oxford and Cambridge), followed by a tough written examination and interviews. During the twentieth century, a small number of Indian-born applicants managed to get in. Family tradition of service in India was commonly passed from father to son, as in the Masters family. John Masters, in 1947, was a lieutenant colonel in 4 Gurkha Rifles. His family had produced Indian army officers in a continuous line spanning every generation since the beginning of the nineteenth century. Although Masters had made a considerable reputation during the Second World War, there was no future for British officers in India in 1947. Most of the regiments remained in the Indian and Pakistan armies, but all the officers were native-born. Masters eventually became an American citizen and an author with a worldwide reputation. A number of his books give a vivid insider view of regiments of the old Indian army, including his own.[1] The title of this chapter comes from Frederick Roberts's memoirs.[2] He had followed his father into the Indian army. As with all such families, the close connection with Britain was carefully nurtured. The land of his adoption did not supplant the land of his family origin. Children were invariably sent to Britain for their education.

Marriage between British and Indians was a sensitive issue. British attitudes were relaxed before the mutiny (an attitude to mixed marriages that continued among the Dutch in the Dutch East Indies until the country, renamed Indonesia, became independent). But after the mutiny, British attitudes hardened, and mixed marriages were actively discouraged. This applied to the 'officer class'. Many NCOs in British regiments on garrison duty in India married Indian wives, and they often stayed in India after their discharge and had well-paying jobs running the Indian railways.

The 'Mere Handful'

The 'mere handful' refers to the capable and dedicated British men who were able 'to direct the administration of a country with nearly three hundred millions of inhabitants, differing in race, religion, and manners of life'. These words were written by Roberts himself.[3] Britain always had reserves of talented and ambitious men who wanted to make careers abroad, and these became explorers and empire-builders.

Frederick Sleigh Roberts was born on 30 September 1832 in India, at Cawnpore, where his father was serving. His family was Irish, members of the Protestant establishment. The only unusual branch on the family tree came from a lady who was the daughter of a Huguenot who had been expelled from France when the Edict of Nantes was revoked in 1685.[4]

The Roberts family provided many officers in the army and navy. Frederick Roberts's father, Sir Abraham Roberts, built his career in the Indian army until he was a major general, when he had to return to Britain for reasons of his health. He ended his service as a full general (known today as a four-star rank). The general's brother, Samuel, was an admiral who had a splendid fighting record and was also knighted. Abraham Roberts married a widow with two children, and they had five children of their own. When Frederick Roberts was two, mother and seven children returned to Ireland to take care of the children's education. During his childhood, Frederick Roberts was considered to be 'delicate', with a supposedly 'weak heart' and digestive problems. In his twenties, he had a number of serious bouts of fever. Nevertheless, he was to have a long and physically active career.

With seven children to be educated, the Roberts family was financially stretched, but they just managed to educate all the children privately. The young Frederick Roberts was given a preparatory education that enabled him to pass into Eton at the age of thirteen. He only spent a year there, too short a period to make any mark, although he won a prize for mathematics.

The next stage of his education was unorthodox. He was removed from Eton, and at the age of fourteen, he entered the Royal Military College, Sandhurst, where he spent two years. The entrance examination was very simple but became much more difficult in the 1870s. At this time, Roberts did not consider a career in the technical branches of the army because all potential officers in the engineers and artillery had to graduate from the Royal Military Academy, Woolwich. (This was the route taken by Roberts's contemporary Charles Gordon, 'Gordon of Khartoum,' whom Wolseley was soon to meet in the Crimea.) When commissions were purchased, cavalry and infantry officers were normally commissioned direct from civil life. Sandhurst was therefore something extra, although the college provided an excellent basic military education. It only became obligatory during the 1870s, when purchase was abolished. Roberts was successful and popular at Sandhurst. He was nicknamed 'Deductions' because of his mathematical skill—a useful accomplishment for a gunner officer.

Roberts had always intended to go into the Indian army, joining the 'mere handful' referred to in the title of this section. To increase his chances of acceptance, he followed his Sandhurst graduation with two years at the East India Company's cadet training college at Addiscombe, near Croyden, Surrey. This establishment was run on rigorous lines, with hard work and plain food. But it did an effective job of preparing young officers for their duties. Addiscombe was dissolved after the East India Company became defunct following the Indian Mutiny. When they left Addiscombe, the young officers normally sailed immediately to India, and they had to expect that their first home leave would only come around ten years later.

In the rank order of graduates, Roberts was in ninth place out of the total of forty cadets. He was duly commissioned as a second lieutenant in the Bengal Artillery of the East India Company. He had just passed his nineteenth birthday. His father gave him a gold watch and a cheque. But there was some disappointment because the young officer did not pass quite high enough to enter the engineers, who received higher pay than the artillery. Roberts's commission was signed by the governor general, Lord Dalhousie. Commissions in the British army were signed by the sovereign. This interesting distinction was perpetuated after the East India Company ceased to exist. Commissions of the British officers in the Indian army were now signed by the sovereign, which meant that they were appointed King's Commissioned Officers (KCOs) or Queen's Commissioned Officers (QCOs). However, the native-born officers in Indian units—about half the officer strength in such units—had their commissions signed by the viceroy. They therefore became the Viceroy's Commissioned Officers (VCOs). VCOs were always junior to KCOs. But after the First World War, a number of Indian-born cadets went to Sandhurst and became KCOs, which made them eligible for the highest ranks.

A Rumbling Volcano

In the mid-nineteenth century, most ships to India made the long journey under sail. However, in mid-February 1852, Roberts took one of the infrequent steamships. He left Southampton and landed at Alexandria, where the passengers made the difficult overland journey to Suez. They then picked up another steamship, and Roberts arrived in Calcutta on 1 April 1852, after a journey that had lasted forty-one days. He had an enjoyable time on board because he was in the company of other cadets from Addiscombe who were also going to India to join their regiments. Roberts and his comrades were all commissioned into an army whose regiments were recruited from separate Indian races. This made for a colourful patchwork.[5] The territory of India—then much larger than it is today because of the breakaways—was under permanent control by the East India Company. However, as a typical example of British pragmatism, the total territory included a number of princely states. Each of these had its own ruler, but with effective control in the hands of a British political adviser from the Civil Service. This system remained until the end of the Raj in 1947, when the entire country was unified, and the princes lost the relics of their political importance. Also at that time, Pakistan broke away, to be followed later by Bangladesh (split from Pakistan). Sri Lanka (formerly Ceylon) was always a Crown Colony.

During the years of East India Company rule, a large army was needed for two purposes. First, it had to wage a number of small frontier wars in Burma and with various disaffected tribes, especially on the North-West Frontier. There was always the possibility of large-scale wars in countries as far apart as Afghanistan, Persia, and China. The second purpose was internal security. The Indian population comprised many different races, and squabbles were always breaking out, and military discipline was needed to pacify them. When Roberts went to India, the total size of the Indian army was 352,000 men (which is, incidentally, *three times* the size of the British army in the twenty-first century). Of the total, 38,000 were British regulars. And 314,000 were members of the East India Company (EIC) army, which also included a small number of regiments of British-born troops as well as many more Indian units. When a serious problem of morale arose in 1857, the much greater numbers of Indian troops under arms provided a decisive push that turned a morale problem into a mutiny. Very quickly, shots began to be fired. The tension below the surface was like a rumbling volcano about to erupt.

Roberts soon experienced again Indian heat, miserable living conditions, inactivity, and disease. At the time, the proportion of British soldiers who died every year of disease was a shocking 10 percent. Later in his career, Roberts made a successful effort to improve matters. The large cantonment of Dum Dum, where Roberts made his temporary home, was half deserted. Many of the permanent residents had gone to Burma, where war was being fought intermittently (and where Wolseley received his baptism of fire). Dum Dum gave its unfortunate name to Dum Dum bullets, which had their points flattened and which caused frightful wounds. In later wars, any soldiers firing Dum Dum bullets received no mercy from the enemy at whom they had been firing. Roberts received no hospitality from the Anglo-Indian community, and on one occasion, the cantonment was in the direct path of a cyclone that caused devastating damage. Professionally, Roberts had few duties. He was attached to a native artillery battery, where morale was low. The officers had no promotion prospects, some subalterns having served for fifteen years in that rank.

The solution for Roberts was to get to Burma, and the best string he was able to pull was held by his father, who was commanding the division in Lahore (in present-day Pakistan). In response to the younger Roberts's plea, his father had an interesting idea. He suggested to his son that he might be able to join him as an ADC, or 'galloper', when Roberts *père* took command of the Peshawar division, the largest in India and the garrison stationed on the North-West Frontier. This was considered a difficult and demanding appointment, and the elder Roberts was almost sixty-nine. In early August 1852, the young Roberts left Dum Dum on an immensely long and uncomfortable journey across northern India to the west. He had firm hopes of a more interesting job and—most important of all—active service.

Roberts made the seemingly endless and difficult journey in three stages. From Dum Dum to Allahabad (760 miles) he went by riverboat, then by carriage over a metalled road. From Allahabad to Meerut (600 miles), he continued by carriage. But from Meerut to Peshawar (another 600 miles), he went by palanquin, a type of enclosed rickshaw pulled and pushed by eight walking men. The teams changed regularly, and speed could be maintained at three miles per hour. Not long afterwards, the Grand Trunk Road speeded things up significantly.

En route, he was entertained by the local commissioner in Allahabad, a friend of his father. He was an Englishman who had spent too many years in the tropics. As an example of his eccentricity, he employed a servant whose sole duty was to attend to his hookah pipe, which he smoked constantly, even during meals. Roberts even came across some members of his own family who were serving in various military garrisons. He also met a number of officers for the first time who would become friends for life. On two occasions, he encountered units of the Bengal Horse Artillery, who wore uniforms that were dazzling even by that day's standards. He immediately resolved to do well enough to be invited to receive his 'jacket'. This was the token of membership of a Horse Artillery regiment, the elite of the Royal Regiment of Artillery because of the great care that was taken to select the best officers and men.

It took Roberts three months to make his journey of just under two thousand miles. This is something that raises a point of general importance. As discussed in chapter 1, an important change in military technology took place during the mid-nineteenth century. The second phase of technology (characterized by primitive firepower) gave way to the third phase (characterized by superior firepower and greatly improved transport). A little more than a decade after Roberts's journey, the strategy of the American Civil War was relying to a large degree on railways to transport troops. And in India, well before the end of the century, the journey that had taken Roberts three months could be made in three days.

During Roberts's early days in Peshawar, Major General Roberts and the civil commissioner (who was also an army officer) were engaged in patient and successful diplomacy: something that they hoped would reduce the need for fighting. They kept close to the ruler—the amir—of Afghanistan, and because of the friendly relations they established, Afghanistan kept its distance when the Indian Mutiny broke out in 1857.

From the viewpoint of the twenty-first century, life in the Indian frontier cantonment in the 1850s was rough and violent. Peshawar was crowded, insanitary, and disease-ridden. The cantonment was kept small to make it easy to defend, and it was surrounded by sentries and pickets. Despite martial rule, the civil commissioner was murdered by Muslim fanatics in September 1853. The murderer was immediately hanged and his body was burned, which Muslims believed would make it impossible for him to enter paradise.

The young Roberts found his life very different from Dum Dum. He had plenty to occupy him, and he was happy. He served in a battery of the Horse Artillery, one that was considered so efficient that it was being converted to mountain artillery, armed with 'screw guns' carried on the backs of mules. The Indian army was famous for these weapons. Roberts had an excellent battery commander, a major who supervised his work carefully. Some months later, the major recommended Roberts to receive his 'jacket' as an officer in the Horse Artillery. The battery commander also showed exceptional ability to maintain discipline, although he was authorized to impose severe punishment. Two British soldiers had been flogged but had soon committed the same offence again. They were just about to have a repeat punishment when the battery commander remitted the sentence if the soldiers promised never to break the rules again. This ability to temper justice with mercy showed a good understanding of the psychology of command. As a result, the two gunners became trouble-free members of the battery.

In addition to his duties in the battery, Roberts became his father's ADC; and in this capacity, he worked with his father's staff. These were outstanding men, and they all, in due course, became generals. Before too long, they were able to offer opportunities to the young Roberts. Restless and aggressive tribes on the North-West Frontier needed, on frequent occasions, to be pacified by small British forces. In November 1852, Major General Roberts moved north to supervise a minor operation. He was happy not to take his ADC because the young officer was too occupied with his battery. The much colder weather in the north was such a contrast to the heat of Peshawar that Major General Roberts was thought to be close to death. He was given medical orders to resign his position and return to England. The son accompanied his father for a short part of his long journey home, but soon returned to rejoin his battery.

Frederick Roberts had, by now, been in India for two years. Everybody from Britain who spent long periods in India suffered from bouts of fever, usually malaria. There were no effective drugs in those days. Roberts now started getting frequent bouts, and he was granted local leave for six months. With a comrade in the battery, he

marched north, with coolies carrying the baggage. This was Roberts's
first opportunity to experience one of the great contrasts offered by
the subcontinent: the contrast between the plains and the hills. They
eventually reached the valley of Kashmir, which was a riot of fruit and
spring flowers. Seventy years after the end of the Raj, the ownership of
Kashmir—with its capital, Srinagar, and its floating gardens—is still
constantly being disputed by both India and Pakistan.

Roberts returned to Peshawar to receive the good news that he
had been awarded his 'jacket'. The Horse Artillery troop he joined
was manned by strong Irishmen who were good riders. He took the
opportunity of improving his own seat on a horse. However, his health
was responsible for another setback. Further episodes of fever forced
him to take another eight months' leave. He spent part of this in
Kashmir and then made his way east to Simla. This was an important
station and was to become the viceroy's future headquarters during
the summer, when the plains were torrid. At Simla, Roberts met the
quartermaster general, who was impressed by him.

The British army Staff College (then known as the Senior Branch)
was not yet in full operation. Staff appointments were nevertheless much
sought by ambitious officers because staff jobs offered the best prospects
of active service. Staff appointments were also open-ended and provided
a long career. Roberts's father had always recommended him to aim for a
staff appointment, especially in the Quartermaster General's Department.
The young Roberts's meeting with the quartermaster general now made
a difference. When Roberts got back to Peshawar, he was unexpectedly
offered a job assisting Peter Lumsden, who had been a senior member of
his father's staff and was now the deputy assistant quartermaster general
(DAQMG), recently appointed as member of a team to conduct a
geographical survey of Kashmir. Roberts's appointment was part-time,
and he continued with his duties with the Horse Artillery. His connection
with the Quartermaster General's Department continued until he left
this branch in 1878, when he was quartermaster general himself.

At Peshawar, the most important event that took place in 1856
was the continued negotiation with the amir of Afghanistan. This
led to a treaty signed in early 1857. The result was peace on the

frontier, engineered by cash subsidies and muskets donated by India to Afghanistan, which would be used in the war that was being waged between Afghanistan and Persia. A handful of British officers were now permitted to visit Afghanistan, and these included Peter Lumsden. In his absence, Roberts temporarily took over the job of DAQMG. Roberts started work, but there was a serious hiccup. The quartermaster general himself refused to confirm Roberts's temporary appointment because he had not yet passed the qualifying examination in Hindustani. He had to find in a hurry a good instructor, a native scholar, a *munshi*:

> 'It was then May 1856, and in July, the half-yearly examination was to be held. I forthwith engaged the best *munshi* at Peshawar, shut myself up, and studied Indian literature from morning til night, until I felt pretty confident of success.'[6]

Roberts passed and his temporary appointment was confirmed, and this marked an important step in his career because he was a very good staff officer, and staff jobs at all levels were now open to him.

Meanwhile, in Afghanistan, negotiations continued between the amir and his officers and the delegation from the British army. The figure who dominated the negotiations was the chief commissioner of the Punjab, Colonel John Nicholson. He was the man who had a magical rapport with the native Indian races, but he was to lose his life during the mutiny.

Roberts's career between the ages of nineteen and twenty-four had been successful—although in comparison with his contemporary Wolseley, his progress had been less than dramatic. Roberts had trodden water during the time he took before he got to Peshawar and during the unfortunate fourteen months of sick leave. However, when he was under the professional aegis of his father, his career moved in a promising direction. He became a highly effective young officer in the Horse Artillery, and he got an entrée into the Quartermaster General's Department. He was about to make much more rapid progress, triggered by the Indian Mutiny. The metaphorical volcano erupted in 1857.

Endnotes

1. Masters, John, *Bugles and a Tiger* (London: Michael Joseph, 1956). *The Road past Mandalay* (London: Michael Joseph, 1961).
2. Roberts of Kandahar, Field Marshal Lord, *Forty-One Years in India* (London: Michael Bentley, 1897), *Volume I,* vii.
3. Ibid., viii.
4. James, David, *Lord Roberts* (London: Hollis & Carter, 1954), 1.
5. Roberts, *Forty-One Years in India.* Most of the details of Roberts's life in India before the mutiny can be found in *Volume I,* chapters 2, 3, 4, and 5.
6. Ibid., 46–47.

CHAPTER 5

HARD MARCHING AND BLOODY FIGHTING: 'PLUCKY WEE BOBS' DURING THE INDIAN MUTINY

'The very serious outbreak in Meerut' (in the words of the 1857 report) was the first unambiguous sign of disaffection among the sepoys in Bengal.[1] In common with a number of other officers, Lieutenant Roberts immediately departed on active service; his experience as an artillery officer was much in demand. What happened in Meerut, an important garrison town, marked a step along the path to the eventual dissolution of the British Empire. This patchwork of territories that covered one quarter of the land mass of the world lasted longer than any other empire in the modern era, and it had been built by an ambitious and restless island race that used its army and navy mainly to protect its overseas possessions. Colonialism has a very low reputation in the twenty-first century, but the British did not leave behind a legacy as bad as the Belgians in the Congo, the Dutch in Indonesia, the French in Vietnam, and the Portuguese in Mozambique, who were all rapidly forgotten after their empires had come to an end. In contrast, the British were remembered with respect—if not affection—in the enormous Indian subcontinent, where the civil law had come from the British

Isles and the *lingua franca* is still English. The regiments of the Indian and Pakistani armies all have strong identities, and they are, without exception, the descendents of regiments of the old Indian army, which, during the Second World War, was the largest volunteer army in the world.

The long growth of the British Empire was not uninterrupted. It received two severe shocks. The first was the revolt of the American colonies following the Declaration of Independence in 1776. This was a permanent loss, and its importance was not fully appreciated until the end of the nineteenth century, when the economic potential of the United States became one of the wonders of the world. The second shock was the Indian Mutiny, which began at Meerut. Although this was suppressed with brutality, trouble rumbled below the surface and emerged in the form of passive resistance before and during the Second World War, and this led directly to the ending of the Raj in 1947.

Life in India for expatriate British men and women offered many attractions to compensate for the heat and disease, the distance from the British Isles, and the rarity of home leave. Indian bungalows could be made comfortable even in the hot weather and during the monsoon, and many families managed to spend the hot season in the comfortable cool of the hill stations. Servants were plentiful everywhere. The average British officer employed more than a dozen. British private soldiers had servants to help with all their chores, acting as barbers, cooks, cleaners to make the bungalows comfortable, and personal valets to look after their kit—but not their arms, which were always securely guarded. The typical memsahib had to devote much time to marshalling her staff to run the household and look after the young children. The Viceregal Lodge in Simla had more than 260 indoor servants. And during the 1920s, when the Prince of Wales visited India, he said that he had at last learned how royalty should live.

Since 1840, British control of the country had been expanded and made firmer. The hereditary rulers of Delhi and Oudh had been removed and pensioned, and the reach of the Civil Service had been extended over the whole country. This meant that taxation increased. A network of telegraph connections was set up, and a small start was made in building railways. These became extremely important by the end of the nineteenth century. Of the total number of troops in the country, 11 percent were from the British regular army—hardy, experienced, and well-disciplined soldiers—who were eventually successful in suppressing the mutiny and restoring order. The other 89 percent, which until 1858 composed the army of the East India Company, were locally recruited. There were two types of such regiments. First—the large majority— were made up of native private soldiers, NCOs, and junior officers, but with British senior officers; second—a smaller number of units—were made up of British-born soldiers in all the ranks. These did not join the mutineers, and after the mutiny, they would all be transferred to the British army.

The obvious disparity between the living standards of the British ruling class and the Indian servant class built a rigid barrier. The British army and the sepoy army were organized in a broadly similar way, but there were important differences, notably the two classes of officers: captains and above were British, while subalterns were Indian and held Indian commissions. In the eyes of the British army, the discipline in the Indian army was much too relaxed.[2] The British thought that disaffection would not be impossible. This was inconceivable in the British army, with its rigid discipline. After the mutiny had been suppressed, very few of the original British commanders were reappointed in the new Indian army.

In 1856, the introduction of the Enfield rifles with their cartridges greased with animal fat was the cause of the immediate crisis. The exaggerated belief that the fat came from oxen (which outraged the Hindus) and the equally exaggerated belief that it came from pigs (which had a similarly devastating effect on the Muslims) very quickly caused alarm that the British were trying to suppress the sepoys' religions and make them Christians. The word spread through the ranks from person to person and via the telegraph, the post, and even in mysterious packages of chupattis that supposedly signaled some important future event.[3] The British claimed that the grease did not come from animal fat. However, the damage had already been done; and by the late spring of 1857, the rumour had spread from regiment to regiment, and there were many more native regiments than British ones. This meant that the British suddenly had a most dangerous situation on their hands. (They invariably described the local inhabitants as natives; this is a description that caused offence after the ending of the Raj.)

When the mutiny exploded, the British military stations in India soon knew about it by telegraph. Frederick Roberts, a junior staff officer in Peshawar in the Punjab, learned quickly about the contingency plans that were being made by his military superiors: plans that would involve Roberts himself, although nobody was able to foresee how quickly events would give him an opportunity to make his name. Roberts, being a junior officer, played his part in tactical operations; but these were part of something much larger. In order to describe Roberts's part in the mutiny, the following section outlines the ebb and flow of British military fortunes in 1857 and 1858. (See **Maps 3 and 4**.) Roberts returns to centre stage in 'From the Punjab to Bengal'.

1857, the Year of Mutiny

Mutinies had sometimes occurred in the past among native Indian troops, and two minor disturbances even took place in early 1857. However, the outbreak that occurred in Meerut in May was of a different order of magnitude, judged by the number of soldiers involved and the extent of support they received from the native population.[4] It started with the mutiny of eighty-five sepoys. They were court-martialled and paraded in chains before their regiment. This caused the rest of the garrison to join the mutiny and open the prisons that contained 1,200 men, including the eighty-five who were serving ten-year sentences. British officers were soon being murdered, and in May 1857, all the mutineers, who were from three regiments, marched on Delhi, forty miles to the south-west. They were joined by mutineers in Delhi itself, and the force occupied the city although the British troops there had blown up the magazines, to make sure that the mutineers could not get to the explosives.

The mutiny quickly spread. When the sepoys slaughtered their British leaders, they took a path from which there was to be no return. Some regiments disintegrated, but those that kept their cohesion were now commanded by their native-born officers and NCOs. By far the largest number of mutinous regiments came from the Bengal army, the main body in the Calcutta military district and the largest army overall in the subcontinent. The Bengal army occupied a number of garrisons along the Grand Trunk Road, a metalled highway that was being built to connect Calcutta in the east and the Punjab in the west, a distance of one thousand miles. Dozens of garrisons were affected by the mutiny, although most were small and were occupied by a single regiment. But two garrisons—Delhi and Lucknow—were of major importance and continued to be vigorously engaged by the British. The Bengal army was composed largely of Bengali troops but included a number of regiments that contained Rajputs and men from provinces in Central India. The sepoys who mutinied were Hindus, and they regarded Christianity as the worst element of British rule. Brahmins—highly respected members of the Hindu priestly caste—saw Christianity as the force behind reforms that the British regarded as humanitarian: the abolition of female infanticide and *sati* (the burning of widows on their husbands' funeral pyres), the spread of education, and various land reforms. The uneducated population never questioned the Brahmins' conservatism and authority, even their opposition to railways and telegraphs. In addition, the Bengali army had grievances that made the regiments particularly prone to mutiny. They had reluctantly agreed to serve abroad, although this was against their religion; and the recent occupation of Oudh had been universally resented. The new rifle cartridges were a final outrage.

Delhi on the Jumna River, a city of 150,000 people, was the ancient capital of the Mughal Empire. After the mutiny, it rapidly grew to an astonishing degree, and in 1912, it replaced Calcutta as the new capital of India. It was adorned, during the 1920s, with the suitably imperial architecture of Edwin Lutyens. The mutineers from Meerut and Delhi itself forced the British out of the old Delhi fort, an ancient building that had been built for defence and was still formidable. The insurgents stopped and devoted themselves to plundering and drink.

Not surprisingly, many of the British who had escaped from the city now began to trickle back and occupy the old cantonment. This cluster of buildings was a short distance from the fort—less than a mile at one end of the cantonment and two and a half miles at the other—and was protected by a long, arid sixty-foot ridge that runs north to south to the west of the fort. (See **Map 3**.) The cantonment was not yet organized or fortified, but on 27 May, a small mainly British formation commanded by Brigadier General Archdale Wilson routed groups of the enemy in two pitched battles. On 7 June, General Barnard, commander-in-chief of the Indian army, led a strong formation that reached the city and won another victory. The British position was now secure. However, on the increasing number of occasions when the mutineers attacked from the fort, the British defences had to be strongly manned. British guns were always well forward and firing over open sights, despite the danger of the enemy capturing them. On 19 June, the British made the first detailed plan to assault the fort, but it was wisely decided to postpone this until there were reinforcements. These included Roberts, who arrived on 28 June. It was September before a major assault was finally made, and it turned out to be a magnificent feat of arms.

East of Delhi, at a distance of two hundred miles, is Cawnpore, Roberts's birthplace. On 4 June, sepoys in Cawnpore mutinied. They were encouraged by a local Indian prince, and before long, the insurgents were in control. The British soldiers and their families had been promised safety if they departed from the city. They were slaughtered. British officers and men were often in the same stations for years. The majority of officers with the rank of captain and above were married and had their wives and children with them, and Victorian families were large. The mutineers murdered 125 women and children, whose bodies were thrown into a well. After the end of the mutiny, the British built a permanent monument out of this well, and during the rule of the Raj, no native Indians were allowed to approach it. On 16 July, a column under Henry Havelock reached the city and put the mutineers to the sword, after a number had been humiliated by being forced to carry out jobs against their religion.

After Cawnpore had been made secure against any further attacks, Havelock established a small garrison and prepared to lead his column on to Lucknow, only fifty miles north-east of Cawnpore. Lucknow had been under siege since June. The city was defended by John Lawrence's brother Henry, who was killed in the defence. James Outram then took command. Two relief columns eventually fought their way through. The first was Havelock's, which got into the city in September but was forced to join the garrison in the city since it did not have the strength to defeat the besiegers. A second column, under General Colin Campbell, got through in November. Roberts was in this column. The mutiny had now been substantially quelled, despite small further outbreaks in Lucknow, Cawnpore, Oudh, and Central India. These lasted until the early months of 1859.[5]

The outbreaks in Central India were suppressed by General Hugh Rose, who had come from Britain. He fought the mutineers with practiced skill, and each insurrection was defeated in turn. The leader of the mutineers in Central India was captured and hanged: the fate of uncounted numbers of mutineers in all parts of the country. Large numbers also suffered the ancient Mughal punishment of being blown from guns. This was the most terrible of all punishments for Muslim soldiers because if their bodies were blown to pieces, they could not get to heaven.

In the Bengal army, more than seventy regiments mutinied, but they were joined by only small numbers of mutineers in the other Indian military districts. There was never any question of a national uprising. Out of the total Indian army strength of 314,000 men, about a quarter were the Bengal mutineers: regiments that were subsequently disbanded.[6] British resolution to quell the mutiny never wavered, but the numbers of loyal troops were initially small: 38,000 men in the British regiments; loyal regiments of Punjabis, Sikhs, and Gurkhas; plus the remaining minority of Bengalis. Help was also on the way from Britain, the Crimea, Burma, Ceylon, Mauritius, Persia, and some men *en route* to China (including Garnet Wolseley, who arrived in Calcutta in October 1857). Transporting reinforcements took a lot of time. Men from Britain had to sail around Africa because the Suez Canal had not yet been built. Those from the Crimea had to make the difficult journey by land.

The combat took place in torrid summer heat, causing heatstroke, and the monsoon rains that arrived during the late summer. India was notorious for tropical diseases (malaria, cholera, and dysentery) and premature deaths. In fact, British casualties during the mutiny totaled two thousand men killed and another nine thousand who died of heatstroke and disease. These numbers do not include the murdered civilians or the mutineers and other natives. The soldiers wore totally unsuitable uniforms—red woollen tunics and the Highlanders' heavy sporrans and thick woollen kilts, although some soldiers replaced their feather bonnets with white cotton caps with neck flaps. The Highland Regiments took a prominent part in the fighting, and 70 percent of them were Gaelic speakers. Fortunately, on a few occasions, soldiers obtained thin white uniforms, which they dyed khaki with coffee and curry powder. Before long, the mutineers discarded their European uniforms and changed to more comfortable native dress.

Much of the fighting was carried out by columns of relieving troops—rarely more than three thousand men. This limitation was important: the troops could move quickly because they carried only ammunition, food, and water. Troop movements in India were traditionally extremely cumbrous because baggage was carried on creaking carts drawn by oxen, and every body of soldiers was accompanied by an additional army of camp followers. This followed the Indian tradition of employing servants, including women and children, to do the cooking, washing, cleaning, water-carrying, grass-cutting, and acting as grooms and personal attendants. Most marches were on roads and tracks, but occasionally, small groups were able to move by riverboat.

The sieges and battles provided opportunities for military glory. Important generals emerged: Colin Campbell, Hope Grant, Henry Havelock, Henry Lawrence, John Lawrence, John Nicholson, James Outram, and Hugh Rose. Nicholson planned and led the desperate but successful assault on Delhi and lost his life in the process. Havelock and Henry Lawrence also died in harness. Campbell, who was the most successful of all, was an educated Scot who had come from a working-class background. He eventually became Lord Clyde.

From the Punjab to Bengal

On the evening of the day of the outbreak at Meerut, Frederick Roberts was learning his job as DAQMG, a plum appointment for such a junior officer. His post was in Peshawar, the army headquarters in the Punjab, a garrison town (now in Pakistan) near the frontier with Afghanistan and five hundred miles, as the crow flies, north-west of Delhi. His duties brought him into contact with the senior officers in the station, some of whom were soon to be famous. The civil and military chiefs quickly acted to suppress the news of the mutiny, to prevent it contaminating the morale of the native regiments. This was really too late because letters that were intercepted in the post office showed that sedition was already spreading. The commanders—notably General Herbert Edwardes, chief commissioner (i.e. civilian head of the district), and his deputy, Brigadier General John Nicholson—immediately made plans for the worst contingency.

In the main stations of the province, there were only fifteen thousand British soldiers with eighty-four guns, while there were sixty-five thousand native troops with sixty-two guns.[7] The first thing that Edwardes and Nicholson did was to contact the native chiefs throughout the Punjab and the Frontier and appeal to their loyalty. This was an important—and successful—move that had long-term consequences. Meanwhile, the British formed a movable column composed of infantry, cavalry, and artillery, and made it ready to suppress any outbreak as soon as news of it arrived. Brigadier General Neville Chamberlain assumed command, and the twenty-four-year-old Roberts was fortunate enough to be appointed his staff officer (the approximate equivalent of brigade major). This was 'the most important piece of good fortune that could have come to me'.[8]

Meanwhile, General George Anson, commander-in-chief in India, a popular officer with excellent judgment—although he had not fought in a battle since Waterloo—had taken steps to pacify the fears of his Indian troops, and he believed that he had been successful. And shortly afterwards he departed for Simla, the hot-weather headquarters of the army. But when he got there, he prepared to move again on hearing of the uprising in Meerut. While Anson was assembling an improvised and poorly equipped force, news came in of a rash of further outbreaks. Anson was keenly aware that his most important task was the relief of Delhi, but he also realized that he did not have a strong enough body of men to do the job decisively. On 26 May, Anson was struck by cholera and immediately succumbed. The responsibility for quelling the outbreak now fell on his successor, General Henry Barnard, who had been chief of staff in the Crimea but had virtually no experience of India. He was less cautious than Anson and took immediate steps to march on Delhi.

In the Punjab, the movable column took some weeks before it reached Bengal, where it was so obviously needed. There were three reasons for this delay. The first and worst problem was continuous disturbances in the Punjab. In Peshawar itself, four native regiments were disbanded, although Edwardes's negotiations with the tribal chiefs paid a dividend before long. Second, since the movable column was an *ad hoc* formation, the various elements in it had to be drawn together. The third problem was the perpetually slow pace of transport, which was governed by the pace of marching soldiers. The railway had not yet reached Bengal. (The American Civil War, which broke out in 1861, was the first conflict that depended on transportation; the Confederate armies won battles because they used railways to operate on interior lines.) In India, the Grand Trunk Road was at an early stage of construction but was not yet carrying much traffic. The headquarters of the movable column was carried in slow and unreliable carts. Headquarters included a telegraphist with his instrument, who called on each of the infrequent telegraph stations to send and receive messages.

Chamberlain and his men marched from Peshawar to Rawalpindi (120 miles to the east), then to Wazirabad (100 miles south), then to

Lahore (a further eighty miles south), which they reached on 31 May 1857. At Lahore—at the time a city of one hundred thousand people and capital of the Punjab—the civil chief Robert Montgomery was alarmed about the loyalty of four sepoy regiments. On his advice, the garrison commander quietly and efficiently disarmed the native troops. There were also doubts about the loyalty of the native troops in the mobile column. This was still very small: two batteries and a British battalion, plus some native infantry. Chamberlain inspected these sepoys and found that two of them had loaded their weapons without orders. They were immediately court-martialled and condemned to death. Roberts witnessed, for the first time, the dreaded punishment of guilty men being shot from guns. It was soon obvious that the only way to control disaffected troops was with the firmest possible discipline. In later years, the uncompromising discipline imposed by the British on the native troops was echoed by the attitudes and behavior of the British rank and file towards the natives, which sometimes verged on the brutal.

Continued trouble in the Punjab still meant that the mobile column had to be retained despite the urgency of the situation in Delhi. A new problem was caused by the departure of Chamberlain, who was promoted adjutant general in army headquarters. His replacement—and Roberts's new chief—was Brigadier General John Nicholson, who was to be the hero (although a tragic one) of the successful assault on Delhi three months later. Roberts was immediately struck by Nicholson's energy and military knowledge, although he was a civil official. (Roberts would meet Nicholson again at Delhi.) In the meantime, an order arrived from army headquarters that artillery officers on detached duties were needed in Delhi, where the small British garrison was in peril. The column was still in Bengal, and Roberts faced a journey of 250 miles. Without delay, Roberts was on his way, carrying the smallest possible amount of personal kit. The rest would be brought by his servant, who would follow him.

On his journey, he noticed plentiful signs of recent small-scale fighting; and as he reached Delhi, the sound of gunfire became louder and louder. He used his initiative to find an ammunition cart that was bound for the cantonment and seized a place in it before a number of other officers who were also anxious to get there. Roberts was delighted to arrive at the Delhi cantonment on 28 June. He was to spend three months there. He was appointed DAQMG for the artillery: a job that could have been made for him. Before his arrival, a siege train got to the cantonment, and this contained a good deal of artillery. This artillery was not totally suitable to assault a well-constructed fortress, and ammunition was in short supply, but Roberts's task was to fight more and more in the front line, deploying small numbers of guns.

Quo Fas et Gloria Ducunt[9]

During the uncomfortable summer months, reinforcements arrived for both the mutineers and the British: many mutineers but smaller numbers of British, who were also losing many from sickness. The British numbered six thousand men in early July. But the insurgents, besides having more men, also had four times as much artillery. Barnard was an effective field commander, but on 5 July, he was struck by cholera and, like his predecessor, soon died. One continuous problem facing the British was that some mutineers emerged from the British ranks to reinforce the openly identified insurgents in the fort. When they were caught, they suffered the rough justice that so many mutineers had already received.

The fighting was a series of soldiers' battles—in most cases fought by British formations of a thousand men composed of cavalry and infantry, with a couple of guns. A recent innovation in the British army was the Victoria Cross (VC). This was first awarded in the Crimean War in 1856, and each bronze cross, which includes a scroll FOR VALOUR was (and still is) cast from the guns that had been captured from the Russian army. In the fighting at Delhi, the first VCs were given outside the Crimea. The Victoria Cross is open to all ranks in the armed services. It takes precedence before any other order or decoration, it can be awarded posthumously, and the initials 'VC' follow the recipient's name whenever he is mentioned. To maintain its special value, the number of awards is severely restricted. In the Second World War, it was estimated that the VC was given to one in twenty thousand of all the soldiers, sailors, and airmen.

Roberts came under fire for the first time on 30 July and was in battle almost every day from then on. On 14 July, he wrote:

> 'So many of the men with the two guns were *hors de combat*, and the horses were so unsteady (several of them being wounded), that there was great difficulty in limbering up, and I was helping the drivers to keep the horses quiet, when I suddenly felt a tremendous blow on my back which made me faint and sick . . . I had been hit close to the spine by a bullet, and the wound would probably have been fatal but for the fact that a leather pouch for caps, which I usually wore in front near my pistol, had somehow slipped round to the back; the bullet passed through this before entering my body . . . Our casualties amounted to fifteen men killed, sixteen officers, and 177 men wounded, and two men missing. The enemy's loss was estimated at one thousand.'[10]

The fighting continued in this unrelenting way, but there was as yet no major attack on the fort. After Barnard had died, Major General Reed assumed command, but his health broke down within days. He was in turn succeeded by Archdale Wilson, who was promoted major general. He had his merits, but he was not an inspiring commander. He was, however, soon joined by Brigadier General John Nicholson. Nicholson commanded the movable column from the Punjab, which at last arrived on 13 August. It contained units of infantry, cavalry, and artillery who were reliable but all under-strength because of disease. The total number of men in the cantonment had increased to eight thousand. This was a strong enough force to mount a serious assault, especially since the estimated total of thirty thousand mutineers were little more than a rabble. They were brave in small groups, but in large numbers they lacked cohesion.

Nicholson immediately advanced to contact the enemy with a brigade made up of 1,600 infantry, 450 cavalry, and sixteen RHA guns. Nicholson's order to the infantry was to hold their fire until within twenty or thirty yards of the enemy. The British swept forward. In the meantime, the force in the cantonment was greatly strengthened by the arrival of a siege train with thirty-two guns and plenty of ammunition. Before the assault, a strong artillery battery was put into a strongly fortified position to control the right of the assault, and this was where Roberts was in control. Engineers constructed large amounts of assault stores: fascines, platforms, scaling ladders, and the like. The attack was to take place early on 14 September. The infantry were formed from fifteen battalions, in five separate columns. There were three on the left, one on the right, and one in reserve. Each column contained three under-strength battalions: one British and two Indian. The total strength of the infantry was reduced to five thousand men as a result of sickness. (Fifteen full-strength battalions had a nominal size of fifteen thousand men.)

After a brief but intense artillery bombardment, the infantry sprang forward. At this stage, Roberts was ordered back to accompany Major General Wilson.

> 'Nicholson gave the signal. The Sixtieth Rifles, with a loud cheer, dashed to the front in skirmishing order, while at the same moment, the heads of the first and second columns appeared and moved steadily forward. No sooner were the front ranks seen by the rebels than a storm of bullets met them at every side, and officers and men fell thick on the crest of the glacis. Then, for a few seconds, amidst a blaze of musketry, the soldiers stood at the edge of the ditch, for only one or two of the ladders had come up . . . Dark figures crowded on the breach, hurling stones upon our men and daring them to come on. More ladders were bought up . . . Nicholson, at the head of a part of his column, was the first to ascend the breach . . . the ramparts which had so long resisted us were our own.'[11]

The spectacular success of the operation was the result of the high quality of the troops and the success of the tactics that had been developed at short notice by Nicholson. There were focused assaults on three strong points on the northern walls of the fort. In **Map 3,** the city walls, oval in shape, are shown in black. The fort is situated in the east of the city, close to the river. When the walls were breached, ferocious hand-to-hand fighting continued, and casualties mounted. These included Nicholson, who died painfully of his wounds. When Roberts entered the fort later that day, he found Nicholson lying in a doolie, unaccompanied by any porters. Roberts saw 'John Nicholson, with death written on his face', and arranged for the doolie to be carried to a hospital.[12] The general confusion was so great that Major General Wilson considered withdrawing his force, but he was dissuaded by members of his staff, including Roberts. Roberts's visit to the fort made it clear that the British position was strong, although the actual area occupied by the British troops was very small. The streets, alleys, and bazaars of the native quarter did not represent a military threat to the British. Roberts and his party had a brush with some enemy in an alley, but these were easily defeated.

The assaulting force had lost sixty-six officers and 1,104 men killed and wounded: a substantial rate of loss from an effective force of five thousand men. Roberts had been actively occupied and spent many hours day and night continuously in the saddle. He had been involved in the initial planning; then in setting up the artillery battery that launched the assault, working there as a gunner officer; and finally, with the commander-in-chief, in the important role of acting as his eyes and ears and strengthening his resolve. On 15 September, the fighting was virtually over, and the army was engaged in reorganizing, restoring peace in the streets, clearing away dead bodies that were in a sickening condition, and smashing liquor bottles to keep them away from ebullient soldiers.

On 21 September, a royal salute of twenty-one guns signaled the victory. This was more than a token. It was a triumphal indication that optimism was now going to replace anxiety in British communities in all parts of the subcontinent. The next tasks were the capture of Cawnpore and Lucknow, after which the worst would be over.

The Martinière and the Residency

On 21 September 1857, a small independent column was formed in Delhi to march on Cawnpore and Lucknow. It contained 750 British and 1,900 native troops and sixteen guns. Roberts was the DAQMG. When the column was on the march, progress was interrupted by rebel forces of different sizes, but they were brushed aside. The soldiers in the column were appalled when they reached Cawnpore on 26 October and saw the evidence of the butchery that had taken place there four months before. (See **Map 4**.)

Roberts's column left Cawnpore on 30 October, taking with it part of the garrison, mainly soldiers who were recovering from wounds. The column was commanded by a dashing Scottish cavalry officer, Brigadier General Hope Grant; but an overall commander was appointed, who arrived on 9 November. He was General Colin Campbell, the new commander-in-chief of the Indian army, a leader of remarkable ability who had earned his spurs in the Crimea.

When the column approached close to Lucknow, messages started getting through from the besieged city. James Outram wrote them himself using the Greek alphabet. How the messages got through became one of the legends of the mutiny. The communications were carried by a civilian called Henry Kavanagh, an Irish clerk in Lucknow who disguised himself as a native and managed to creep through the lines. After the end of the mutiny, he received a unique recognition: the only Victoria Cross awarded to a civilian. There were fewer than three thousand men in Lucknow, plus fourteen guns. Campbell's force was not large: 3,500 infantry, 600 cavalry, and forty-two guns, including some heavy naval pieces. He formed three brigades from detachments from nine mainly British regiments. They were all under-strength.

The force set out on 11 November and soon met resistance, which also did not stand in its way. As they were approaching Lucknow—a city of 250,000 inhabitants, plus about 50,000 mutineers from the province of Oudh—General Campbell wished to avoid a direct attack, which would have meant that his men would be caught up in streets and alleys. (This was the route taken by the previous relief column in September

1857.) Campbell decided to find an indirect approach, which had to have a wide and solid enough path to carry artillery. Roberts had met the commander-in-chief two days before, and Campbell decided that Roberts was the man to reconnoitre this circuitous route. He employed a native guide and carried out the job skilfully. The route would follow a wide swing to the right (i.e. to the north-east, north, and north-west) and bring the force between the Gumti River and the city walls. The troops followed Roberts's route, which involved no problems, and Campbell made his headquarters in the Martinière, a mile east of the city. The Martinière was an elegant building that had been erected in 1800 as a school. It had been built by Claude Martin, a French soldier who had been a prisoner of war when the British fought the French in India during the 1760s. He had remained in the country and had become extremely successful. At the Martinière, Kavanagh was able to point out the landmarks of the city, and Campbell set up a signaling post to semaphore messages to Outram.

The British army had by now taken up firm positions as a springboard to assault the city. This had been done efficiently on short notice, and an attack by the enemy on the centre was easily brushed off. What worried Campbell most at this time was the shortage of small-arms ammunition. He talked to Roberts, whose opinion he had soon learned to value, and asked whether Roberts could again find the approach route and follow the track backwards by night to collect more ammunition. Roberts, with more enthusiasm than confidence, said that it could be done. He immediately departed, accompanied by a troop of native cavalry. He found the camp from which the advance had been made and where there were ammunition stocks. He requisitioned 150 camels, loaded them with small-arms ammunition, and escorted them back, arriving at dawn. This was a *coup de théâtre.*

Campbell's planned attack was made on the right, preceded by a feint on the left. But before it could reach its objective, the Residency government quarter, it was held up by ferocious fire from a native fort called the Sekundar Bagh. This was bombarded and assaulted with heroism by the British and Indian infantry. After this position was cleared, the attack on the Residency immediately began. There was another major artillery barrage, and then the infantry moved forward. On a signal from the commander-in-chief, the attack was led by none other than Captain Garnet Wolseley, with a company of the Ninetieth Regiment. The relief of the Residency was in two phases and took two days. Wolseley distinguished himself, and Campbell personally promised him a brevet majority.

Roberts, who by now had been in the saddle for sixty continuous hours, soon followed the assaulting troops. He met, for the first time, both Havelock and Outram (who had been a friend of his father) and conducted both generals to meet Campbell and then into the battered Residency. A few days later, Havelock died of exhaustion from his long months of stressful command in the torrid Indian climate. The relief of Lucknow had been a victory. But it had not been a permanent victory. Wounded soldiers and women and children had to be evacuated, and in General Campbell's absence, General Outram was left to command a relatively small garrison. All the insurgents had not been subdued, and it took more than another three months before another relief column under General Campbell arrived to secure the city permanently.

Lucknow was in ruins. On 27 November, Campbell led his men back to Cawnpore, where a large force of mutineers had appeared. It took a series of small battles to defeat them. Roberts fought on horseback in a number of these actions, and wielding his sword, he engaged the enemy hand-to-hand. The recommendation for Roberts's Victoria Cross referred to these small but bloody fights. In carrying out his main military tasks, Roberts had demonstrated many instances of outstanding ability and devotion to duty, and these had already earned him a number of mentions in dispatches. He had been appointed as a staff officer, but by instinct, he was happiest when he was at the 'sharp end'. The Highlanders with whom he fought called him 'plucky wee Bobs'. At the age of twenty-five, Roberts had made his name throughout the army in India.

Roberts received a surprise in the form of a cash reward of £500 'prize money', a type of remuneration that has not been given in the British army since the end of the First World War. Roberts's health had also suffered, and he received a number of medical certificates recommending fifteen months of leave. Roberts's staff appointment had come to an end with the final relief of Lucknow, and he was shortly to sail for Britain. Campbell arranged a similar job for Wolseley, who was still a captain but was shortly to be a brevet major. Roberts embarked for Britain in June 1858, secure in the knowledge that he had received a brevet majority and the Victoria Cross.[13] When Roberts returned to India, a major change was under way in the composition of the Indian army.

The officers of the old East India Company army were always regarded as the poor relations of the regular officers of the British army. This lower status applied both to the East India Company regiments, whose rank and file were from native Indian races, and those whose troops were British born. This was a situation that was inevitably damaging to military efficiency.

In 1858, the army of the East India Company was formally transferred to the Crown. A number of Bengal regiments had already been disbanded. In the original EIC army, the regiments recruited from British-born men—always independent of the British regulars in India—were now transferred to the British army. *Inter alia*, the First Bengal European Cavalry became the Nineteenth Hussars, and the Second Bombay Light Infantry became 2 Durham Light Infantry. The plan was to boost the proportion of British soldiers in India to at least 50 percent of the total troop strength. Each infantry brigade would now be composed of two British and two Indian battalions, the British being the senior.[14] As Roberts's career developed and he was commanding larger and larger formations, half his soldiers were going to be British.

The lessons of the mutiny had not been forgotten. The armies of the Bombay and Madras Presidencies would maintain a watching brief over that of Bengal, a situation neatly expressed as 'using half the Indian army to watch the other half, and using one-third of the British army to watch them all'.[15]

Endnotes

1. Roberts of Kandahar, Field Marshal Lord, *Forty-One Years in India* (London: Michael Bentley, 1897), *Volume 1, 63.*

2. Wolseley, Field Marshal Viscount, *The Story of a Soldier's Life*, (London: Archibald Constable, 1903), *Volume 1, 253.*

3. Roberts, *Forty-One Years in India, Volume 1, 62.*

4. Mollo, Boris, *The Indian Army* (Poole, Dorset: New Orchard, 1981), 87–89. A succinct description of the various phases of the mutiny.

5. Harris, John, *The Indian Mutiny* (London: Book Club Associates, 1973), 199–202.

6. Mollo, *The Indian Army,* 64–70.

7. Roberts, *Forty-One Years in India, Volume 1,* 66–67.

8. Ibid., 70.

9. 'Whither Fate and Glory Lead.' Motto of the Royal Artillery.

10. Roberts, *Forty-One Years in India, Volume 1,* 194.

11. Ibid., 228–229.

12. Ibid., 236.

13. James, David, *Lord Roberts* (London: Hollis & Carter, 1954), 49–54.

14. Heathcote, T. A., *The Indian Army. The Garrison of British Imperial India, 1822–1922.* (London: David & Charles, 1974), 202.

15. Ibid, 101.

CHAPTER 6

WOLSELEY IN INDIA AND CHINA: 'STORM AND STRESS, HORRORS AND GLORY'[1]

Garnet Wolseley, still only twenty-three, had returned to Britain after his service in Burma and the Crimea, where his gallantry had been recognized with promotion: he would become a brevet major as soon as he was eligible, in 1858. This move up the ladder laid the foundation for his military career. After a spell of leave, he returned to his regiment in early 1857, where he heard exciting rumours: the Ninetieth would shortly depart on active service as members of an expedition to the Far East.[2] The Chinese government was giving British traders a difficult time in Peking and other cities on the mainland. The plan was for a number of battalions to sail to Hong Kong, which would be a springboard for a punitive foray against the Chinese army. The invasion of Burma, where Wolseley had received his baptism of fire, had, in a similar way, been carried out to protect the interests of British merchants.

In the expedition, Wolseley commanded a company of one hundred men, all young, fit, and enthusiastic. Most had served in the Crimea, where they had fought against the well-trained and hardy soldiers of the czar's army; they judged that the Chinese would be amateurs in comparison. The men of the Ninetieth were not even deflated when they boarded the ancient troop ship that was to carry them to the East, a hybrid with steam power supplemented by sails. They embarked in Portsmouth on 8 April 1857, and the ship soon showed herself to be alarmingly unfit for sea. She had to return to Portsmouth for repairs, and when she was finally under way, she had to make a landing in Spain, where Wolseley spent an instructive time visiting the battlefield of Corunna. The ship then proceeded down the west coast of Africa and round the Cape. In the Indian Ocean, she more than once came close to foundering and disappearing under the waves.

Worse was to come. While the Ninetieth was sailing east, alone and out of touch with the outside world, the military situation in Bengal was causing alarm, and British regiments in India were on the march to quell the mutiny. Wolseley's ship was approaching the Dutch East Indies when disaster struck. In inadequately charted waters near Sumatra, she struck a large rock and was skewered by it and immobilized. She was clearly sinking, but the ship's crew and the soldiers on board were calm and disciplined and got into small boats with food and water. Fortunately, they were not far from a reef near the coast of an island, where they landed, and the soldiers got to work establishing a camp. They were soon in contact with the outside world, and a ship was sent for them. They landed in Singapore on 23 July 1857. The mutiny was still flaring, and it was immediately decided that the Ninetieth should go to India. China would have to wait.

The Ninetieth Regiment travelled north as quickly as possible, but it took them a month before they reached Calcutta. They then marched forty miles further north, where the men were given new uniforms and replacement rifles for the firearms that had been damaged in the shipwreck. Wolseley found the men and women in the British garrisons jumpy, mainly because of the stories they had heard about the fighting in Delhi and Lucknow—and, in particular, the massacre in Cawnpore. Because of the attitude of the British in Calcutta, some native regiments were disarmed because of doubts about their loyalty. In mid-August, General Colin Campbell arrived as commander-in-chief and, without delay, went on to Lucknow. The Ninetieth Regiment followed shortly afterwards.

Wolseley had only spent a short time in India before he had departed for Burma in 1853. He did not know the subcontinent and did not have a high regard for the native troops in the Indian army: a view shared by many British army officers and men. They all deplored the slack discipline of the Indians, which they thought was a result of the quasi-civilian control exercised by the East India Company. Wolseley later wrote:

> 'I thought in 1857, and think so still, that the Mutiny was the direct outcome of the foolish mode in which the Bengal sepoy had been over-indulged by the Indian military authorities.'[3]

The soldiers in the British army were demonstrably better, as was evident when the British and Indians met in battle. The British troops had longer experience and better training, they had more robust discipline that strengthened unit cohesion, and, not least, they had their regimental pride.

Until late in the nineteenth century, when bolt-action rifles were introduced, much fighting was hand-to-hand: soldiers using their bayonets and officers their swords. The new Enfield rifles that came into service before the mutiny were more accurate than smooth-bore muskets. However, they were still muzzle-loaded, which meant a rate of fire of only one round a minute because the rounds had to be rammed individually down the barrel. The major advance in musketry came from breech loading, which was introduced long after the mutiny. But soon afterwards breech-loading rifles had magazines holding ten rounds, and these were fed into the breech with a simple bolt manipulated by the soldier. This advance made it possible to fire ten aimed shots a minute. Bolt-action rifles were the reason why battlefield casualties increased, with most coming from musketry and artillery. The low rate of fire of the rifles and muskets used during the mutiny meant that the number of men killed in battle was much lower than in later wars. Two thousand men lost their lives in battle, but more than *four times* as many British soldiers died of disease and heatstroke.

Heat, Monsoon Rain, and a Desire for Vengeance

In August 1857, in the torrid climate and monsoon rains, a force of 1,200 infantry and six guns began their march to Cawnpore and Lucknow. The soldiers were from the Ninetieth Regiment (with Wolseley as one of the company commanders) and the Fifth Northumberland Fusiliers. They encountered minor opposition and wisely marched by night to avoid the heat of the day. Bullock carts carried supplies and parties of men who were permitted, for a few hours, to ride rather than march. Some miles of railway had been built in north-east India, and the British troops had the luxury of railway transport for part of their journey. The men and their transport marched between twenty and thirty miles every night: a pace that would take them a month to reach Cawnpore, which was being approached by General Havelock from a different direction. Wolseley's men had no interest in looking at the temples and mosques on their line of march; all ranks were focused on avenging the murder of British women and children, especially those at Cawnpore.

Parts of the British column had been separated on the march, and Wolseley forced the pace of his detachment although he had problems with unruly bullocks and also a tiger that emerged from the jungle. On 10 September, they reached the holy city of Benares (where there was no mutiny). And on 13 September, they reached Allahabad, an important town that controls the junction of the two large rivers, the Ganges and the Jumna, and which was also peaceful. By this time, British forces were marching against the mutineers. Sir John Lawrence's column from the Punjab was besieging Delhi, and General Havelock's force had taken Cawnpore. At Futterpore, forty miles from Cawnpore, Wolseley's column was halted, much to the disappointment of the troops. However, Wolseley's men were soon ordered to the town; they merely had to wait the departure of Havelock's force that was on its way to Lucknow. When Wolseley and his men got to Cawnpore, they were devastated by the bloody scene of the massacre, and their thirst for revenge became even greater.

There were still disturbances in Cawnpore, and this was where Wolseley fought his first action in India. He was part of a force led by the colonel in command of the garrison, an ancient warrior who had fought in the Peninsular War. Wolseley was very unimpressed by the colonel's military knowledge. The young Wolseley had no time for conventional politeness towards senior officers and thought that the colonel 'had the good fortune to be subsequently killed in action'.[4] This encounter with the enemy did not impede Wolseley and his men, who busily prepared to march north to Lucknow, the largest city in the province of Oudh. They crossed into Oudh *en route* to Lucknow. (See **Map 4**.) He was to serve in this province for the next eighteen months. He had by now acquired a horse and hired three Indian servants. He had very little personal kit because of what he had lost in the shipwreck. One of his servants carried this kit tied in a roll, and another carried various cooking pots on his head.

On 24 October, the British column was on the march, and Wolseley's company was the rearguard. On occasion, he ordered volleys of small-arms fire aimed at groups of sepoys who were harassing his progress. And there were constant problems with the primitive carts and their native drivers. When these men did not show enough energy, the British soldiers would lay into them with walking sticks. Wolseley's matter-of-fact description highlights Victorian attitudes to physical violence towards subject races: attitudes that were one of the many causes of the mutiny. The column had soon covered the fifty miles to Lucknow, where it had to kill time to await General Campbell with his larger force. Wolseley's column was established—and virtually besieged—in the large Alum Bagh Palace on the southern edge of the city. The British soldiers, especially the many who had fought in the Crimea, were frustrated that they were held back from assaulting the enemy. But they did not have long to wait. On 10 November, Campbell's advancing troops made contact with the city as a result of Kavanagh's daring exploit in getting through the mutineers' lines. The two forces advancing on Lucknow would shortly be amalgamated.

Campbell's force of under 4,500 men were now about to attack 50,000 mutineers. The British advance guard was commanded by

Brigadier General Hope Grant, a cavalry officer much admired by Roberts and who would later appoint Wolseley to his staff. Wolseley was in a force of six hundred men, commanded by his friend Major Barston, and was in the Alum Bagh, preparing for action. Campbell's total force circled around the east of the city (as explained in chapter 5) and prepared for the next day's assault. Wolseley's company bivouacked in the grounds of the Martinière (a building he did not much admire), where they were close enough to the enemy to hear them talking.

Before the British had discovered the enemy's strong position in the Sekundar Bagh fort, Barnston's men were advancing on the right of the British infantry, where they faced increasing small-arms fire. They were soon in the streets and alleys of the outskirts of the city, and Wolseley found that his personal servant was a brave man and was vigorously looting all the houses they came to. Under increasingly intense fire, Wolseley's company then hauled up a heavy gun from a nearby battery that was soon at work, firing effectively on the walls of the Sekundar Bagh. Soon afterwards, one of the guns in the battery misfired, and shell fragments mortally wounded Wolseley's friend Major Barnston. One of Wolseley's best sergeants was also badly wounded but later won a commission in the field and ended his career as a major. Another of Wolseley's senior NCOs had no stomach for the fight and was later demoted.

Many small and vicious combats continued in the Sekundar Bagh, but the fighting was dying down in that sector of the battlefield. During the night, the British soldiers dug two long and deep trenches. These were filled with the dead bodies of enemy soldiers, laid crossways. The number was counted, and it was the same number as the year: 1857. All the troops needed ammunition and food. This meant that the final assault was delayed to the next day. This was aimed at the last major obstacle before the relieving force reached the Residency, the administrative district. This obstacle was the former officers' mess of the Thirty-Second Regiment, a cluster of buildings known as the Mess House. The main mess hall was well built and surrounded by gardens and other buildings, and it was approached by a drawbridge over a ditch, which had already been lowered.

General Campbell took Wolseley aside and asked him to lead the assault. At the back of Wolseley's mind was the thought that the job would be too difficult for his men and that the general would ask one of his beloved Highland battalions to take over. Wolseley was not going to let this happen. After a short and powerful artillery bombardment, Wolseley's company formed a line and doubled forward, followed by another company of the Ninetieth led by Captain Irby, a cheerful officer who had a rich command of strong language. With unexpectedly light opposition, the soldiers went into and through the main mess hall. Wolseley and his men got over the garden wall beyond, but they were then confronted by a formidable obstacle before they could get to the Residency.

This was the Moti Mahul (Pearl Palace), surrounded by a thick masonry wall twenty feet high and with a detached 'tambour' wall in front of it. The palace was loopholed, and the Indians inside kept up a heavy fire on Wolseley's men. The only way out of the *impasse* was to try and dig a hole through the wall, and crowbars and pickaxes were brought up to do this. The soldiers bashed the wall and started to make some progress. Wolseley then moved along the obstacle to find another vulnerable spot:

> 'As I approached, I caught sight of the soles of a pair of boots and the lower part of a man's legs, the rest of his body being through the small hole just made, which others were still working hard to enlarge. I asked who it was: "Ensign Haig" was the answer. I have seen many a reckless deed done in action, but I never knew of a more dare-devil exhibition of pluck than this was. In any other regiment, this young ensign would have had the Victoria Cross, but to ask for that decoration was not the custom of the Ninetieth Light Infantry. The hole grew rapidly bigger, and one by one, we crawled through it.'[5]

As Wolseley's men were moving forward, they were met with an explosion. This announced the arrival of a company from the garrison.

This also belonged to the Ninetieth Regiment and was commanded by Captain Tinling. The two companies of the Ninetieth Regiment successfully got through to the Residency.

Wolseley had only been ordered to capture the main building, and a message was passed that General Campbell was furious with him for pressing on. However, after a night's rest, he discovered that the general was in the neighbourhood:

> 'Sir Colin saw me in a moment, and shaking his fist at me with a pleasant smile, he said, "If I had but caught you yesterday!" His anger had left him, and no man ever said nicer or more complimentary things to me than he did then. He ended our conversation by telling me that I should have my promotion. He did not know that two years before, I had already been promised it as soon as I should complete the regulation period of six years' service required for that rank.'[6]

General Campbell's force now had large numbers of sick and wounded, and they were also responsible for five hundred women and children in the Lucknow garrison. Campbell therefore decided to abandon the city temporarily, and this had to be concealed from the enemy, who still numbered many thousand mutineers. One thousand sick and wounded, together with the women and children, were very quietly evacuated. This was the time when General Havelock died of exhaustion (as explained in chapter 5). A pressing problem for Campbell was that Cawnpore was being besieged again by ten thousand insurgents. He was soon on his way to Cawnpore, and General Outram remained in command of the garrison on the outskirts of Lucknow. He had to await Campbell's return. Wolseley and his men were in Outram's force, which totaled fewer than 4,500 men. He formed two under-strength brigades of experienced and reliable troops, but these were commanded by ancient colonels who did not impress Wolseley. Outram's force occupied a strongly defended camp at the Alum Bagh, south of the city, and Wolseley and his men were on constant picket duty. The mutineers had grown to a hundred thousand men, but the two sides followed the policy of 'live and let live'. The British were often entertained by the bands of the mutinous regiments playing British airs.

General Campbell returned from Cawnpore in March 1858. He had by then suppressed the mutineers in Cawnpore, and the town was finally pacified. When he returned to Lucknow, the relieving force comprised thirty thousand men, including ten battalions that had newly arrived from Britain and wore new uniforms. These were a contrast to the Ninetieth Regiment and the other British troops whose clothing was tattered and battle-stained. Campbell did not waste time, and he immediately planned an artillery barrage to enfilade the rebels in Lucknow, followed by two attacks coming from different directions. The plan worked flawlessly, and there was very little infantry fighting. This was not surprising in view of the passive attitude of the mutineers who had been facing Outram's men for the previous three months. Lucknow was in British hands by mid-March, and the city remained British.

At this time, in the idiosyncratic way of the British army, the Ninetieth Regiment, also known as the Ninetieth Light Infantry, became known as the Scottish Rifles. Rifle regiments always had a special *cachet*. They all wore dark green uniforms, and when they were first raised, they were skirmishers and sharpshooters. In 1881, the title was changed to Cameronians (Scottish Rifles). Lucknow was one of its most important battle honours. The regiment was disbanded in 1968, during one of the War Office 'rationalizations' after the Second World War.

Sir Hope Grant and the Pacification of Oudh

Shortly after Lucknow was firmly in British hands, Campbell, who was now Lord Clyde, started making plans for the future. In consultation with the governor general in Calcutta, Campbell's focus turned to the entire Oudh province. He formed a division to pacify Oudh, commanded by the newly promoted and knighted Major General Sir Hope Grant. Wolseley was given the key job of quartermaster general (QMG) of this division, although his higher rank had not yet come through. Sir Hope Grant was accustomed to officers much older than Wolseley, but they soon worked well together. Wolseley was to serve in Oudh for his final eighteen months in India. Oudh is a large province: 150 miles from Cawnpore in the south to the lower slopes of the Himalayas, and 120 miles stretching east from Cawnpore and Lucknow. The province is flat and highly cultivated, and it was the home of powerful local chieftains who lived behind the walls of their rough but strong forts. The population is mostly Hindu. (See **Map 4.**)

Major General Sir Hope Grant, who had served in the Ninth Lancers, was a fifty-year-old Scot, tall, lithe, and muscular. He was an excellent horseman, devoted to his profession, and popular with all ranks. With much fighting experience, he was a good delegator who realized (as did Montgomery during the Second World War) that after a general had given his orders, he had little to do except allow his subordinates to get on with their jobs. He was not particularly well educated, but he enjoyed playing the cello. Hope Grant was not very articulate (a deficiency he shared with Haig). This meant an important role for his staff officers, particularly Wolseley and Grant's ADC, Captain Augustus Anson, nephew of General Anson, who had died of cholera when the mutiny first broke out.[7]

The division made its presence felt by carrying out a number of very visible marches across the country. The troops and camp followers formed a single column that reached for many miles. It was organized in the normal Indian fashion: marching infantry, mounted cavalry, and mounted artillery, followed by large numbers of bullock carts, camels (Wolseley had five to carry his kit), many Indian servants (Wolseley had two for his horse), doolies, tents, a portable hospital, and much more. The marching started at 3:00 AM and finished at 8:00 AM, when the weather became too hot. The column marched for about ten miles a day. Wolseley's job was to ride ahead every day, to reconnoitre the next day's march and, in particular, determine the locations for the advanced guards for every few miles of the march. On the next day, Wolseley rose at 2:00 AM, was in the saddle at 2:30 AM, and had reached the position for the first advanced guard, which the troops reached at 3:00 AM.

Wolseley was always impressed by the marching ability of the soldiers, particularly during the hot summer months.

The massive, slow-moving human crocodile was a striking presence in the province and an unmistakable reminder of the strength of British arms. The important point was that the British remained concentrated, although sickness was always taking its toll. On more than one occasion, there were rumours of huge numbers of mutineers: numbers comparable with those that had been talked about in Cawnpore and Lucknow before those cities were finally relieved. The fact that such large numbers did not generate serious resistance to the British forces indicated that the mutiny was losing its impetus.

Local tribal forces were generally concentrated in forts. Three of these were destroyed by the British column. The forts were open spaces of about two hundred acres, enclosed behind strong clay walls and high towers. In front of the walls were ditches and clumps of thorns, both of which were difficult to penetrate. The walls themselves were not designed according to any scientific plan: in particular, they had no acute angles to enable the defenders to enfilade the attackers. There were a few primitive guns, and the defenders were armed with smooth-bore muskets. The British were getting the upper hand since the defenders of the forts were easily defeated and the forts themselves destroyed. On the line of march, enemy skirmishers were easily brushed off.

Many of the tribal chiefs were neutral—or at least biding their time until there was reliable news about the success (or failure) of the mutiny—and the British column visited them in turn. The chiefs were greeted with gun salutes and other marks of respect, which were, of course, another reminder of the British presence. Sir Hope Grant and the civil authorities in Lucknow had many disputes about the cost of the military presence in Oudh, something that came from a misunderstanding of the British role. The point of all this activity was not to defeat a strong existing enemy. It was to deter potential enemies who could not fail to appreciate the disastrous consequences of taking arms against the British.

Over the months, there was a good deal of activity with the column on the march virtually every day. The infantry were burdened by their heavy loads, which included sixty rounds of ball ammunition. But the cavalry also suffered:

> 'I came upon a squadron of the Seventh Hussars on outlying picquet. The general appearance was appalling. Two of its three officers lay helpless under trees with wet towels round their heads, and the men in an exhausted condition lay about in twos and threes under whatever shelter they could find. I had a good helmet with an unusually long turban wound round it, yet the sun seemed to gimlet a hole through it into my brain. My very hair seemed to crackle from the burning heat, and the nails of one's fingers became as if made of some brittle material that must soon break.'[8]

Darkness arrived quickly in the latitude of Oudh, and there were false alarms and casualties from what is now called 'friendly fire'. There was occasional panic, and Wolseley noted that it was always the young officers who set an example and pulled their men together. The column had to cross rivers that were sometimes swollen with monsoon rains. There were also large numbers of crocodiles in the muddy water and the riverbanks. Crossing the river was always a matter of improvisation, with rafts and swimming horses—although on one occasion, the soldiers built a bridge of boats that took five weeks to complete.

Wolseley was educated to make good freehand sketches, and Sir Hope Grant gave him the job of sketching the ground in which the more important actions took place. Wolseley himself occasionally took part in the fighting. A squadron of the Seventh Hussars made a charge that won its commander the VC. Wolseley and Anson both took part in this charge, wielding their swords.

The shock effect of charging cavalry is something as old as war itself. But a technological change before the end of the nineteenth century made cavalry dangerously irrelevant. This change was the growing weight of defensive firepower, which came from rapid-fire musketry and machine guns. This change was hardly noticed during the last three decades of the nineteenth century because all the conflicts at the time had seen little use of cavalry. However, in the Second Boer War of 1899–1902, mounted infantry was effectively replacing traditional cavalry. This is something that Wolseley was thinking about in 1859. While he was engaged with the large marching column traversing the province of Oudh, he began to consider the concept of mounted infantry: columns of one thousand foot soldiers who would move around the battlefield on ponies and be responsible for their own supplies of ammunition, food, and water. The tactical value of mounted infantry became obvious on the high veldt during the Second Boer War, although Wolseley had foreseen it forty years before.

Wolseley's thoughts about mounted infantry showed that he—a young and decisive man of action—was developing a speculative turn of mind. In military terms, this meant that he was becoming a strategist as well as a tactician. As he grew older and more experienced, his vision broadened even further. The end of this chapter gives two quotations summarizing how Wolseley saw the contrast between Japan and China in 1903. They provide remarkable pointers to what was to happen during the century that followed.

On 23 May 1859, the last skirmish in Oudh marked the end of the Indian Mutiny. Major General Hope Grant returned to Lucknow, and Wolseley accompanied him. The year-long expedition had paid off. Hope Grant's services would shortly be needed in China, and this meant the next step in Wolseley's career.

The 1860 Expedition to China

European countries were interested in China for a single reason: the desire to open the country to trade. Even in the middle of the nineteenth century, China had the largest population in the world. The 1858 Treaty of Tientsin between the British and the Chinese Manchu Empire promised a permanent British diplomatic presence in Peking, a total of sixteen treaty ports (i.e. those open for trade), and protection for missionaries. The Chinese went back on their word.

In 1859, a British naval squadron was sent to open the mouth of the river that connected Peking with the sea, but this incursion was defeated with some loss. The British government immediately made plans to send an army to do the job. In August 1860, eleven thousand men—mainly Punjabis and Sikhs from Indian army regiments—landed in Hong Kong, where they were joined by a French contingent of 6,500. The French were there because France was equally determined to open up China to trade with the West. The French were under a separate commander, which caused some problems.

Sir Hope Grant had been promoted and given command of the British expedition. Wolseley, now a brevet lieutenant colonel, joined him as DAQMG, third in the 'Q' hierarchy. Hope Grant wanted him to have the senior job, but Lord Clyde did not think that Wolseley had enough experience yet. The staff arrived in Hong Kong in mid-March and spent their time exploring the Chinese mainland—Kowloon and beyond—where, in the future, they might be fighting. They found the climate delightful after India.

However, the fighting was actually going to take place further north: at Tientsin, twenty miles from the coast, and the capital, Peking, eighty miles further inland. (See **Map 5**.) This is 1,200 miles north of Hong Kong, where the force had landed, because it was a British possession. The men, without delay, had to make the long journey north by sea and river, using 120 transports and seventy smaller vessels. The British troops had by now been built up to fourteen thousand men, and they and the French landed in the swampy country in the mouth of the river leading to Peking. Wolseley gives the delightful picture of one of the first senior officers to laud:

> 'He was an old campaigner, well-known for his swearing propensities and famous as a great game shot in South Africa. I shall never forget his appearance as he struggled through that mud, knee-deep in many places. He had taken off trousers, boots, and socks, and slung them over his brass scabbarded sword, which he carried over one shoulder. Picture a somewhat fierce and ugly bandy-legged little man

thus accoutered in a big white helmet, clothed in a dirty jacket of red serge, below which a very short slate-coloured flannel shirt extended a few inches, cursing and swearing loudly."[9]

The landing was a joint Anglo-French operation, and Wolseley foresaw troubles with this arrangement. The British force comprised two under-strength infantry divisions, a cavalry brigade, and more than six artillery batteries. The weather was unpleasantly wet with the onset of winter. Wolseley rode ahead three days before the departure of the main force. His job was to make freehand maps and sketches, some of which would eventually be included in Hope Grant's official dispatch.

The army's first job was to smash the Taku forts that controlled the route to Tientsin. This was a tough assignment. Hope Grant and the French commander had a dispute about the plan of attack, but the British plan prevailed. The Manchu Empire was plagued by rebel insurgents, and a force of Tartar horsemen attacked the advancing Anglo-French force. The force, nevertheless, got through and, on 21 August, attacked and smashed the Taku forts. The artillery played a major role, especially the new Armstrong twelve-pounders with rifled barrels. (Similar weapons would be used by the Union troops in the American Civil War a couple of years later.) Despite the efficiency of these guns, no more were acquired by the War Office on the grounds of their expense!

The next day, the Chinese garrison surrendered all the territory up to and including Tientsin. The British expected a complete surrender of all the enemy forces, but this did not happen because the Chinese feared that a triumphant conquest of Peking would bring down the Manchu Dynasty. On 8 September, the Anglo-French force marched ahead, with Wolseley again in advance of the troops and equipped with his sketching pad.

North of Tientsin, a Chinese party arrived to talk about surrender. This involved an entrance without fanfare into the city. Prisoners had been taken by the Chinese; the living prisoners were immediately returned, and money was promised as compensation for the families of prisoners who had died. Meanwhile, the French troops had been diverted in search of loot from the houses of rich Chinese. The French were soon joined by the British. However, to ensure fairness, the artifacts looted by the British were valued and the money added up. The total was then shared between the troops according to their ranks. The peace treaty was signed in Peking on 24 October 1860. The army was to remain until 8 November. It is fortunate that the fighting had finished because the snow and ice of the Chinese winter would have been hard on the Indian troops.

It was a short, well-planned, and brilliantly executed campaign. It was, in particular, a tribute to the skill and experience of the British officers and the discipline of the men in the ranks. Although Wolseley developed a high regard for the Chinese people, the Chinese army was outclassed. Wolseley's men in the Ninetieth Regiment, who embarked for China in 1858 and were diverted to India, had a very low opinion of the Chinese. This was justified.

The occupation of Peking did not finish the troubles of the weak and disorganized Manchu Empire. Another serious rebellion broke out after the departure of Sir Hope Grant, and this was not quelled until the end of 1864. The British commander sent out put down the rebellion with such efficiency that he later received the well-merited nickname of 'Chinese Gordon'. He was Charles Gordon, the young officer of the Royal Engineers whom Wolseley had met in the Crimea in 1855, and who impressed everyone with his single-minded Evangelical Christianity. Both Gordon and Wolseley had been considered for the job for which Gordon was chosen. After Colonel Gordon had pacified the country, he volunteered to stay on for some months to get to know the Chinese people better. They were not a martial race. He trained his soldiers intensively, and was popular and successful.[10] When he left China, he departed with the affectionate cheers of the men he had trained. On his return to England in 1865, he and Wolseley met, and in Wolseley's words:

> 'I said to him laughingly, "How differently events might have turned out had I been sent on that mission instead of you.

I should have gone there with the determination of wiping out the rebellion and of becoming myself the Emperor of China!" How much loftier and nobler were the objects he sought after.'[11]

After Hope Grant and his staff had returned to Shanghai, they hired a steamer to take them to Japan. This was only six years after Commodore Perry and his Black Fleet had entered Tokyo Bay and effectively opened up the country. Wolseley saw Japan as a medieval society, but in 1903, he made the following comment about how Japan had changed during the forty-odd years since his first visit.

'In the winter of 1860–1861, when I visited Japan, it was not recognized as a power to be counted with in the list of nations by any Foreign Office. She then possessed nothing one could dignify with the name of an army, and she owned no ship for either peace or war that could sail safely beyond the sight of land. But when I review my impressions, and strive to compare Japan's then position in the world with her present power and eminence among the nations of the earth [*i.e. in 1903*], I realize what being strong on land and sea means to a nation.'[12]

When he wrote these words, Wolseley was looking into the near-term future—in particular into how Japanese military power would develop during the first half of the twentieth century. In contrast, when he looked at China, he was visualizing a far distant future. He was making uncertain guesses about secular change, but such changes are becoming increasingly evident in the twenty-first century:

'To me, they are the most remarkable race on earth, and I have always thought and still believe them to be the great coming rulers of the world. They only want a Chinese Peter the Great or Napoleon to make them so. They have every quality required for the good soldier and the good sailor, and in my idle speculation upon the world's future, I have long selected them as the combatants on one side at the great battle of Armageddon, the people of the United States of America being their opponents. The latter nation is fast becoming the greatest power of the world. Thank Heaven, they speak English, are governed by an English system of laws, and profess the same regard as we have for what both understand by fair play in all national as well as in all private business.'[13]

Wolseley would not have been surprised that the nations on the Pacific Rim would be dominated by Japan during the first half of the twentieth century, or that China would come into its own during the second half.

Endnotes

1. Wolseley, Field Marshal Viscount, *The Story of a Soldier's Life, Volume I, Volume II* (London: Archibald Constable, 1903), *Volume I*, 390–391:

    'It was a period of storm and stress, of horrors and of glory. Its history abounds in military events of transcendent national importance, and in brilliant instances of individual prowess. Surely, a great fighting reputation is a most valuable item when we estimate the strength of any State.'

2. Details of Wolseley's experience in India and China came from Farwell, Byron, *Queen Victoria's Little Wars* (New York: W.W. Norton, 1972); Harris, John, *The Indian Mutiny* (London: Book Club Associates, 1973); Kochanski, Halik, *Sir Garnet Wolseley, Victorian Hero* (London: Hambledon Press, 1999); Wolseley, Lieutenant Colonel G. J., *Narrative of the War in China in 1860* (London: Longman, Green, Longman and Roberts, 1863); Wolseley, *The Story of a Soldier's Life, Volume I, Volume II.*

3. Wolseley, *The Story of a Soldier's Life, Volume I*, 253.

4. Ibid., 274, 281–282.

5. Ibid., 313–314.

6. Ibid., 316–317.

7. Ibid., 342–344.

8. Ibid., 364.

9. Wolseley, *The Story of a Soldier's Life, Volume II*, 23–24.

10. Nutting, Anthony, *Gordon. Martyr and Misfit* (London: Reprint Society, 1968), 75–77.

11. Wolseley, *The Story of a Soldier's Life, Volume II*, 90–91.

12. Ibid., 89.

13. Ibid, 2–3.

CHAPTER 7

ROBERTS CLIMBS THE STAFF LADDER

Roberts left India in early May 1858 and arrived in Britain at the end of June for an extended period of leave. After his six years of campaigning in the subcontinent, he found the autumn, winter, and spring in England and Ireland wonderfully refreshing. He made the most of his time, visiting friends and family and fox-hunting in Ireland. He was also summoned to Windsor to receive his Victoria Cross from the hands of the Queen, who would get to know him better in later years. Roberts, during his long career, received many honours from the British Crown. His last meeting with Queen Victoria, a one-hour audience, took place only a few days before the Queen died, in January 1901.

There was another important event for Roberts in 1858. He met and fell in love with a young lady, Nora Bews, daughter of a retired officer in the Forty-Second Royal Highland Regiment, the Black Watch, named for its dark green tartan. Fred and Nora Roberts married in May 1859, and shortly afterwards, they embarked for India. They travelled by the Mediterranean route, with a land crossing in Egypt. During July, his wife found the heat of the Red Sea oppressive, but worse was to come in the years ahead.

Roberts had not been able to extend his leave because he had a job waiting for him on the quartermaster general's staff at the headquarters of the Bengal Army in Calcutta. He arrived in Calcutta on 30 July

1859, having been away for fifteen months. He was about to begin a long career as a staff officer, and unlike many Indian army officers who favoured a quiet life, he remained dedicated to his work on the staff for almost two decades before he himself received an important independent command as a major general.

The Staff College in Camberley moved into its own premises in 1858. From the 1860s, it became increasingly clear that attending the Staff College was an important key to senior rank. The initials *psc* *(passed staff college)* then appeared with the officer's name in the Army List. There were three grades of staff officer: general staff officer third grade (GSO 3) for captains, second grade (GSO 2) for majors, and first grade (GSO 1) for lieutenant colonels, typically chief of staff of a division. When an officer passed his two-year course at Camberley, he generally received a job as GSO 2, e.g. deputy assistant adjutant general (DAAG), or deputy assistant quartermaster general (DAQMG). The normal pattern was for an officer to alternate staff and regimental duties at three-year intervals. Most but not all officers commanding battalions and regiments were *psc*. And with rare exceptions, all generals (brigadiers and upward) were graduates. During the second half of the nineteenth century, the ethos of many historic regiments was based on loyalty to the regiment. As a result, officers in these regiments were actively discouraged from applying to the Staff College. This attitude—which deprived the army of a number of outstanding potential leaders—took a long time to change.

Eight places at the Staff College were reserved every year for the Indian Army. However, these were not all taken up, because serving in England meant that a student would sacrifice his Indian rates of pay and special allowances, which brought his income down to the British level. The relative dearth of Indian Army officers who carried the *psc* initials meant that a number of officers served an inordinately long time on the staff. As a result of Roberts's outstanding services during the mutiny, he was given a permanent staff position when he returned from England in 1859, and this would be a job with promotion prospects. There was never any question of his attending the Staff College. Roberts spent nineteen years as a staff officer, and his protégé, Ian Hamilton, who also did not attend the Staff College, spent twelve years.

Military historians usually believe that a top staff officer is unlikely to become a successful general. Staff officers and commanders need brains and a strong character, but there are differences between the personal qualities needed for the two appointments. A number of famous cases exist that demonstrate that a good staff officer should remain at the job: Berthier under Napoleon, Ludendorff under von Hindenburg, Weygand under Foch, Bedell Smith under Eisenhower, and de Guingand under Montgomery. American experience from the wars of the second half of the twentieth century showed that generals who did not perform well in battle were those with a background in staff work; they had not been regimental or battalion commanders in the front line.[1]

Roberts—who was an exception to the general rule that staff officers have different qualities from field commanders—became a divisional commander in his mid-forties and never looked back. It was soon evident that he was a good strategist. His long years on the staff had given him wide experience of the working of military formations carrying out different tasks: knowledge that was more valuable to him than regimental service. On the other hand, Hamilton (who reached four-star rank) demonstrated in the Gallipoli expedition that he was a tactician rather than a strategist, which is the quality demanded of an outstanding general.[2] The Indian army received a much larger supply of qualified staff officers after its own Staff College was established at Quetta during the early years of the twentieth century. This now supplies staff officers to the Pakistan army.

After the Indian Mutiny, all officers entering the Indian army were posted to the Indian Army Staff Corps. This was a misnomer. The Staff Corps was merely a pool of officers who served in civil posts, military headquarters, and individual regiments. Before the mutiny, British officers were promoted according to their regimental seniority, which led to anomalies, e.g. rapid promotion for surviving officers in regiments that had lost many officers in action and from sickness. In the Staff Corps, officers were promoted on the basis of their years of service, which meant many transfers between regiments. Indian-born officers, who were all of junior rank, were also promoted by length of service and tended to be old for the job.[3] At this time, the barrier between civil and military jobs was porous; but gradually, the Indian Civil Service (ICS) developed separately. It very soon garnered a formidable reputation for ability, largely because it was recruited from the pick of the graduates of Oxford and Cambridge Universities.

India was divided into three presidencies—large regions, each with its own lieutenant governor and army commander-in-chief—based in Calcutta, Bombay, and Madras. Calcutta, the headquarters of the Bengal army, was the most important, and the commander-in-chief there was head of the Indian army as a whole. Each of the commanders in the three military districts served a five-year term, and each had a full staff of 'A' and 'Q' officers. Roberts, on his return to India, joined the staff in Calcutta as a DAQMG; and shortly afterwards, he was promoted to brevet major.

The Grandeur of the Raj

While Roberts was on leave in Britain, Queen Victoria had made a proclamation that the British government would take over the government of India, which would no longer be involved in trade. This marked its final separation from the original activities of the East India Company. From 1858, the ruler of India, the Queen's Representative, became known as the viceroy and governor general, a title conveying its association with the British Crown. The governor general, Lord Canning, was promoted to be the first viceroy. When Roberts returned from England, he was given an important job that put him directly under Canning; organizing a great display of British power. The viceroy planned a procession and tour to visit the most important garrisons in Northern India and to preside over Durbars, at which he would receive tributes—valuable gifts for the British Crown—from the Indian princes whose palaces were in each district. This large public display, as it proceeded along the recently completed Grand Military Road, was carried out to impress all races and ranks of the Indian population.

Before the massive procession began, Roberts had to locate, inspect, recondition and replace vast numbers of tents, because the viceroy would live in a tent city at each stopping place. The transport was provided by 120 elephants, 1,000 camels, 500 bullocks, and enormous numbers of horses: a column twenty-four miles long and containing more than twenty thousand people. At every stopping place, a temporary city was set up, with avenues of spotless white tents with glass windows, street lamps, a native bazaar, post and telegraph offices, workshops, secure storage for the impressive jewels that were the gifts of the princes, a commissariat, and many other organizations needed to maintain the progress on time. The viceroy was accompanied by the commander-in-chief, Lord Clyde, with a body of troops the size of a brigade: infantry, cavalry, and artillery, with large numbers of camp followers. The vast procession creaked along at a speed of twelve miles a day.

To complicate matters even further, the whole inhabited area had to be dismantled as soon as the viceroy and commander-in-chief departed, and it had to be reassembled in precisely the same form before the arrival of the august personages at the next stopping place.[4] In the absence of mechanical transport and lifting equipment, the whole thing was an astonishing achievement. Roberts was in total control, reconnoitering the vast spaces of the stopping places, supervising all details of the journey, and ensuring discipline among the native drivers and *mahouts*. He even had to cope with a serious fire that destroyed many of the possessions of the viceroy and his wife. The journey across Northern India was an almost medieval spectacle, but within a few years, it would have been made in greater comfort by train.

The procession started on 18 October 1859 and ended on 9 April 1860. It covered one thousand miles and stopped at thirteen different locations, starting in Lucknow and ending in Simla. At each, the viceroy made a state entry, and a number of days were spent on ceremonies of dazzling splendor. At the durbars for the native princes, these wore heavily jeweled tunics and turbans and gave tributes to the Queen with gifts of diamonds, rubies, sapphires, emeralds, and pearls. Even greater durbars were to be held in the years ahead, the greatest of which being the durbar in Delhi for King George V and Queen Mary in 1905.

Simla, which would become the hot-weather headquarters of the Indian government and Indian army, is a delightful hill station in the foothills of the Himalayas. Shortly after the end of the viceroy's great procession, Roberts acquired a modest house in Simla called Mount Pleasant. It was in a particularly hilly location, and the track up to it was especially difficult for carriages. While Roberts rode his horse and sometimes walked, his wife and their newborn daughter travelled in a *jampan*, a vehicle like a sedan chair carried by four porters who were relieved at regular intervals. Roberts's description of the house, which was the first home of the Roberts family, carried an obviously emotional message:

> 'Our house, "Mount Pleasant", was on the very top of a hill; up and up we climbed through the rhododendron forest, along a path crimson with the fallen blossom, till we got to the top, when a glorious view opened out before our delighted eyes. The wooded hills of Jakho and Elysium in the foreground, Mahasu and the beautiful Shalli peaks in the middle distance, and beyond, towering above all, the everlasting snows glistening in the morning sun.'[5]

It was not long before Roberts was ordered to organize another highly visible journey through the various garrisons for the viceroy. This was a three-month expedition through Central India, beginning at Benares on 6 November 1860. The viceroy's party was almost as large as before, but it was not accompanied by the commander-in-chief and his sizeable military detachment. There was, of course, a large menagerie of animals to carry the men and women with their tent city and all their supplies. Crossing the Ganges was a major operation because there were no bridges. The 180 swimming elephants must have been a remarkable sight. The smaller animals were carried across on rafts.

Roberts was back in Simla at the end of February 1861. Within days, his infant daughter died, a reminder of the ever-present diseases that were endemic to India. A few months later, the viceroy's wife died of 'jungle fever', and Roberts's wife became gravely ill, and it was touch-and-go for three weeks. Lord Canning returned home in 1862, having ruled India firmly during the turmoil of the mutiny, but he died three months after arriving in England. He was replaced by Lord Elgin, who also died prematurely.

During this period, Roberts had been offered well-paid positions in the Indian Civil Service, but he turned them down without much hesitation. He was anxious to continue his career as a soldier. From early in 1861, Roberts's work was to arrange journeys for Canning and, later, for the commander-in-chief, Sir Hugh Rose. During the winter of 1861–1862, Rose led a number of visits to the North-West Frontier, during which he and his staff rode for up to forty miles a day. They spent much time with the troops in the cantonments and were occasionally entertained by the Indian princes who lived not far away. This region was to play a major role in Roberts's career when he was a general.

In 1863, an order limited the length of staff appointments in India to five years. However, this did not prevent an officer who had come to the end of one five-year appointment from accepting another, which gave him another five years on the staff. In 1863, a promotion and subsequent vacancy at the top of the Quartermaster General's Department led to a chain of promotions. Roberts became assistant quartermaster general (AQMG), which put him fifth in the departmental hierarchy and in line for promotion to lieutenant colonel.[6]

Tribal War on the Frontier

After the mutiny, India—with a population of about three hundred million—was garrisoned by fewer than three hundred thousand troops under British command. The troops were spread over the country in cantonments, many housing only a single regiment. These men were keeping their eyes on the population, with the average soldier effectively responsible for a thousand Indian men, women, and children. The British control of India was relatively relaxed and tolerant, but the

British soldiers in the garrison were there to provide internal security, to stamp out any flicker of civil unrest and law-breaking. This was essentially a police function. However, there was frequent tribal warfare along the frontier between India and Afghanistan. Today this is Pakistani territory, and the frontier is known in the twenty-first century as Af-Pak.

The frontier fighting was, to some extent, welcomed by British commanders, who saw it as an opportunity to keep the soldiers in fighting trim. Their everyday life on the plains encouraged inactivity, and the troops became rusty. The frontier is appalling terrain for combat because of the mountains and ravines. The tribesmen are hardy, ruthless, and brave, with an instinctive 'feel' for ground. They could ambush parties of troops sent to pacify them. The tribesmen were short of rifles, but they were extremely ingenious in devising ways to steal and smuggle British weapons. The British kept the frontier quiet by punitive expeditions. On rare occasions, an Indian army force would advance further into hostile territory, into Afghanistan. This was dictated by a general strategic doctrine: the need to meet a potential threat from a Russian force advancing into Afghanistan. The British strategy was known as the 'forward policy' and was assumed effective in pre-empting aggressive Russian moves.

Afghanistan is mountainous and barren and is extremely difficult fighting territory. The amir, the ruler of the country, held the balance between British and Russian interests, and he was courted by both sides. The British attempted to buy his loyalty with annual subsidies. The Russian armies kept within their frontier, but the situation was always tense, and it was to lead to the Second Afghan War in which Roberts was to play a leading role.

The frontier incursions after the mutiny did not cross into Afghanistan. However, they involved some difficult fighting. Roberts, being an officer on the staff of the general commanding the army of the Bengal Presidency, did not march with any of the punitive columns; but on one occasion, he made a decision that turned failure into victory.

A small army of tribes of religious fanatics had been terrorizing much of the frontier population since 1857 (a time when the British had other things on their hands). After the mutiny was quelled, the British planned to suppress the rampaging tribes, and a column was mounted in 1859 to advance against them. This force was not strong enough, and the British planned a more formidable operation to be launched in 1863. This was commanded by Brigadier General Sir Neville Chamberlain, with Roberts as one of his staff officers. Chamberlain was the leader who had formed the movable column in the Punjab at the beginning of the mutiny. For the 1863 frontier expedition, Chamberlain commanded a reinforced brigade of six thousand mostly Indian troops and nineteen guns. One of the main problems they faced was logistics. Supplies had to be carried by mules since the country was so mountainous. The column would have to move very slowly.[7]

The force that marched out of Peshawar was split into two columns. The stronger of the two got to Umbeyla, on the frontier, on 20 October 1863. It soon ran into trouble as a result of the slow pace of its movement: it took two days for the rearguard to enter Umbeyla. Because of this delay, the tribesmen—who were lightly armed and extremely nimble—closed in on Chamberlain's force and carried out a series of small assaults. These were serious enough to force the column into defensive positions; and to make matters worse, Chamberlain himself was badly wounded in the middle of November. In such a situation, a well-trained military force will not wait long before command is automatically taken by the next senior officer. Since Chamberlain was not evacuated, there is no sign that anyone came on the scene with a firm grip. However, the troops' morale was strong enough for them to win a number of successful defensive battles at a company level, for which two Victoria Crosses were awarded.

Word of the trouble had got back to army headquarters in Peshawar, where steps were taken to send forward reinforcements. However, the commander-in-chief needed a firsthand view of what was going on. He immediately dispatched two experienced staff officers to act as his eyes and ears. They were Lieutenant Colonel Adye, DAG, and Roberts, AQMG, both Gunners. It took them two days to arrive at Umbeyla, and they got there on 25 November. It did not take them long to make up their minds that the expedition should go forward. Reinforcements were on their way, and Major General Garvock had been nominated to take command from Chamberlain. Garvock would be expected to push the force forward immediately on his arrival.

Adye's and Roberts's recommendations were endorsed by both the commander-in-chief and the viceroy. In the meantime, Roberts made himself useful in planning the next phase of the operation. The tribesmen had suffered many casualties, and it appeared that their morale was sinking (as would later become evident in the battle of Umbeyla Hill). The hostile tribesmen numbered about fifteen thousand, spread all over the frontier, but the most formidable position on the route to be taken by the column was the conical hill at Umbeyla. This rises more than one thousand feet, and there was no path at the top, just scrub and rough grass. The sides are steep everywhere and precipitous in places. The heights were defended, at the time, with stone fortifications known in India as *sangars*. There were three thousand tribesmen on the hill, and Garvock deployed 7,800 troops for the attack. These were carefully positioned around the lower parts of the hill, and mountain guns were set up to support the infantry attack. On 15 December, the infantry assault was launched, and the men had to swarm up the hill in full view of the enemy. However, they could not be stopped, and the final storming was made by the 101st Regiment (Bengal Fusiliers), who took the hilltop in hand-to-hand fighting.

The attackers suffered eighty-three casualties, killed and wounded. The defenders lost four hundred men. In infantry assaults, it is normally expected that attackers suffer far more casualties than defenders— because the attackers are in the open and the defenders are in protected positions. The fact that the casualty figures in Umbeyla were the reverse was a tribute to the discipline, tactics, and bravery of the attacking soldiers. After the battle, the expeditionary force continued making progress against occasionally strong opposition. Roberts was as usual with the fighting troops. On one occasion, he and another staff officer were with a large party of soldiers who were being assaulted by enemy cavalry, and they were visibly shaken. Roberts immediately shouted to the men in Urdu and rallied them. The defenders held their ground, and after the battle, they counted the bodies of two hundred enemy tribesmen they had killed.

At the end of the two-month war, the tribesmen had been defeated but not crushed. A treaty covering a few simple points was signed with the tribal leaders, and the men returned to their homes, having learned a lesson. However, tribal antagonisms remained, and conflicts flared up regularly on the frontier. Roberts had once again impressed his military superiors. The commander-in-chief recommended promotion to the rank of brevet lieutenant colonel. However, Roberts would have to wait because the viceroy considered that, since he was only thirty-two, he was too young to move up so quickly.

Abyssinia and Lushai

The next step in Roberts's career took him to the Allahabad division, where he spent his time with troops, many of whom were in isolated camps attempting to avoid a virulent outbreak of cholera, which was cutting a swath through the army. He was in Allahabad in 1867 when he was appointed AQMG of a brigade that was shortly to join an expeditionary force to invade Abyssinia. Abyssinia (now Ethiopia) is a large, mountainous country in the Horn of Africa. The population follows an ancient Christian faith, and the country is barren and extremely poor. (In the twenty-first century, *per capita* income is only two dollars a day.) In the nineteenth century, the country was then a kingdom ruled by an autocratic royal house. The king, Theodore, who was thought to be mad, had recently imprisoned sixty British, French, and German citizens whose future was uncertain. The British government was determined to use force to release these prisoners, and since India is closer to Abyssinia than Britain is, the task was given to the Indian government. Lieutenant General Sir Robert Napier, head of the army of the Bombay Presidency, was given command, and fourteen thousand men were earmarked for the expedition.

Roberts was immediately set to work to arrange efficient transportation for his brigade across the Indian Ocean to Abyssinia. This is more complicated than it seems. Roberts was experienced enough to know that large military movements usually had chaotic results. Separate ships were generally used to carry the various individual parts of an army: men, ammunition, equipment, horses, mules, and so on. Doing it this way means that much time is wasted at the receiving end sorting things out. The Gallipoli expedition of 1915 was a prime example of such chaotic inefficiency.

Roberts quietly got to work to ensure that the individual parts of the brigade that would have to fight together landed together. A single cavalry regiment in the brigade included nine British officers, thirteen native officers, 450 NCOs and men, three native doctors, 489 horses, 322 mules, and 590 camp followers. Each regiment required a number of ships, and altogether, the brigade needed a fleet. Roberts was in Calcutta, working out these complicated arrangements, and he and his wife were living with his chief, Colonel Donald Stewart. An astonishing stroke of ill luck now occurred when the house was struck by a cyclone that threatened the lives of the inhabitants and washed away the contents of the house. As soon as the cyclone had passed, Roberts immediately went to the docks to inspect the transport ships, which he found substantially undamaged, although the cyclone had ripped out many large trees and flattened the native bazaar.

By this time, the main expedition commanded by Napier had left India. Stewart and Roberts departed in early January 1868, in advance of the rest of Stewart's brigade. Roberts's wife accompanied him for part of the way and then sailed on to England. Stewart and Roberts arrived in Abyssinia on 9 February. They established their headquarters at Zula, near the coast—an unpleasant place where the temperature was 117 °F during the day, and where fresh water had to be condensed from seawater. Roberts had a heavy load of administrative work in Zula, but his time there was short. In April, Napier defeated the Abyssinian forces in the Battle of Magdala, the prisoners were released, and King Theodore killed himself.[8]

After Roberts had supervised the embarkation from Zula, he had a pleasant meeting with Napier, who ordered him to carry out an important and prestigious duty. He was to take the official dispatches of the campaign to London and deliver them personally to the commander-in-chief, the Duke of Cambridge. At the meeting, the duke was accompanied by the Prince and Princess of Wales, and Roberts was treated warmly. A few years later, Roberts was to meet the royal couple again, in India. In August 1868, Roberts at last became a brevet lieutenant colonel.

On his return to India, Roberts's five-year appointment as AQMG came to an end. While he was preparing to return to regimental duty as a battery commander, he was offered a higher staff appointment, as first AQMG, which permitted him to spend another five years on the staff. He carried out many months of routine work in the heat and stickiness of Calcutta, which was not good for his health. It was 1871 before he received an appointment that was to be decisively important to his future career. He was given the job of senior staff officer to a force that would be deployed in Lushai, a district in South-East Bengal, on the border of Burma.[9]

For a number of years, the local Lushain tribes had made destructive raids on private tea plantations in the province. During one of these, a young English girl, Mary Winchester, had been abducted—an event that prompted the lieutenant governor of the Calcutta Presidency to order a punitive expedition to set out at the end of 1872. This was of brigade strength, divided into two columns. The terrain is extremely difficult because of the humid climate, thick jungle, and mountains that were five thousand feet high. Roberts was responsible for building a narrow road and arranging all transport. He had coolies for road building, and 110 miles were constructed during the four-month campaign. He had no horses and mules, but thirty-three elephants carried enormous loads. Although Roberts had been promised 157, most of them did not appear. Roberts brought brains and energy to his job. Cutting through the jungle was a much more formidable task than dealing with the tribesmen who had caused the trouble. Roberts joined the senior of the column commanders, Brigadier General Bourchier. Everyone had to march in single file, and the officers and men were ordered to reduce their baggage to the lowest possible amount (and even this was reduced later). There were some outbreaks of cholera; but fortunately, these did not spread.

The opposing tribes were among the most primitive in the world and, with their ancient muskets, were hopelessly unskilled in fighting an organized enemy. Roberts described one engagement as follows:

'As soon as we began to draw in our picquets, the Lushais, who had never ceased their fire, perceiving we were about to retire, came down in force and entered one end of the village, yelling and screaming like demons, before we had got out of the other. The whole way down the hill, they pressed us hard, endeavoring to get amongst the baggage, but were invariably baffled by the Gurkhas who, extending rapidly whenever the ground was favorable, retired through their supports in admirable order, and did not once give the enemy the chance of passing them. We had three men killed and eight wounded during the march, but the Lushais confessed afterwards to a loss of between fifty and sixty.'[10]

As the columns reached tribal villages, these were burned by the soldiers. At last, Mary Winchester was discovered unharmed and was repatriated. She died in England in 1950, an extraordinary link with the British Empire before it reached its apogee. The expedition continued for a further month, the time it took for the tribes to be adequately punished. The troops then withdrew, to the great relief of the officers and men. Roberts was well rewarded for his services. He was moved up an important notch in his staff department, becoming deputy quartermaster general (DQMG). He also became a Companion of the Order of the Bath, and so he would be known officially as Lieutenant Colonel Roberts, VC, CB.

Between 1873 and 1878, Roberts, in common with other senior officers in the Indian army, was closely concerned with the Russian menace and the relationship between India and Afghanistan. This was tense but did not lead to war. However, in 1877, plans began to be drawn up for a large Indian army field force to invade Afghanistan. Roberts was scheduled to command a column, with the local rank of major general. This was an unusual promotion for a staff officer, but it indicated Roberts's outstanding success at his job.

As discussed in chapter 1, on every occasion an officer is promoted, he works his way up a pyramid, broad at the bottom but narrow at the top. As an officer is appointed to a rank higher in the pyramid, many of his contemporaries fall by the wayside. This is especially true when a major becomes a lieutenant colonel and, later, when a field officer reaches a general's rank. What is the reason for one man to be chosen ahead of many others? How is potential ability recognized?

In the nineteenth-century British army, an officer was promoted as a result of five factors: seniority, the funds to purchase the next rank, his professional ability, patronage (i.e. how he is recognized and supported by senior officers), and luck. (Napoleon prized luck above all other qualities.) Roberts managed to advance his seniority because of his two brevet promotions. The money for purchase was not relevant for him because this system was not used in both the Royal Artillery and the Indian Army. Roberts was demonstrably a man of outstanding ability, and since he had worked directly for a number of senior officers who valued his services, he attracted patronage. He also had his share of luck, and more was to come—in particular, when he eventually rose to command the Indian army.

Roberts's long years on the staff were spent exclusively in the 'Q' department: a job concerned with what is described today as logistics. These were always important and became increasingly so as armies grew in size and complexity and became more technically oriented. During the Second World War, Churchill always complained about the length of an army's administrative 'tail', and his generals had to describe patiently the complexities of modern logistics. A recent American analysis discusses 'an old military saying that amateurs talk tactics, while professionals talk logistics'.[11] Tactics are normally thought to precede strategy. However, an effective strategy demands effective logistics before it can be implemented. Roberts's extensive knowledge of logistics was almost certainly the main reason for his first spectacular achievement as a general: the march from Kabul to Kandahar in August 1880.

Roberts, during his twenty-five years of service, had progressed from ensign to major general. Of his contemporaries, only Wolseley had moved up faster and had been promoted a local major general five years before Roberts. However, at the end of 1879, Roberts became a lieutenant general and moved ahead of Wolseley. Roberts's ability had been recognized by his brevet promotions, his VC and CB and many mentions in dispatches, and the extent to which he had impressed important generals who all supported his promotions. At the heart of his professional ability was his particular specialty: he had become an expert in logistics. To Roberts, work in the 'Q' department was always practical and 'hands-on'. He always tried to escape from his office to spend time with his troops. These were attributes of a successful general. Wolseley, not surprisingly, shared the same qualities.

During Roberts's first ten years of marriage, his wife was not in good health, and they tragically lost four children in their infancy. This was hard on Roberts and his wife, although he did not in any way neglect his military duties. But when he was in his late thirties and a senior staff officer, his worries about the family's health disappeared. Three children arrived, and all survived: a girl in 1870, a boy in 1872, and another girl in 1875. Roberts's son became a soldier in the Sixtieth Rifles but tragically lost his life in the Second Boer War, in an action in which he was awarded a posthumous Victoria Cross. At the time, Roberts was just about to become commander-in-chief in South Africa. His success in that campaign led to his appointment as the last commander-in-chief of the British army.

Endnotes

1. Ricks, Thomas E., *The Generals* (New York: The Penguin Press, 2012), 170–172.
2. Jones, *Johnny. The Legend and Tragedy of General Sir Ian Hamilton*, 171, 216, 234–235.
3. Heathcote, T. A., *The Military in British India* (Barnsley, South Yorkshire: Pen & Sword, 2013), 129–145; also Heathcote, T. A., *The Indian Army* (Newton Abbot, Devon: David & Charles, 1974), 24–26, 136–138.
4. Roberts of Kandahar, Field Marshal Lord, *Forty-One Years in India* (London: Michael Bentley, 1897), *Volume 1,* 456–478.
5. Ibid., 479.
6. Ibid., 483–501.
7. Roberts of Kandahar, *Forty-One Years in India, Volume II*, 1–24.
8. Ibid., 27–38.
9. Ibid., 53–68.
10. Ibid., 62.
11. Ricks, *The Generals*, 274–275.

CHAPTER 8

WOLSELEY IN NORTH AMERICA. ON THE STAFF IN LONDON. THE SOLDIER'S POCKET-BOOK

Wolseley left Hong Kong for Britain in May 1861, the month that saw the fall of Fort Sumter. The opening salvoes of the American Civil War rapidly echoed throughout the world: Roberts, in India, heard them at about the same time. Wolseley was due for an extended period of leave. He was just short of twenty-eight, he had been commissioned for eleven years, and was a brevet lieutenant colonel. Roberts, at the age of thirty-two, had been put up for a similar promotion; but he had been told to wait because the viceroy of India considered him too young. In Wolseley's case, his promotion was in recognition of his active service in Burma, the Crimea, India, and China. And in all these conflicts, his work had come to the notice of his military superiors, who marked him as a coming man.

Extended leave in Britain was normal in the nineteenth century for officers who had spent a number of years in tropical countries. Roberts spent fifteen months in Britain after the Indian Mutiny. Wolseley had saved most of his pay since, on active service, he had nothing to spend it on. He began his eighteen-month leave with some weeks in Paris; and then he went to England and Ireland, where he enjoyed fox-hunting, as Roberts had done. While he was engaged with this, he received a telegram to return to duty. This shortened his leave to seven months.

At the end of 1861, Wolseley was appointed AQMG in an expeditionary force bound for Canada, commanded by Colonel J. Gordon, who had fought in the Crimea with Wolseley. The British government sent the force to Canada to establish a British military presence in North America, where a crisis had already taken place. The president of the Confederate states intended to establish a separate nation, unconnected to the United States. For this reason, it was important for the Confederacy to send diplomats to a number of European countries, notably Britain. Early in the war, two Confederate diplomats travelled in a British merchant ship, the *Trent*. They must have hoped for an untroubled passage. However, the *Trent* was boarded by a ship of the United States Navy, and the envoys were arrested.

After strong British protests, President Lincoln realized the danger of a conflict with Britain, and the envoys were returned, with apologies. This solved the immediate problem, but the British government was convinced that future troubles were likely, and this meant that a permanent British force had to be established in Canada. The troops were already on their way, and the officers and men of the headquarters, together with a battery of field artillery, sailed by steamer in early December 1861. They had a terrible crossing, with constant seasickness. They arrived in Nova Scotia before the end of the year to find thick snow on the ground and a population that mostly spoke Gaelic. A battalion of Scots Guards—many also Gaelic speakers—had recently arrived and received an unexpected but appropriate welcome.

The British North American force was to have its headquarters in Montreal, but most of the soldiers would be billeted further north, at the railway terminus of Rivière de Loup. At that time of year, the best route was to sail from Halifax to Boston, and then take the train north to Montreal and Rivière de Loup. Wolseley's assignment was to set up the accommodation for the troops, with semi-permanent heated barracks. The men were already in Nova Scotia and were arriving in parties by sledge across the snowy landscape. Rivière de Loup was French Canadian, and Wolseley had to learn some of that language. He found that the local landowner was totally French Canadian although he had a Scottish name. His ancestor, who had been given the property, was one of Wolfe's soldiers during the taking of Quebec a hundred years before.

When the troops were settled, Wolseley returned to the headquarters in Montreal. He spent a quiet winter there, although he was snowed in for much of the time. He took the opportunity to visit the United States on a few occasions, and he was to make a more extended visit in 1862.[1]

The War Between the States

The Southern States still use this description of the war—which, in the North, is usually called the Civil War or the Rebellion. Since Wolseley's visit was to the Confederate armies, it is appropriate to call the war by its Southern name. The ultimate cause of the war was slavery, but the immediate trigger was Lincoln's determination to prevent the Union from falling apart. The Southern States were agricultural—an activity that, in the mid-nineteenth century, was labour-intensive. The labour was provided by slaves, and since they were bought and sold, their cash value represented an overwhelming proportion of the capital possessed by the farmers and plantation owners who owned them. If slavery were abolished, this would mean that their capital value would disappear, and all slaveholders would become much less rich than before. Slavery, therefore, underpinned the way of life of the Southern States.

Slavery was opposed on humanitarian grounds by the population of the Northern States, not to speak of European nations—notably, the British, who had abolished slavery in the early part of the nineteenth century. This widespread hostility to the Southern States forced them into a corner. They therefore seceded from the Union and set up the Confederate States of America, with their capital in Richmond, Virginia, and a president, Jefferson Davis. The Confederacy fired the first rounds of the War in May 1861, when they captured Fort Sumter, in the harbour of Charleston, South Carolina.

The United States was never a militaristic power, and it had an army of only sixteen thousand men in 1861. However, the officer corps was strong since commissioned officers were graduates of the United States Military Academy, West Point, on the River Hudson, New York. The academy graduated about fifty officers per year after a rigorous four-year program and a degree. The academy was widely regarded as providing the best military education in the world.

When war was declared, the first duty of the United States military leaders was to boost the small force of regular soldiers to an army of a number of divisions of well-trained volunteers. The most important force was the Army of the Potomac, commanded by Major General George McClellan. Nearly all the officers who supervised the training had graduated from West Point. As the war progressed, regiments were added on a state-by-state basis, and eventually, conscription became necessary despite its unpopularity.

The Confederate troops were mainly farmers who were used to a country life and were practiced shots. The Southern officers were drawn from members of sometimes prominent Southern families, and many had graduated from West Point. Others had come from the Virginia Military Institute (VMI) in Lexington, Virginia, an organization with a strong ethos:

> 'VMI had a moral culture that brought together several ancient traditions: a chivalric devotion to service and courtesy, a stoic commitment to emotional self-control, and a classical devotion to honor. The school (in the twentieth century) was haunted by the memories of Southern chivalry: of the Civil War general Stonewall Jackson, a former professor there; of the 241 cadets, some as young as fifteen, who marched out on May 15, 1864, to turn back a Union force at the Battle of New Market; and by the ghost of the Confederate hero Robert E. Lee, who served as a *beau idéal* of what a man was supposed to be.'[2]

McClellan was a practiced organizer and trainer of men, but he was astonishingly reluctant to commit them to battle: something that Lincoln found insupportable. The Confederate generals were much more aggressive, and their skill and energy became obvious as early as the First Battle of Bull Run in July 1861, where the Confederate army won a dramatic and surprising victory. This was where Brigadier General Jackson, commanding the Virginians, stood upright against the enemy fire, 'like a great stone wall', and won his immortal name. It is no coincidence that Wolseley was anxious to meet Lee and Jackson.

The Union and Confederate armies comprised infantry, cavalry, and artillery. The Union infantry were armed with British Enfield muskets and (the more accurate) rifles. But the rate of fire was slow—one round per minute—because the weapons were muzzle-loaded, with the bullets rammed down the barrel one at a time. The cavalry had an important but non-dominant role, and some cavalry generals, notably J. E. B. Stuart, became famous. The artillery used nine-pounder and twelve-pounder field guns that fired directly at a range rarely more than a mile. They also had a low rate of fire because of muzzle-loading. They were smooth-bore, but rifling was later introduced. It was not until later in the war that the industrial superiority of the Northern States tilted the war against the Confederacy. In Springfield, Massachusetts, the armory was eventually producing machine-made rifles with replaceable parts at a rate of one thousand a day.

As the war continued, the North became stronger and the South became weaker, although two years of bloodshed and destruction did not lead to any conclusion. It took President Lincoln two years to find, at last, Grant and Sherman, who were generals with the military skills and determination to fight an industrial war. This focus on leadership is a reminder of Napoleon's maxim that what matters in war is not the men, but the *man*.

From the beginning, the war was carefully studied by armies in all parts of the world. A number of British officers in Canada travelled south to visit the Northern troops, but these were not doing well, despite their large numbers and their superior equipment. McClellan had made a skillful plan to land his army by sea at the base of the

Yorktown Peninsula and then advance up it to Richmond. This had been blocked by Robert E. Lee, the head of the Army of Northern Virginia and Confederate commander-in-chief. Lee boosted his strength by bringing Stonewall Jackson by rail across country from the Shenandoah Valley, where he had been operating successfully against substantial Union forces. McClellan was defeated and relieved of his command. His successor also attempted to take the war into the South and was equally unsuccessful.

Robert E. Lee now seized the initiative and advanced into Northern territory. In early September 1862, he crossed the Potomac and moved into Maryland to threaten Washington. His army totaled only thirty-five thousand badly equipped men, and was met by a Federal force of seventy thousand commanded by McClellan, who had been reappointed. The bloody Battle of Antietam stopped Lee's further advance, although he had the better of the fighting. But McClellan made little effort to catch the Confederates as they marched away, accompanied by fourteen thousand prisoners, fifty guns, and large quantities of supplies. It was a tactical victory for the South but a strategic victory for the Union. But because Lee had given McClellan a bloody nose, it is not surprising that Lincoln finally ran out of patience.

Wolseley was determined to visit the scene of the war, and he applied for a two-month leave to do so. He intended to visit the Confederate army, who were clearly making the running. But Wolseley had very little idea how he was going to get through the Northern lines. He traveled from Canada and reached Baltimore—a city with strong Southern sympathies—arriving there before the Battle of Antietam. He had a letter of introduction that ensured that he was welcomed by a number of prominent citizens. He soon learned that there was a good deal of communication with Richmond, and indeed there was a large trade in smuggled goods that were scarce in the South. Wolseley now met a correspondent of the *Times*, a well-connected Englishman, and they decided to make the journey south together.

They hired a buggy driven by a Southern sympathizer. It took them some days to reach Harpers Ferry, bumping into a number of Northern cavalry patrols. They eventually found a quiet stretch of the

Potomac and spent the night in a rat-infested hut on the riverbank. They paid a high price for places in a smuggler's boat full of contraband tea, coffee, and sugar, and slipped across the river. On the Virginia side, they encountered a Southern cavalry patrol and were taken to its headquarters in Fredericksburg. From there, they went to Richmond by rail, accompanied by many wounded men who were all in pain. In Richmond, Wolseley met the Confederate war minister, whose offices were full of Union battle flags that had been captured. (The British army at the time still carried battle flags, with each regiment's two colours acting as a rallying point for the soldiers. However, this came to an end in 1880.) Wolseley gave his word that he would not disclose any military secrets to outsiders, and this completely satisfied the minister.

Wolseley was in plain clothes, and he was given a warm welcome everywhere because of his credentials as a lieutenant colonel in the British regular army, particularly since he had made such an effort to pass through Northern territory and smuggle himself across the Potomac. The war minister arranged for Wolseley to visit a number of battlefields, something of the greatest professional interest to him. He walked over the positions around Richmond where McClellan was defeated in what became known as the Seven Days Battles. The terrain was wooded and favored defence, and the forests were pockmarked with scars from bullets and widespread destruction from shellfire. A young officer explained Lee's strategy of moving Jackson's army to the east 'on interior lines', which enabled Jackson to attack the enemy in the flank and thus reinforce Lee's frontal pressure. During the battles, the Confederate soldiers seized quantities of badly needed arms, equipment, and clothing.

The war minister also arranged for Wolseley to meet Robert E. Lee, and he went to Lee's headquarters in the beautiful Shenandoah Valley. This was no more than a group of tents, and there was an absence of military pomp. The tents were stencilled with the initials *U.S.*, which showed them to be war booty. Wolseley talked to Lee long enough to appreciate his abilities and personal qualities. Lee was 'a thoroughbred gentleman':

'He was the ablest general, and to me, seemed the greatest man I ever conversed with; and yet I have had the privilege of meeting von Moltke and Prince Bismarck, and at least upon one occasion had a very long and intensely interesting conversation with the latter. General Lee was one of the few men who ever seriously impressed and awed me with their natural, their inherent greatness. Forty years had come and gone since our meeting, yet the majesty of his manly bearing, the genial winning grace, the sweetness of his smile and the impressive dignity of his old-fashioned style of address, come back to me amongst the most cherished of my recollections.'[3]

Wolseley next met Stonewall Jackson, who was Lee's *alter ego*. Jackson also made a powerful impression, and Wolseley considered him an Ironside like Cromwell, and compared him with Lee, a Cavalier like Prince Rupert:

'More than anyone I can remember, Jackson seemed a man in whom great strength of character and obstinate determination were mated with extreme gentleness of disposition and with absolute tenderness towards all about him.'[4]

Like the Roundhead warriors of the English Civil War, Jackson was a militant Christian. He had visited England, and the incident that made the strongest impression on him was the 'seven lancet windows in York Minster'. Wolseley also spent an afternoon with General James Longstreet, Lee's most important cavalry commander. As his division marched by, Wolseley could not fail to be impressed by their fighting spirit, although their clothing and equipment were in tatters.

Wolseley's leave was only for two months, and he managed to return on time, although he had great difficulty in crossing the Potomac into Northern territory. Until the end of his life, he remained impressed with the patriotism of the Confederate soldiers. He believed that if trade had been opened between the Southern states and Europe—something that was impossible because of the Northern blockade—the Confederate States would have benefited from strong economic growth, and they might have won their independence. This was not to be. And even more importantly, the Union's strategic victory at Antietam gave Lincoln the political confidence to issue the Emancipation Proclamation that liberated the slaves. This meant that the Confederate States were ultimately doomed.

Wolseley used his time visiting the Southern army very productively. His first-hand acquaintance with this army—and, in particular, its leading commanders—made him a unique figure in the British army. The War Between the States was the first conflict of the industrial age, and Wolseley was the only British officer to receive an early glimpse of it.[5]

Fenians and the Red River

Wolseley returned after his two-month visit to the opposing sides in the American Civil War. By now, he was convinced that 'the United States people have become the foremost nation in the world, far greater than Washington and his able colleagues could ever have hoped for or even dreamt of'.[6] In the 1860s, not many people in Britain, France, or Germany would have agreed with him; but every year that passed would confirm the wisdom of Wolseley's judgment.

When he was back in Canada, he was given an assignment that helped lay the foundation for the future successes of the Canadian army. This force provided regiments during the Second Boer War, and divisions and corps during the First and Second World Wars, and even an army in North-West Europe in 1944–1945. When Wolseley was in Canada, it was a British colony and did not become self-governing until the end of the nineteenth century. The population was made up of two groups. The larger group was British: immigrants and descendants of immigrants, many of whom were Scottish Presbyterians. The smaller group was French. (In the twenty-first century, these represent more than 20 percent of the population.) Members of the French-Canadian population are concentrated in Quebec, which has helped preserve their identity and their Roman Catholicism, and also their distinctive *patois*.

In the 1860s, the British government decided to organize and train a Canadian militia, a part-time military force. The British army commander-in-chief, the Duke of Cambridge, was charged with making this happen. It was modeled on the British Militia, which was based on the regular regiments: a militia battalion was attached to each, and the small permanent staff came from the regular regiment. Before the First World War, the British Militia was phased out and replaced by the Territorial Force, which had different terms of service. The part-time force in Canada is still, in the twenty-first century, called the Canadian Militia.

Canada has never had a large regular army, although it has the distinguished Royal Military College in Kingston, Ontario. Canada's enviable military reputation has therefore been based on the militia regiments that were mobilized during the First and Second World Wars. The force contains infantry and cavalry (and later, armored) regiments, as well as artillery, engineers, and services. Many of the infantry regiments soon became affiliated with established British regiments. The Governor General's Bodyguard is linked to the Coldstream Guards, and a number of Canadian infantry units are affiliated with Scottish Highland and Lowland regiments.

Before the system was drawn up to create a national militia force, a number of Canadian cities and towns had independently set up militia units, although there was no standard system of organization and training. The Duke of Cambridge appointed an experienced British officer, General Sir Patrick MacDougall, to command the force. The officers and men were enthusiastic but untrained. Wolseley was given the key job of setting up a camp for militia officers and to supervise their training. He established two battalions with their own commanding officers, one British and one French-Canadian. Wolseley was well qualified to inculcate the qualities that the young officers needed to develop the power of command:

> 'Anyone can learn in a few weeks to shout out the drill-book
> words of command required for any military movement . . .
> but not so the art of commanding men . . . good pleasant

manners, closely allied to firmness, a genial disposition, a real
sympathy for the private soldier, and an intimate knowledge
of human nature, are essential qualifications for the man who
would command soldiers effectively anywhere.'[7]

On one occasion, Wolseley compared British regulars with his
young Canadian officers. The British were inclined to follow orthodox
procedures, while the Canadians were more pragmatic and relied on
their plentiful common sense.

One of the most important reasons why an efficient Canadian
Militia was established was because of the danger of an armed incursion
by a quasi-military body of men called the Fenians. The Fenians,
founded in 1858, were a league of Irish people in the United States,
many of whom had immigrated during the Potato Famine of the 1840s.
The members were Roman Catholic and passionately hostile to the
British, who had governed and often oppressed the people of Ireland
for four centuries. In later years, the Fenians' cause was adopted by the
persistently militant Irish Republican Army (IRA). The Fenian leaders
hoped—unrealistically—that if they invaded Canada, large numbers
of Canadians would rally to their cause. They also believed—equally
unrealistically—that the United States government would assist them.
Many Fenians had been Irish recruits who had fought in the ranks
of the Union army during the Civil War. The Fenian leaders were
optimistic enough to believe that they would persuade the United States
government to support them, especially since the British had been
inclined to favor the South because of the importance of the Lancashire
cotton industry, which had slumped because of the lack of raw cotton.

Two groups of Fenians gathered in Upstate New York, in Buffalo
and Ogdensburg, with the intention of advancing into Canada in
the summer of 1866. The Canadian government, who had received
information about what was going on, mobilized ten thousand members
of the militia. When the Fenians moved into Canada from the Niagara
Peninsula, they had no chance of success. The response of the Canadian
Militia was confused, but the Fenians were even more so. One step

that the government took was to dispatch Wolseley to pull the defenses together.

In the heat of early June 1866, the Fenians lost many men in inconclusive skirmishes. They made no forward progress and, before long, withdrew into United States territory. The whole enterprise was a fiasco. However, to prevent any further Fenian incursions, Wolseley set up a camp on the Niagara Frontier. It was manned by a regular British battalion and an artillery battery. Militia battalions were cycled in four or five at a time, and Wolseley made a good deal of progress in training these men, whom he regarded highly.[8]

It was a busy time for Wolseley, especially since in 1868, on his thirty-fifth birthday, he married. His wife was a handsome Irish lady called Louisa Erskine, whom he called Loo and who would receive an endless stream of letters from her husband in future years.

The Fenian incursion of 1866 was not the end of the military disturbances. Canada is a very large country, and in 1869, a much more serious outbreak occurred at the Red River. Wolseley was closely involved in this, and his success added greatly to his reputation. The Red River Expedition was organized to suppress a rebellion in the enormous undeveloped province then known as Prince Rupert's Land. This region had been controlled by an independent commercial organization, the Hudson Bay Company, whose business was based on trade with the local Indian tribes to buy furs, selling them to wholesale and retail customers in regions of Canada that had been settled for generations. The Hudson Bay Company ran the territory that it occupied (in a similar way to how the East India Company ran the Indian subcontinent). However, the Canadian government eventually stepped in, and on payment of the modest sum of £300,000, it took over Prince Rupert's Land, which became the Province of Winnipeg. (See **Map 7**.) The commercial activities of the Hudson Bay Company continued to prosper.

Fort Garry was half a mile south of the village of Winnipeg. As this grew into a city, it incorporated Fort Garry, which, in the 1860s, was a strong edifice with four high stone walls. It stands on the Red River, which runs north from the United States through 120 miles of Canadian territory until it empties into Lake Winnipeg. It is 350 miles west of Lake Superior as the crow flies. The Red River Expedition left from Lake Superior, and it had to march through wild countryside and had to cover a distance far longer than 350 miles.

The rebellion in the Red River Province had a complicated cause. Five separate parties were involved: the Canadian government, the Hudson Bay Company, the English-speaking settlers, the local Native Indian tribes, and the French-Canadians. The most important was the Canadian government based in Ottawa, which could not accept any more separate French provinces. The Hudson Bay Company had a major commercial interest in the prosperity of the province, and political tensions would depress this. The English-speaking settlers were Scottish Presbyterians who had arrived during the first two decades of the nineteenth century, and many more settlers arrived later. The many local Indian tribes had an important position in the region, especially since the French-Canadians embraced them as allies. The direct originators of the conflict were the growing numbers of French-Canadians. These were Roman Catholics who were organized locally by their churches, under the powerful overall leadership of their bishop. Their explicit intention was to establish a second province, like Quebec, on the western Canadian prairie. Aligned against them were the increasing numbers of English-speakers, whose political authority in Parliament had increased and who were forcefully supported by their local press. When surveyors were sent to map out the virgin land for individual farms, they invariably favored English-speaking Canadians over French-speaking ones.

A leader of the French-speaking faction now emerged. He was Louis Riel, who had worked in the United States and had learned to speak English. In October 1869, he demonstrated his powers of leadership over French-speaking Canadians and half-castes as he led them to open rebellion. Riel declared a republic with himself as president, and the rebellion soon demonstrated its seriousness. The rebels arrested one of the land surveyors, tried him by court martial, condemned him to death, and shot him. Meanwhile, the government in Ottawa appointed a governor general of Winnipeg Province. He travelled north from the

United States, but his passage was blocked before he reached Fort Garry. The rebels were now in control.

Ottawa took decisive action. Wolseley was quartermaster general of the British force in Canada and was a senior enough figure to be appointed to command a stripped-down brigade of 1,400 men, which was now ordered to the Red River to suppress the rebellion. The expeditionary force comprised a British regular battalion of the Sixtieth Rifles and two battalions of Canadian Militia—one English and one French, which were both specially embodied. There was also a small British regular detachment of artillery and engineers. The brigade travelled from Toronto by rail and later by steamboat, where there were unfounded fears that the Fenians would cause trouble. Wolseley's base was at Thunder Bay, on the western shore of Lake Superior, where Wolseley set up his camp on 25 May 1870. (See **Map 7**.) Preparation for the expedition took three weeks.

The expedition demanded rigorous logistical planning, and Wolseley was well qualified to do this because of his years of experience in the 'Q' department. The approximate distance the force would travel between Thunder Bay and the Red River is more than 600 miles (compared with the direct distance of 350 miles). The brigade would traverse rivers and lakes, but between the waterways, a way had to be cleared through forests and around and between hills. The greatest difficulty would be these stretches of rough country. The whole journey called for manual labour to clear the way and then haul the boats—a process called 'portage'. The boats were thirty feet long and held a dozen men, including French-speaking Indian 'voyageurs' whose job was to row and steer the vessels. (Fourteen years after the Red River Expedition, Wolseley commanded the British army that had to advance rapidly up the Nile to reach General Gordon, who was besieged in Khartoum. The Nile has patches of rough water called cataracts, and Wolseley organized Canadian-style portages to haul the boats overland parallel to the cataracts.)

The 1,400 men of the Red River force had to be totally self-sufficient because they could not expect any further supplies after they had embarked on their journey. They had to transport provisions for two months, and also medical supplies, ammunition, tents, equipment to repair boats, tools for clearing the countryside, fishing nets, and anything else that would be needed for such a venture. Wolseley was proud that it was his first independent command, and his job was to do much more than supervise. He had to instill a sense of urgency into all the men under his command. Wolseley aimed to get the job done quickly since the battalion of the Sixtieth Rifles had to return east before the winter, when the lakes in the Red River Province were solid ice. One of the British officers who made a mark on Wolseley was Captain Redvers Buller of the Sixtieth Rifles. He was built like an ox, he could wield an axe, repair a boat, and carry a hundred-pound barrel of pork on his back. He later became a *protégé* of Wolseley and a prominent member of the group of officers known as the Wolseley 'Ring'.

When the force set off on its outward journey, only the first forty-eight miles were on partially constructed roads. These took the force to Lake Shebandowan. From then on, the transport had to be mainly by boats. From Lake Shebandowan to the Lake of the Woods was a distance of 310 miles, which demanded seventeen portages, some a mile long. The weather became hot, with frequent thunderstorms, and there was a troublesome plague of flies for which Wolseley provided face veils for the troops. But despite the discomfort and the hard manual labour, the morale of the soldiers was high. Wolseley also had to meet the chiefs of the Chippewah Indian tribe, who wanted to be paid to allow the troops to march through their land. Wolseley had to do some fast talking to persuade the Indians that there would be great long-term benefits although no short-term ones!

When the column was fully underway, its length stretched for 150 (*sic*) miles. Putting it together was a remarkable feat, particularly since fewer than 40 percent were regular soldiers. The portage operations were run with a high standard of discipline. Each company commander was responsible for all the boats carrying his company and all their supplies. The company commander was personally responsible for

> 'the opening out of all the "portages" and cutting down and laying the rollers along them. The poplar of about six or eight

inches in diameter made the best rollers, as the boats could be hauled most easily over their soft and juicy bark. As a rule, when each company reached a "portage" the company immediately in front had not yet quite cleared away from it. But until all the stores of the company in possession of the "portage" had been taken across, the newly arrived company was not allowed to begin discharging provisions, etc.'[9]

The men were enthusiastic and in robust health. Everyone worked from dawn to 7:00 PM and lived on monotonous food: salt pork, hard tack biscuits, and any wild fruit they could find. Tents were carried on the boats, but they were only rarely pitched because the men preferred to sleep in the open air even in the frequent rain. Wolseley's sense of urgency infected all ranks.

Wolseley acted like a scout for his whole force, marching in advance and marking trees to indicate the route to follow. News of the expedition had reached Fort Garry, but Riel and his so-called republic did not know how they were going to respond. Wolseley was aware of what was happening in the fort because he had put in place a remarkable young intelligence officer, Lieutenant William Butler of the Sixty-Ninth Regiment, who travelled via the United States and reached Fort Garry from the south. He managed to get messages through from Fort Garry to the relieving brigade. On one occasion, Wolseley made preparations to advance on Fort Garry from the east, using a primitive road. Riel moved some of his men to block this move, but it was nothing more than a ruse.

Wolseley had always intended to follow a different approach: an advance north-west along the Winnipeg River until it debouched into Lake Winnipeg, from which the route would turn to the south to reach Fort Garry from the north. The Winnipeg River is beautiful but fierce, with many rapids, whirlpools, and falls. This makes for very difficult progress, but the 'voyageurs' did their job well, and no one was drowned. Despite these difficulties, the regulars in Wolseley's force reached Lake Winnipeg by 20 August 1870.

Riel requested an amnesty, and the Roman Catholic bishop went to Ottawa to try and arrange this. However, the governor general would not consider it in view of Riel's responsibility for the murder of the land surveyor. Riel and his six hundred men were a thoroughly disorganized force. In heavy rain and thick mud, Wolseley rounded them up in what is best described as a police action. Riel was captured and, after a time, released; but he caused more trouble in the future and was eventually hanged.

The Red River Expedition was a model operation on a small scale. Everything went right, and there were no casualties. The total cost was estimated to have been £100,000 (about £10,000,000 in twenty-first-century money). This was thought a small expenditure of public funds considering the outcome, which was that Canada west of Quebec would, in future, be substantially English-speaking. Wolseley's contribution was recognized by a public dinner in Montreal. This was followed by his appointment to the War Office in London, the center of Britain's worldwide military establishment.[10]

The Soldier's Pocket-Book

Wolseley made his mark during his service in Canada. However, this did not mean that his life was one of continuous activity. He had time to think, and his thinking led him to write a book that was published and very well received. Despite his sketchy education, Wolseley eventually became a prolific author. *The Story of a Soldier's Life* has been quoted extensively in this book, and this was not the first work that came from his pen. Even more remarkable was *The Soldier's Pocket-Book for Field Service*, published in 1868 and written in Canada over the course of five years. As Wolseley received further promotions, new and expanded editions of *The Soldier's Pocket-Book* came out. It was bought and used by more than one generation of British regular, militia, yeomanry, and volunteer officers. Tens of thousands of copies were sold, and although these did not make Wolseley a rich man, they helped make him the best-known officer in the army.[11]

'Pocket-Book' is a misnomer, because no normal pocket would be large enough to contain it. This was particularly true of the later editions. The fourth edition—published in 1882 when Wolseley was adjutant general—was five hundred pages long, with more than 250,000 words (the same size as one of Dickens's larger novels). Wolseley's language is brisk and businesslike: clear, direct English. The work concentrates on all the details of how military units and formations are run: the 'plumbing' that keeps them in smooth operation. The book contains an eclectic collection of 180 brief chapters, e.g. 'Field Equipment for Officers,' 'Table of Bulk of Rations,' 'Fitting a Ship for Horses,' 'Medical and Surgical Hints,' 'Wars with Savage Nations,' 'English and French Weights and Measures'. There are many tables and sixty-two clear line drawings, e.g. 'Camp of a Battalion of Infantry on War Establishment'. But there are a few important omissions. The book has little to say about tactics; it describes drills but not a commander's grip on a battlefield and his ability to exploit speed and surprise. And on a larger scale, there is no discussion of strategy at all.

The Soldier's Pocket-Book was really a small encyclopedia, an excellent source of information for officers who were ambitious about efficiency. Indirectly, Wolseley's book was an inspiration for manuals written in the twentieth century by J. F. C. Fuller and B. H. Liddell Hart, authors who were much more concerned with tactics and strategy. During the Second World War, the War Office issued many practical pamphlets, each devoted to a single topic (e.g. the three-inch mortar), and which provided accurate and practical help to junior officers and NCOs whose duty was to instruct the men in the ranks.

After Wolseley's book was published in 1868, most senior officers learned about it. Although many were impressed, others felt that Wolseley should have confined himself to the organization of regiments of infantry and cavalry and similar-size units of artillery and engineers. They believed that he should have stopped short at the level of brigades and larger formations.

Wolseley arrived at the War Office in May 1871. He found it 'as full of life as an upturned beehive'.[12] The former somnolent atmosphere in that institution had completely disappeared. Wolseley's success in commanding the Red River Expedition brought him to the notice of his superiors in London. Shortly after his arrival there, he had a very friendly meeting with the commander-in-chief of the British army, the Duke of Cambridge. The duke, who was Queen Victoria's cousin, was a popular figure and looked every inch a commander-in-chief. But he was a figure out of the past, the most conservative officer in a notably conservative officer corps. To Wolseley, the duke and his closest colleagues 'had forgotten nothing and learnt nothing since Waterloo'.

The duke's headquarters was at the Horse Guards, which backs onto Whitehall. The Secretary of State for War was at the War Office, then in Pall Mall. He was Edward Cardwell, appointed by Prime Minster Gladstone as part of his Liberal administration that came to office in 1868. Cardwell was to be the major reformer who transformed the War Office into the 'upturned beehive'. The physical separation of the uniformed head of the army and its political head made for tension. The two jobs were not equally important. In a parliamentary democracy, the Secretary of State for War had the weight of responsibility, and the commander-in-chief reported to him. However, it took more than thirty years for the post of commander-in-chief to be abolished. After the weaknesses disclosed by the Second Boer War, a general staff was set up, and the Chief of the Imperial General Staff (CIGS) became the main military advisor to the Secretary of State for War. The last soldiers to be commanders-in-chief were to be Wolseley and Roberts.

In 1871, Wolseley, by now a colonel, was appointed to the adjutant general's staff as deputy adjutant general (DAG), with responsibility for courts martial and other aspects of military discipline. He spent his time in the War Office 'beehive'. Two outside events added force to the need for reform. The first was the lingering memory of the Crimean War, which exposed terrible deficiencies in army organization and staff work. The miserable conditions of the soldiers besieging Sebastopol were widely known, as were the shocking conditions of the military hospitals, vividly described by William Howard Russell, the *Times* newspaper correspondent. Even the heroic Charge of the Light Brigade was known as a disaster because of confused orders—in the words of Tennyson, 'someone had blundered'.

The second event was nearer in time: the Franco-Prussian War. The unexpected but total defeat of France was the outcome of the Prussians' high standard of training of their conscript army; their weapons (notably, their breech-loading rifles); and, most importantly, the talents of that concentration of military brainpower, the Great General Staff of the Prussian army.

Cardwell began a programme of reform that was also carried on by his successor, Hugh Childers, who was responsible for the introduction, during the early 1880s, of the 'linked battalion' system. The initiative taken by Cardwell from the time of his appointment ensured that the centre of military influence had decisively moved from the Horse Guards to the War Office. The army in which Wolseley rose so swiftly was not only based on its robust regimental tradition, but it was also made more efficient by the reforms of the 1870s:

- The widespread use of the breech-loading rifle. The first models were single-shot, but the rate of fire increased spectacularly to ten rounds a minute. Since muzzle-loaded rifles could only fire one or two rounds a minute, breech loading transformed the battlefield—the higher rate of infantry fire caused enormous casualties among charging cavalry. In 1888, a rifle was introduced with an eight-round magazine. This increased the rate of fire even further to at least fifteen rounds a minute, and sometimes twenty-five rounds in the hands of a highly trained marksman.[13]
- The reduction in the sizes of all the overseas garrisons except India, where the garrison was maintained at a higher level than before the mutiny.
- The purchase of commissions was finally abolished, which meant an improvement in the quality of leadership because candidates eligible for promotion were judged on their talent rather than their ability to pay.
- Short service was introduced. Traditionally, soldiers in the ranks could serve for extended periods, even as long as twenty years. Short service meant seven years with the colours and five years in the reserve. (Both periods could be extended.) This change

meant that the average age of the rank and file was reduced. And, most importantly, a reserve was quickly built up. When the British Expeditionary Force (BEF) went to France in 1914, half the soldiers were reservists. They were trained men, and their only difficulty was the time it took them to get used to marching on the *pavé* of French and Belgian roads.

- The Childers Reforms made infantry regiments larger in size. Each was given the name of its regimental recruiting area: something that provided an additional source of loyalty. Each regiment was made up of two linked battalions, with one serving overseas at full strength and the other training at home and dispatching men to the overseas battalion. This was the system that made it possible to garrison efficiently a widespread empire.

- The part-time home defence forces were a long-term problem, with the regiments of cavalry (the old yeomanry) and infantry (the old volunteers) operating rather like private armies. The difficulties were finally solved by the Haldane Reforms in the early twentieth century, when the Territorial Force was set up, with each individual unit forming part of its parent regular regiment.

These six reforms were implemented, although some time passed before the linked-battalion system was in operation, and even more time before the yeomanry and volunteers were reorganized. Short service was quickly put into effect, but it caused controversy. Many experienced officers wanted to retain long service because they considered it was important to have large numbers of old soldiers in the ranks to provide 'ballast': something that steadied young soldiers when they came under fire. Short service was introduced into the Indian army some years later than in the British. Roberts was not in favour of the change, and he had his own ideas about reforming the terms of enlistment. This was a subject he thought and wrote about when he was in command at Madras, and his views are discussed when his time in Madras is examined.

Wolseley was a newly promoted colonel in the War Office and worked on all these issues. Cardwell liked him and took him into his confidence. However, Wolseley was only there for a little over two years, although he was to return in 1880 as quartermaster general. Trouble was brewing in the unhealthy British possessions on the West African coast, and as another indication of Cardwell's confidence in him, Wolseley departed in September 1873 to command an expedition against the Ashanti tribe.[14]

Endnotes

1. Wolseley, Field Marshal Viscount, *The Story of a Soldier's Life, Volume II* (London: Archibald Constable, 1903), 101–116.
2. Brooks, David, *The Road to Character* (New York: Random House, 2015), 107.
3. Wolseley, *The Story of a Soldier's Life, Volume II*, 135.
4. Ibid., 139.
5. Ibid., 117–144.
6. Ibid., 144.
7. Ibid, 154.
8. Ibid., 152–164.
9. Ibid., 197–198.
10. Ibid., 181–226.
11. Wolseley, Lieutenant General Sir Garnet, *The Soldier's Pocket-Book for Field Service,* Fourth Edition (London: Macmillan, 1882).
12. Wolseley, *The Story of a Soldier's Life, Volume II*, 240.
13. Duckers, Peter, *British Military Rifles, 1800–2000* (Princes Risborough, Buckinghamshire, 2005), 17–25.
14. Wolseley, *The Story of a Soldier's Life, Volume II*, 228–256.

1. Garnet Wolseley (1833–1913). This photograph shows him in full-dress uniform as a field marshal (with his baton in his right hand). The image dates from 1896, when he was commander-in-chief of the British army.

National Army Museum (NAM), London, negative 50400

2. Frederick Roberts (1832–1914). This photograph shows him in his serviceable field uniform. The image dates from the 1880s, when Roberts was commander-in-chief of the Indian army. He is accompanied by his Indian orderly.

NAM negative 92784

3. Duke of Cambridge (1819–1904). This painting shows him in his full-dress uniform as a field marshal. He was Queen Victoria's cousin and was commander-in-chief of the British army, 1856–1895. The duke was famous for the length of his period in office, and also for his extreme conservatism.

NAM negative 132577

4. Charles Gordon (1833–1885). He was one of the great heroes of the British army during the nineteenth century. As a major general and governor of the Sudan, he was killed by the dervishes when they stormed Gordon's headquarters in Khartoum.

NAM negative 32506

5. British trenches at Sebastopol, 1854–1855. Trench warfare became increasingly important during the second half of the nineteenth century and the beginning of the twentieth. A major influence on this was the growing volume of small-arms and artillery fire that troops could only avoid by digging trenches.

NAM negative 97423

6. The Martinière, Lucknow, 1857. This photograph, despite its poor quality, is an important relic of the siege of Lucknow during the Indian Mutiny.

NAM negative 105864

7. Peiwar Kotal, Afghanistan, 1878. This photograph shows the formidable terrain over which Roberts's troops had to clamber and fight to win their notable victory. Note the small number of British soldiers in the foreground. *NAM negative 126421*

8. Kandahar Gate, 1880. The capture of Kandahar concluded the heroic march of Roberts's ten thousand men from Kabul in the fierce heat of August. *NAM negative 121237*

9. British camp in Ashanti, 1873–1874. The figures are war correspondents who sent despatches on the expedition to the British and American press. They included Henry Morton Stanley, the Anglo-American journalist who subsequently became a major explorer of the African continent.

NAM negative 162775

10. Gordon Relief Expedition, 1884–1885. Unloading whalers that transported troops of the river column up the Nile towards Khartoum.

NAM negative 126538

11. Gordon Relief Expedition, 1884–1885. Guards Camel Corps, being inspected by Wolseley, who was wearing a Wolseley helmet.
NAM negative 22881

12. Battle of Abu Klea, January 1885. This battle was fought by Wolseley's desert column. A few days later, Khartoum was taken and Gordon killed by the dervishes. Abu Klea was too late.
NAM negative 8169

13. Redvers Buller (1839–1908). Buller was a member of the Wolseley 'Ring'. He commanded the British army in South Africa at the beginning of the Second Boer War. His lack of success led to the appointment of Roberts in overall command.

NAM negative 116102

14. Herbert Horatio Kitchener (1850–1916). This photograph shows him in the full-dress uniform of a field marshal, holding his baton. Kitchener had an obvious air of command. In the Second Boer War, he was Roberts's chief of staff and assumed command when Roberts returned to England at the end of 1900.

NAM negative 108494

15. South Africa, 1900. Roberts with his staff. Roberts (with his arm in a sling) sits in the front row. Sir Alfred Milner, governor of Cape Province, is in plain clothes. Ian Hamilton is seated at the far right. Among the officers who are standing, seventh from the left is Lord Stanley (later the Earl of Derby), who succeeded Kitchener as Secretary of State for War in 1916. Henry Wilson is sixth and Henry Rawlinson is eighth: both achieved high rank during the First World War.

NAM negative 85379

CHAPTER 9

THE ASHANTI INVASION AND THE GENESIS OF THE WOLSELEY 'RING'

The Gold Coast—the British colony in West Africa now known as Ghana—is an unhealthy place, especially for Europeans. It was worse in the nineteenth century than today because during the last 150 years, there have been great improvements in the eradication of pests and immunization against tropical diseases. The region is hot and humid, densely forested, and the home of plagues of mosquitoes carrying malaria. It has long been called 'the white man's grave'. In the second half of the nineteenth century, it was inhabited by a number of tribes under British protection. The British occupied the territory for the main purpose of clearing the country of the slave trade, which had been outlawed in all British possessions in Africa in 1833.

The region was called the Gold Coast for a good reason. Precious metals were found there, and members of the Ashanti tribe were skilled craftsmen in the use of gold, silver, and wood. But the Ashanti were better known for another reason: they were ferocious fighters. They were independent of British rule and lived north of the British protectorates. They numbered about four million people and had the justified reputation of being much stronger fighters than the tribes to the south, whose lands they had invaded on a number of occasions. The Ashanti—who sometimes dispatched eighty thousand marauding warriors—lived in a wide territory 150 miles north of the coast. They were ruled by Kofi Karikari, a tribal chief with the title of king. He reigned from his palace in his capital, Kumasi, and was very rich as a result of the slave trade. This enabled him to buy small arms for his tribesmen: weapons that did not do much damage because of their small amount of gunpowder and short range. The king's support of the slave trade naturally made him an enemy of the British. The Ashanti exploited the opportunity of capturing slaves by invading the British protectorates to the south. They had done this in 1801, and in 1823–1824, when the British were soundly defeated.

In 1863, the Ashanti invaded the British protectorates again. The British had no strong garrison to impede the invaders, who took yet more territory and seized more slaves. This caused ripples of discontent in London, but no action. In 1873, the Ashanti attempted to push further, and twelve thousand armed warriors moved slowly and with deliberation south towards the coast. As they got nearer, the British provided an effective block. A small force from the Royal Navy, the Royal Marines, and the West India Regiment from Barbados held their ground at the two towns of Elmina and Cape Coast Castle. (The Royal Navy had, for years, roamed the West African coast and shelled the villages of natives who were thought to be engaged in the slave trade.) In 1873, this small British force proceeded to push the enemy back about ten miles from the coast, and it set up a strong position there and established a garrison. The eight hundred British soldiers and sailors—146 of them prostrated by fever—held their position while they waited for reinforcements.

These events prompted the British government to act at last to suppress the Ashanti invasion, although the Liberal government under Prime Minister Gladstone worried about the likely cost of the expedition. The tribe had to be defeated in battle. Natives in all parts of the colony feared that if the British did not take steps to crush the invaders, the tribes in the protectorate would regard this as weakness, and this would encourage more Ashanti aggression. Quelling the invasion would provide Wolseley with his first experience of commanding an expedition against a foe who substantially outnumbered his own force.

Wolseley had spent the two years 1871–1873 as an assistant adjutant general in the War Office, which was, at the time, a ferment of activity because of the energy of the Secretary of State for War, Edward Cardwell. He was totally dedicated to reforming the army and carried through a number of measures that led to important improvements. All this time, he was supported by Wolseley, who considered Cardwell to be

> 'the greatest minister I ever served with at the War Office. He was the only civilian Secretary of State I ever knew who understood what military administration meant, or who had any fixed ideas of the principles upon which an army should be organized for rapid mobilization. It was a pleasure to work with so able a statesman, and one could always trust him implicitly.'[1]

Cardwell, in turn, had great respect for Wolseley, who had been studying the situation in West Africa for some time. It was not surprising that Cardwell invited him to draw up a plan to defeat the Ashanti. After some disputes between the War Office and the Colonial Office, Wolseley's recommendation was accepted, and he was instructed to sail immediately to West Africa to command the expedition. Since he would be reporting to both the War and Colonial Offices, he was given both military and political responsibility. He welcomed this, since it would greatly simplify how he conducted his campaign. Just before Wolseley's departure, the Colonial Office had sent out a naval officer, Captain Glover, with orders to operate in the basin of the River Volta—to the east of where Wolseley would be operating—and, if possible, to recruit local levies. Wolseley was also recruiting natives, and Glover was ordered to report to him. In the event, although Glover managed to raise a large army of tribesmen, they had little effect on the campaign because his native army melted away because of wholesale desertion.

Shortly before leaving England, Wolseley had just become the father of a daughter, Frances—who would be his only child and to whom he would always be devoted. It was therefore not easy for him to leave his family to take up his new appointment, but in September 1873, he finished his work at the War Office and departed for West Africa. He was a brevet colonel and local major general, the same rank Roberts reached when he commanded the Kuram Field Force in November 1879 in the invasion of Afghanistan. Before Wolseley left England, it was planned that he would be commanding a mixed force about a division in strength, but including only a few regular British troops. The number of British soldiers was kept low because of the widespread feeling that the West African climate and the diseases endemic to the colony would reduce their effectiveness. Additional forces would have to be recruited locally.[2]

An increasingly common practice during nineteenth-century wars was press reporting that described to the public what was taking place on the battlefield. A number of war correspondents accompanied the Ashanti expedition, and their dispatches helped to make Wolseley a household name at the end of the war.

The Wolseley 'Ring'

Wolseley had not yet had the time to select and appoint a formally structured staff. But in West Africa, he was able to set one up using a number of officers whom he knew and who were anxious to join him. At the time, Wolseley was forty. His chief of staff, Lieutenant Colonel John McNeill, was badly wounded during the first exchange of fire during the campaign, but he eventually recovered and rejoined Wolseley after the end of the Ashanti campaign. He was replaced by Colonel George Greaves, who provided a colourful picture of Wolseley as he appeared at the time:

> '. . . a man free from nerves, with clear, penetrating, observant blue eyes, spare, light frame, and brisk, active step' with a 'strong but suave voice.'[3]

McNeill and Greaves were the same age as Wolseley. The other senior men were all at least five years younger: Captain Henry

Brackenbury, military secretary; Captain Hugh McCalmont, ADC; Captain Redvers Buller, chief of intelligence; Lieutenant Colonel Evelyn Wood, a supernumerary officer and soon to be a battalion commander; Brevet Major Baker Russell, also soon to be a battalion commander; Captain William Butler, another supernumerary; and Major George Colley, transport officer for the British troops. In addition, Wolseley had a private secretary, Lieutenant John Frederick Maurice, who was in his early thirties. These officers later became the central figures in the celebrated group known as the Wolseley 'Ring'. McCalmont, Russell, and Wood came from the cavalry; Brackenbury and Maurice from the artillery; and the five others, like Wolseley himself, from the infantry (Buller from the socially exclusive Sixtieth Rifles).

All these men were experienced, and during the campaign they continued to perform well. Their careers subsequently blossomed, keeping pace with Wolseley's own advancement. He gave them jobs, which meant increases in rank. The ten all became generals: four major generals (two-star rank); one a lieutenant general (three-star); four generals (four-star); and one five-star, Field Marshal Sir Evelyn Wood. However, not all the officers whom Wolseley favoured were ultimately successful. In particular, Colley (at Majuba Hill in 1881) and Buller (in South Africa in 1899–1900) were examples of overpromise and under-delivery.[4]

Shortly after Wolseley's arrival and while he was setting up his staff, he appointed three senior officers to command columns—Baker Russell, Evelyn Wood, and Brigadier General Sir Archibald Alison, who had been sent from London and was not highly regarded by Wolseley, although in the final battles he did good work. Wolseley immediately sent them out to recruit local levies. This was extremely difficult because there were very few natives who were courageous and well enough disciplined to face the Ashanti warriors. Wolseley also summoned all the tribal chieftains to a meeting. Few of them turned up, and those who did admitted that they had no control over their tribesmen. This made it very important to bring in British troops. Three high-quality regular battalions were earmarked: 2/23rd Regiment (Royal Welsh Fusiliers), 2/ Rifle Brigade, and the Forty-Second Highlanders (the Black Watch).[5]

On 13 October 1873, Wolseley sent an ultimatum to the Ashanti king, setting strict controls on his future conduct. There was no response, and this cleared the way for Wolseley to draw up his plans for a measured advance to the north and an invasion of Ashanti territory, 150 miles away. To make this possible, Wolseley decided to build a road. A railway would have been better, but it was not possible to construct one because the ground was too uneven and there were too many streams. A road was feasible as far as Prahsu on the Prah River, halfway to Kumasi. However, north of Prahsu, there was thick bush: dense forest and brushwood through which the troops had to cut their way. Building a road beyond Prahsu was therefore impossible. (See **Map 8**.)

While the road was being constructed, there were a number of sharp engagements in the difficult marshy terrain just north of the coastal region. Wolseley was anxious to clear the tribal protectorates of all the Ashanti invaders, and the Ashanti obliged. Parties of them, with their customary aggressiveness, attacked all the British garrisons they could locate. They were everywhere defeated, although with great difficulty. They were confronted by well-trained British officers, mostly of junior rank, who suffered many casualties in their efforts to boost the morale of the natives under their command. Wolseley was himself on the scene when he could get there, but the ground, which was sometimes reduced to a swamp, was too difficult for him because of his old wound from the Crimean War. He was therefore carried in a wicker sedan chair.

He was anxious to observe these native troops in action because he wanted to judge their fighting value. He realized that the British officers were doing an excellent job, but the men were very unimpressive: they lacked soldierly qualities and could not be relied on in future. Since these native levies would not be capable of carrying out a disciplined large-scale operation, they would be increasingly used as porters.

As a result of much intense activity in the tropical sun, Wolseley's health gave out. He was struck with a fever that lasted for a week, and his recovery was largely due to the ministrations of his private secretary, Lieutenant Maurice. Wolseley's description of this unpleasant experience brings it vividly to life:

'In the worst night of my waking fever, I remember well how
my puzzled brain tried repeatedly to work out a quadratic
equation which no amount of transposition would enable me
to solve. Existence in the narrow borderland which intervenes
between sanity and insanity in such cases is always a fearful
experience . . . the worst moments come from a feeling of
inability and want of strength, both mental and physical.'[6]

The three British battalions arrived at the end of 1873. Wolseley
immediately gave them some practical help. He designed an improved
type of tropical uniform: light, loose-fitting grey homespun, and cork
helmets to protect from the sun. The soldiers also received a daily
dose of quinine, which helped to prevent malaria. In preparation for
the troops' gruelling march in the tropical heat before they contacted
the enemy, Major George Colley arranged transport companies from
the local levies: three thousand men and women to carry regimental
baggage, including rations. The soldier's daily ration was crude but
generous, one and a half pounds of bread, one and a half pounds of
salt meat, vegetables, and extras, which included rum and lime juice.
Another five thousand men and women carried army supplies and
wounded men. Each native, for a small wage, was expected to carry the
weight of fifty pounds, which was rather more than the British soldiers
were carrying, including their ammunition. The porters carried their
loads on their heads. Huts were also built along the road, and men could
temporarily rest in these.

Although many of the natives deserted, the job was done more or
less on time. Wolseley had spent time with Colley while the natives were
being organized into companies of porters. This experience reinforced
Wolseley's low opinion of them, and the way he described the black
races is offensive to twenty-first-century readers. This was in sharp
contrast to how Roberts described the Indian sepoys who fought for
him. His ability to get the best out of them was one of the secrets of his
success. Wolseley's attitude to the black races was also quite different
from how he treated British soldiers.

'Your Soldiers Are Powerless before an Army of White Men'[7]

This quotation is from a letter from Wolseley to the king of the Ashanti. It was not mere bravado. Wolseley would assemble a force to turn it into reality. By the end of 1873, the three battalions from England had arrived, and before long, these received their tropical kit. They were now ready for battle. Since the tribal protectorates had at last been cleared of Ashanti invaders and the road north had been almost completed, Wolseley was able to finalize his plan to march towards the Ashanti. The first problem he faced was how to defeat a much more numerous enemy army when the native levies he had recruited were so obviously unreliable. With some difficulty, he solved it.

Wolseley moved rapidly up the road to Prahsu, travelling for part of the time in a rather unmilitary way: in a small horse-drawn buggy. His first operational task was to establish a bridgehead at Prahsu, across the Prah River. The force contained a number of engineers, who managed to improvise a bridge with the use of various types of pontoon. The remaining men marched north during the following days, but their pace was slow because the natives carrying the supplies had to catch up with the fighting troops. Fever also struck many men. The Ashanti king soon learned that his kingdom was under threat, and he sent a delegation to try and arrange a peace treaty. This was not acceptable to the British, not least because the king had imprisoned a number of European hostages. Wolseley had also been quite clear before he left London that his task was to defeat the Ashanti decisively in battle. The Ashanti king continued to send messages to Wolseley, who was unyielding.

Wolseley's plan was to assault Kumasi from four separate directions. The most powerful was from the south, using the mainly British force that was under his direct command and was approaching Prahsu. When the Ashanti delegation arrived at his headquarters, he made sure that they were kept there long enough to see—and be impressed by—the disciplined and businesslike regular British troops in the bridgehead. The four-part attack was criticized after the war because it disregarded the traditionally important principle of concentration of force. However, it had a psychological effect on the enemy. The king did not realize that the four attacking columns differed in strength, and Wolseley quite reasonably hoped that the king would believe that four columns would be four times as strong as one column. But the reality of Wolseley's position was that the sole force that he could rely on was the brigade of mainly British battalions under his own command. The other three attacks, including Glover's from the east, were unlikely to be effective because of the mass desertions of the native levies who would be doing the attacking. None of the three reached Kumasi before Wolseley.

Wolseley's plan was to make the main attack with his own force. This had been concentrated at Prahsu on 15 January 1874, then crossed the Prah and started to cut its way through the bush. On 26 January, it reached Moinsi, twenty miles north of Prahsu. The spring rains would shortly arrive, and these would make marching and fighting particularly difficult.

Wolseley's command was an unbalanced brigade, heavy in infantry but light in supporting arms. It comprised the following components:

- 2/Rifle Brigade, Forty-Second Highlanders, and 2/23rd Regiment. (The 2/23rd was initially kept in reserve except for one hundred men who marched with the main force.)
- The naval detachment and West India Regiment that had blocked the Ashanti invasion earlier in 1873.
- Wood's native battalion and Russell's native battalion.
- Detachment of eighty scouts commanded by an enterprising officer, Lord Gifford. These were a reconnaissance group that kept ten miles ahead of the main force.
- Artillery troop of light guns, rockets, and one Gatling gun.
- Detachment of Royal Engineers.
- Ammunition column.
- Field hospital.

An infantry brigade normally comprised four battalions. Wolseley had six in the main force, with a nominal size of four thousand, but they were all under-strength because of sickness. The Gatling gun was an American design and was the first weapon that could fire rifle-calibre bullets automatically and repeatedly. It did not fire a stream of bullets from a single barrel. It had a clutch of separate barrels that were rotated so that the repeat fire came from this rotation. The Gatling was effective but clumsy, and it needed a large carriage with wheels. During the 1890s, it was totally outclassed by the Maxim/Vickers Medium Machine Gun (MMG), which was used by the British army for six decades. MMGs, like Gatlings, fired from static positions, generally concealed from the enemy, and infantry advancing in the open were totally vulnerable to their enfilade fire. During the First World War, the increasing number of machine guns—which greatly boosted the strength of the defence—led to the deadlock of trench warfare.

All the units except the Wood and Russell battalions were well-trained regular British troops. Wolseley was relying on quality rather than quantity. This advantage was reinforced by his well-planned logistics that kept a constant flow of supplies from the coast, one hundred miles away. This was especially difficult because of the thick forest and the dense scrub. The roads constructed by Wolseley's men were of some help, but were barely adequate. The final advance towards the Ashanti was not a smooth progress because the country was even worse and the road had petered out. However, Wolseley forced the pace. His objective was to get to grips with the enemy, defeat him, and stamp out slavery. After doing his main job, he wanted to get his troops away from the harsh climate, the spring rains, and the omnipresent disease. He planned to march his soldiers back to the coast and away to Britain. The Ashanti soldiers soon realized what Wolseley was trying to do. They called him 'the man who would not stop'.

There were not many large wild animals in the places where Wolseley's men were marching. Some soldiers found a crocodile, others found an elephant. Wolseley himself was given the gift of 'a little bush deer, the size of a rabbit, very prettily marked with spots and stripes'. However, 'creepy-crawlies' were everywhere.[8]

Wolseley Journal, 16 January
'A very hot night. I sleep under a small mosquito net to prevent beetles, spiders, etc. etc. falling on my face from the

roughly thatched roof. The consequence is that I am bathed in perspiration every night and wake up from its effects and the stinging of the prickly heat caused by it.'

The route passed through low ground where the heat was oppressive. However, there was some high ground, where the temperature was mercifully cooler.

Wolseley Journal, 22 January
'Marched at 6:15 AM. A cool morning for marching. Reached Wood's camp under the Adansi Hills a little before 10:00 AM. We have been always told that this was only a hill and not a range, but it is a range, closely covered throughout with forest: the regular path up is very, very steep, but we have zig-zagged a very fair road up it. There was a pleasant cool breeze on top, where our fortified post is, but although vistas had been cut looking both north and south, there was no view to be obtained to any great distance, owing to the heavy haze.'

The most continuously serious problem was disease. On 22 January, so many men from the Rifle Brigade had fallen out that Wolseley had to order up two hundred men from the 2/23rd Regiment, which was in reserve. One of Wolseley's own staff was also struck down. He was Captain George Huyshe, whose father was one of Wolseley's friends. The young man contracted dysentery, a particularly debilitating disease. He appeared to be recovering when the disease suddenly attacked his brain and drove him mad. Without realizing what he was doing, he attacked his servant. He lingered on for another day. By this time, Wolseley and his staff had continued their march. Buller and Maurice were left behind to make sure that Huyshe was properly buried. This young man would probably have become a member of the Wolseley 'Ring' if he had lived longer.

Besides the number of men who had to drop out of the column because of disease, there was another reason why many men had to be held back. This was because of the need for small garrisons over the whole course of the route to protect it from enemy attacks. Men of the West India Regiment were also quartered in native villages to intercept deserters who were trying to get back home.

On 27 January, Wolseley's force was approaching Kumasi. During the march, Wolseley had received messages from the Ashanti king, who was alarmed by the prospect of battle. While Wolseley responded with perfect courtesy, he was quite unyielding about abandoning his mission—in particular, eliminating slavery. About this time, he came across a wounded slave woman who had been shot twice by her master. Wolseley's medical staff picked out all but one of the 'slugs' that had hit her. (The bullets fired by the feeble small arms of the Ashanti warriors were called slugs.) She was naked, and Wolseley instructed that she should be given a cloth to make her decent.

> *Wolseley Journal, 27 January*
> 'I am now only about thirty-three miles from Kumasi. My difficulty is food: I have frequently to halt to bring it up from the rear. I am now over 100 miles from the coast from whence all my supplies must come on the heads of men and women, and then I have to protect my line of communications by fortified posts every ten or twelve miles.'

> *Wolseley Journal, 29 January*
> *Wolseley had been in touch with a Mr. Dawson, a civilian trader of mixed blood who was in Kumasi, acting as an interpreter. Dawson sent a coded message back to Wolseley containing a quotation from the Second Letter of Paul to the Corinthians. Wolseley saw the point:*
> 'This is evidently intended as a warning to us to beware of treachery. The king evidently means to fight.'

'The Enemy Fought like Men'[9]

The village of Amoafur, almost twenty miles south of Kumasi, was where the king concentrated his army of five thousand men and where he would stand and fight. Buller, Wolseley's intelligence officer, sent a spy into the enemy's camp, and he reported back the size of the enemy force and their intentions. South of Amoafur, Wolseley's headquarters had spent four days concentrating supplies. The road south to Prahsu was secure as a result of eight small garrisons that had been set up on the way, which meant that future supplies could get through. Wolseley decided to attack the enemy early in the morning of 31 January 1874.[10] The enemy positions were in a dense forest, which Wolseley described as follows:

> 'How sobering to the highest spirits was its dim, shadowless gloom. Rank earth-smelling dampness pervaded it, and soft slimy depressions in the ground, whence oozed black, oily mud, marked the course of streams at times.'[11]

The strength of Wolseley's force had now fallen to 1,500 British and 780 natives. In the nineteenth century, the British army defensive formation was the square, which was normally effective in providing all-round cover. Wolseley now deployed his entire attacking force in a square, with one (under-strength) battalion on each side. With the Forty-Second Regiment in the lead, moving forward to the sound of the pipes, the square advanced through the thick forest. They were soon greeted by a semicircle of hostile fire, with the enemy attacking in rushes in many places. Wolseley's guns and rockets caused great carnage. Two newspaper correspondents, in plain clothes, joined the battle and kept up a hot fire with their rifles. One of these was Henry Morton Stanley. He was a United States citizen who had been born in Wales, and he had fought in the American Civil War. He was to become a world-famous explorer of Africa and would find the missing missionary Dr. Livingstone.

During the sometimes ferocious fighting, Wolseley kept his calm and smoked many cigars. After some hours, the fighting became too much for the Ashanti, who had all faded away by 2:00 PM. The enemy army did not lack courage; the problem was the weakness of their small arms. Wolseley's native carriers had, unfortunately, all deserted while the fighting was taking place, which meant that he was unable to exploit his victory immediately. However, a victory it was. British casualties were twenty-two officers and 176 men. Most were wounded and not killed because the enemy fire was too feeble to cause anything but flesh wounds. The enemy casualties were probably five times as great.

Although the enemy had been driven from the field, they had not been vanquished. It was not long before Wolseley reclaimed the initiative and finished the job. Early on 2 February, Wolseley's force set out to march the fifteen miles to Kumasi.[12] They carried five days' rations in the soldiers' packs and the regimental transport. Progress was slow because of the country: they made only three miles on the first day. While the men were advancing, the enemy attacked the supply line. However, Colley soon had this under control and successfully prevented the porters from running away. The force reached the village of Aggenmanu, from where there was a usable road to Kumasi that would make for speedier progress.

On 3 February, the force encountered and soon engaged the enemy in a strong position on high ground. Some prisoners were taken, and these reported that there were ten thousand warriors blocking the road to Kumasi. The king kept sending messages to Wolseley, but this did not influence Wolseley's own plans. As it was the start of the rainy season, a massive cyclone now arrived, bringing sheets of rain. In these arduous conditions, Wolseley's engineers put up a serviceable bridge over a twenty-yard stream that the troops would have to cross.

On 4 February, the weather became much more cheerful. The Ashanti king had a large force and soon confronted Wolseley's advancing men. Wood's native battalion was in the lead and was rather shaken and fired wildly. Wolseley immediately ordered the Rifle Brigade to take over the lead and added a light gun to reinforce the firepower of the battalion. A pitched battle followed, during which Wolseley had to keep the enemy at bay and, at the same time, bring forward his supplies to keep them out of enemy hands. The enemy army, despite its large numbers, did not fight with the same resolution as at Amoafur. In the afternoon, the battle started turning in Wolseley's favour. An advance force, led by Brigadier General Alison, moved into Kumasi.

The two native battalions and the naval detachment formed a rearguard to protect the supply line.

At 6:15 PM, Wolseley himself arrived at Kumasi with the rest of his force, which was mainly British:

> 'The whole road was strewn with abandoned war-trappings. The numbers of state umbrellas, of royal litters, drums of various shapes and sizes, were evidences of the hurry and confusion of bewildered flight. Just before I entered the city, Sir Archibald Alison had drawn up the troops on a wide open place in the city, where he received me with a general salute. We gave three ringing cheers for the Queen.'[13]

As at Amoafur, the numbers of casualties were very light, and the enemy lost more men. The king and his immediate followers had by now bolted; but while they were still alive, slave-trading would remain a curse.

By the evening, the city was peaceful although there were some fires. The Ashanti people, some carrying firearms, greeted the British soldiers with the words 'thank you' (the only English words they knew!). The royal palace at Kumasi was surprisingly opulent, and much was in the Moorish style, because the Arab Empire once stretched as far as the southern Sudan. But the palace showed signs of brutality: hostages had been butchered every day. On 5 February, Wolseley's wounded and sick were on their way back to the coast. He sent messages to the Ashanti king offering a peace treaty on strict conditions, e.g. the abolition of slavery. There was no reply. The treaty was left in abeyance because Wolseley refused to keep his troops any longer in the West African climate, particularly after the onset of the spring rains, which made many roads impassable.

Wolseley began his return journey on 6 February. He left orders that prize agents should collect gold and other valuables, which would become the property of the British Crown. He also left engineers with instructions to burn part of the city. And as Wolseley travelled south, he destroyed a number of the villages through which he had passed. Wolseley arrived at the coast on 19 February and embarked for Portsmouth on 4 March. It was calculated at a later date that 71 percent of the white troops had fallen sick during the campaign, and 43 percent had been invalided home.

The Conquering Hero

When Wolseley arrived in Britain, he found that he had become a national hero.[14] His victories at Amoafur and Kumasi were decisive, but they were small operations because Wolseley was commanding only a single brigade. His antagonists were an army of native troops—brave but not highly disciplined, and armed only with out-of-date weapons. It is therefore surprising that these battles made the reputation of Wolseley in the eyes of the British public. Wolseley's military skill was in an unspectacular field. It was logistics. In West Africa, his base was on the coast, yet he managed to supply his troops and evacuate his wounded and sick soldiers over a distance of a hundred miles or more over rough and contested ground. He obviously had no mechanical transport, very little animal transport, and only long lines of natives carrying loads on their heads. These natives were still in their villages until Wolseley arrived in West Africa, when he recruited them. The logistics of the campaign were quite remarkable, and it could never have succeeded without Wolseley's meticulous planning.

Wolseley's fame in Britain was immediate. Perhaps this was because of the journalists who had accompanied the expedition and sent back regular dispatches. And it is possible that some members of the public were struck by the romantic idea that Wolseley was commanding a crusading army marching across hostile territory to free the slaves. The Queen ordered a grand review in Windsor Park of her soldiers who had fought under Wolseley. He received the thanks of both Houses of Parliament. He was given a large banquet at the Mansion House by the Lord Mayor of London. He received two major decorations, both carrying knighthoods. These were the Grand Cross of the Order of St. Michael and St. George (GCMG), normally given to senior diplomats and civil servants, and Knight Commander of the Order of the Bath (KCB), usually awarded to senior soldiers and sailors. Both were accompanied by imposing stars to wear on the breast of his uniform. His rank of major general was made substantive. He was offered a baronetcy, but (unlike Roberts) he declined this, presumably in the hope of a peerage, which he received some years later. Not least important, he received a cash grant of £25,000 (perhaps the equivalent of £2,500,000 in twenty-first-century terms).

The campaign was warmly regarded by Gladstone and his government as a military success that also kept within its budget. This was and still is something that happens very rarely. The main reason was that the campaign had been brought to a successful conclusion so rapidly. Wolseley pressed forward unrelentingly because he wanted to win the war and get his soldiers away from the West African climate. On his return to England, Wolseley received some bad news: he learned that a fire had consumed all his possessions, including his papers, in the warehouse where they were stored. His wife and daughter had fortunately been elsewhere.

Five years after the campaign, audiences at the Savoy Theatre in London enjoyed *The Pirates of Penzance* and saw George Grossmith adopt the mannerisms and clothing of Wolseley, singing, 'I am the very model of a modern major general.' This ensured that Wolseley's memory would last for as long as Gilbert and Sullivan's ever-popular work is played. Wolseley was amused by how he was described. Another phrase also became widely popular: 'All Sir Garnet,' which conveyed the idea that everything was in good order. This was indeed an accurate reflection of Wolseley, the invariably careful military planner.

Endnotes

1. Wolseley, Field Marshal Viscount, *The Story of a Soldier's Life, Volume II* (London: Archibald Constable, 1903), 271–272.
2. Beckett, Ian F. W. (ed.), *Wolseley and Ashanti. The Ashanti War Journal and Correspondence of Major General Sir Garnet Wolseley, 1873–1874.* (Stroud, Gloucestershire: The History Press, for the Army Records Society, 2009).
3. Ibid., 16.
4. Wright, William, *Warriors of the Queen. Fighting Generals of the Victorian Age.* (Stroud, Gloucestershire: The History Press/Spellmount, 2014), 31, 42, 44, 124, 179, 181, 216, 288.
5. Beckett, *Wolseley and Ashanti* (October 1873) 93–188. Wolseley, *The Story of a Soldier's Life, Volume II*, 274–302.
6. Wolseley, *The Story of a Soldier's Life, Volume II,* 307–308.
7. Ibid., 355.
8. Ibid., 341–358.
9. Ibid., 361.
10. Wolseley, *The Story of a Soldier's Life, Volume II*, 330–345.
11. Ibid., 340.
12. Ibid., 346–370.
13. Ibid., 356–357.
14. Kochanski, Halik, *Sir Garnet Wolseley. Victorian Hero* (London: The Hambledon Press, 1999), 72–73.

CHAPTER 10

THE GREAT GAME: THE SECOND AFGHAN WAR. ROBERTS'S STAR IN THE ASCENDANT

When a twenty-first-century reader comes across the name *Afghanistan*, what comes immediately to mind is the indecisive war that has been waged in that country for sixteen years, with no end in sight. (In sharp contrast, the campaign in Western Europe that ended the Second World War lasted for *eleven months* from the invasion of France to the surrender of the formidable German army.) Today's Afghan war is being waged by the American army with small detachments from allied countries and a growing number of Afghan troops trained by the Americans. What is very difficult to understand is why—despite the high standard of training of the Americans and their tactical skills, not to speak of their superb equipment—the campaign has not been brought to a decisive conclusion.

The Afghan War has two characteristics that go some way to explain the present *impasse* (and they certainly should have been considered when the decision was made to go to war in the first place). The first characteristic is evident from all major wars since Vietnam in the 1960s and 1970s. Warfare is no longer *bipolar* and has become *asymmetrical*:

'*bipolar*, fought between nation states of roughly comparable strength . . . *asymmetrical* and diverse, with potential antagonists spread in pockets rather than formed into compact armies.'[1]

Asymmetrical warfare (see Chapter 1) demands that political activity should become much more important than military. This is because of the need to search for, identify, and constantly monitor potential enemies, and to establish a government that outlaws and eliminates terrorists. This is something that makes unusual demands on commanders in the field.

The second characteristic of fighting in Afghanistan is the difficulty of the terrain itself. It is large, mountainous, and arid, with a relatively small population of often hostile tribes. Communications are poor. Troop movements are slow because of the rough ground and inadequate roads, although air power has improved matters in the twenty-first century. During the nineteenth century, the British never confronted in battle their major *bipolar* opponent, Russia. The object of British policy was to pre-empt any Russian move into Afghanistan that would open the door to India. India was the 'jewel in the British Crown', and its defence was Britain's number one priority. The North-West Frontier provided the route into India and had to be kept firmly in British hands. Afghanistan provided access to the North-West Frontier, and it had to be denied to the Russians. This often meant fighting the Afghans to keep them out of the Russian orbit.

This is the reason why the British were constantly on the lookout for Russian moves over their border into Afghanistan, because any expansion of the Russian frontier towards Afghanistan would bring Russia uncomfortably close to India. By the end of the century, as a result of continuous expansion in small bites, the Russians were only thirty miles away from the North-West Frontier. Although Britain and Russia had fought the Crimean War of 1853–1856, the tension in Afghanistan was never allowed to bring the two countries to blows in that country. However, the mutual watchfulness became widely known as *The Great Game*.[2]

For centuries, Russia's national policy was to extend her enormous territory: pushing out from the Caspian to the Aral Sea, from Siberia to the independent countries at the northern border of Afghanistan, and to the east towards China and the Pacific. The North-West Frontier of India (now known as Af/Pak because it divides Afghanistan and Pakistan) was the only part of the long frontier of the Indian subcontinent that was vulnerable to assault from an aggressive outside enemy. The North-West Frontier, with its impressive Khyber Pass (the west in Afghanistan and the east in India), was the home of restless tribes: those on the Indian side fighting among themselves and also with tribes on the other side of the Afghan border. To pacify the region, the British regularly mounted infantry columns to burn tribal villages and teach the tribes a lesson. The British also appointed political agents (PAs), who had their headquarters in tribal territory and had the authority to control the headstrong natives, whom the British half-admired as natural soldiers. The system worked surprisingly well in maintaining the peace in this sensitive region. And many tribesmen from selected frontier districts were recruited into the Indian army, mainly in regiments of Muslim Punjabis.

Afghanistan was never regarded as Britain's direct foe. But it was the most important buffer state between Russia and India, and British military activity in Afghanistan was aimed at keeping the Russian Bear within its borders. The Indian army troops that fought in Afghanistan served in units of well-disciplined and trained regulars, in infantry battalions, cavalry regiments, and artillery batteries. Larger formations—columns the approximate size of brigades and divisions—were built from these individual units and reinforced their endemic strength. Their opponents in battle were large formations of Afghan soldiers, loosely organized from different tribes and not held together by the bonds of discipline and *esprit de corps*. They generally disappeared into the hinterland if they were defeated in the field.

Because of the differences between the two armies, battles in nineteenth-century Afghanistan were less and less symmetrical. The invading forces packed a greater punch than the Afghans and were concerned with the political organization of the country, e.g.

appointing, subsidising, and supervising amirs. In contrast, the fighting in Afghanistan in the twenty-first century is totally asymmetrical, with the large difference in the size of the opposing forces. Substantial formations under American leadership and with state-of-the-art equipment, including drones, are continuously (but unsuccessfully) engaged in searching for small numbers of elusive terrorists. This is why the war has lasted so long.

Over the course of the nineteenth century, British policy resulted in two Afghan wars. In the first, the British suffered a severe defeat; but they recovered from this and eventually re-established the *status quo*. The second war was successful at a tactical level but did not bring permanent peace. It did, however, demonstrate the heroism and military skills of Roberts's Indian army troops. In both wars, the British forces engaged the Afghans with the sole ambition of establishing a strong presence on the ground to discourage Russian incursions. The Afghans were a formidable enemy. The tribesmen had never known luxury, but they were hardy soldiers, armed with accurate long-barreled rifled jezails. An experienced British officer rated the Afghans as the best marksmen in the world. The Indian army used smooth-bore muskets until the 1840s, and it was the late 1860s before they received rifles of an advanced design, with breech-loading and metal cartridges.

Afghanistan is a relatively large country, with an area about the size of France (but only half the population). It has always been desperately poor, and even in the twenty-first century, it is one of the poorest countries in the world in per capita income. It is landlocked and has an oval shape pointing from south-west to north-east: 850 miles long and 600 miles wide. (See **Map 9**.) The temperature has extremes: torrid in the summer and frigid and snowy in the winter. It is mountainous, and much of it is barren; the fertile land is cultivated, and one of the most important crops is poppies, a major worldwide source of illegal drugs. In the nineteenth century, communications were exceptionally poor, with unpaved roads winding between the mountains. It was difficult country for attackers but helpful to defenders, who had the advantage of high ground from which they could direct fire at enemy troops below them. The country contained a number of strong fortresses, notably in the capital, Kabul, more than sixty miles west of the Indian frontier, and Kandahar, 320 miles south-west of Kabul. The population was, and still is, made up of independent tribes, 90 percent of whom are devout Sunni Muslims. In overall control there was the amir, whose grip on the country was weak because of the strength of the local tribes. To the east and south was India (now Pakistan); to the west, Persia; and to the north—the dangerous frontier—the various once-independent countries that were being taken over by the Russians.

The First Anglo-Afghan War was fought between 1839 and 1842, and it was started by a British invasion of Afghanistan. The underlying reason was to contain any Russian move, but the immediate *casus belli* involved direct interference by the British in the governance of an independent country with its own tribal leader and titular ruler, the amir.[3]

In 1838, the Afghan army, with a British adviser, managed to defeat an invasion from the west by a Persian army, with a Russian adviser. The governor general of India, Lord Auckland, now decided to invade Afghanistan, to 'save the country' from being overcome by Persians and Russians. The invading British army, commanded by General Sir John Keane, was instructed to depose the amir, Dost Mohammed Khan, who had developed a close relationship with the Russians. He was to be replaced with someone more docile who had for long been in British pay, Shah Shujah. Keane commanded a division of 15,500 British and Indian troops, many of whom were untrained. The army was accompanied by thirty thousand camp followers—an even larger number than was normal at the time—with thirty thousand camels to carry the baggage. The army included Sikhs, a race who were heartily detested by the Afghans.

As the army advanced toward Kabul, it attacked and subdued a large fortress at Ghazni. The Ghazni tribes would shortly become troublesome to the British columns when the British, in turn, retreated. The British soon entered Kabul and installed Shah Shujah, who was no improvement over his predecessor. The British entered the fortress easily, then spent some months marching around the country demolishing fortresses and other defensive works. The Afghans scorned the new amir and also the British and Indian soldiers who had put him in his place. Shah Shujah was soon riddled with bullets and his predecessor restored. The British soldiers were then subjected to considerable abuse and, before long, were besieged in their inadequate cantonments northeast of the city. The British commander was indecisive but eventually decided that the force had to be withdrawn and marched back to India. By this time, British forces were also besieged in Kandahar and Ghazni and were in no position to come to the aid of their comrades in Kabul.

The Kabul garrison of 4,500 men and more than ten thousand camp followers departed in the winter snow on 6 January 1842. The column was sniped on the way by Ghaznis in the hills, and the men were virtually all killed or captured. The most poignant image of the war was a lone horseman, slumped over his exhausted steed, as he entered Jalalabad. He was a regimental surgeon called William Breydon, who was thought to be the sole survivor of the troops from Kabul. A few sepoys arrived later. Jalalabad was very soon also besieged by the Afghans.

Jalalabad—sixty miles east of Kabul and close to the Khyber Pass—had a crumbling fort that was held by two thousand British soldiers led by General Robert Sale, a soldier with an excellent fighting record but who was in his sixties and whose power of command had faded. However, he was supported by a number of strong subordinates. Jalalabad held out and was eventually relieved on 17 April 1842. The relieving force from India was commanded by General George Pollock, who fought his way through the Khyber Pass, reached Jalalabad, and got to Kabul in September 1842. The British, Indian, and Sikh prisoners were released, and Pollock ordered the great bazaar to be burned down as a punishment. Honour had been restored; but after the British force had marched back to India, Afghanistan returned to the *status quo*. The war had achieved nothing except a considerable loss of life. However, it provided lessons for the next conflict in Afghanistan, in which Frederick Roberts played the leading role.

Indian Army Columns March West

During the 1850s and 1860s, there was tribal warfare in Afghanistan but no major confrontation. The Russians, meanwhile, were absorbing more territory beyond the northern border and kept gradually moving their frontier towards India. However, in 1877, Russia declared war on Turkey. As a tentative replay of the Crimean War, Britain transferred five thousand Indian army troops to the Mediterranean, where they remained without going to war. In response to this move, Russia sent a mission to Afghanistan, where it was enthusiastically received. The viceroy, with the approval of the British government, proposed also sending a British delegation to Kabul—a mission specifically described as friendly.

A year had now passed since Russia had declared war on Turkey, and during that time, the Afghan government had moved into the Russian orbit. The proposed British mission to Kabul was a problem, and the amir dragged his feet about accepting it. Eventually, the British lost patience, and the mission set out and marched as far as the Afghan frontier. It was led by a senior political officer, Major Cavagnari, who had French, Irish, and English blood and was a strong character. He was a former officer in the Indian army but had transferred to the political service, where he demonstrated great diplomatic skills. At the Afghan frontier, his party was threatened and refused entry.[4]

Earlier, while the political mission was being organized, a military force was also being set up, since this would be needed if the negotiations with the Afghan government finally broke down. The military force was organized in three over-strength brigades of varying sizes. They were called field forces, to be directed at Kandahar (commanded by Major General Stewart), Peshawar Valley (under Lieutenant General 'Sam' Browne), and Kuram (under Roberts). The total strength was 706 officers and 35,002 men. Roberts, after his long and successful career on the staff, had been selected for a field command, the Kuram Field Force, with the local rank of major general. This was his greatest professional opportunity to date. On 30 October 1878, an ultimatum was sent to the Afghan government, which was set to expire three weeks later.

On 20 November 1878, the three columns began to march.[5] Roberts commanded 5,335 troops—one quarter British and three quarters Indian—plus eighteen guns. (During the next few days, he was forced to detach some of this small force to the other British columns.) Roberts's men crossed the frontier through a pass south-west of the Khyber. His destination was the Kuram Valley that led to Kabul, and the route passed through formidable mountainous country, the highest peak being fifteen thousand feet. The men had been marching for some days along a river between the mountains when surprising information arrived that an organized enemy force, including artillery, was entrenching a strong defensive position at the pass of Peiwar Kotal, above the Kuram Valley. The defenders, who outnumbered the Anglo-Indian force by six to one, occupied positions two thousand feet higher than the approaching attacking force, who set up a camp to prepare an attack. (See **Map 9**.) The enemy had a surprising amount of artillery and used their small arms effectively, but they lacked the disciplined cohesion of the British and Indian troops.

Roberts decided early to keep the initiative over the enemy and maintain a tight grip on the battle, which meant carefully deploying his men and artillery and devising a detailed tactical plan for an assault that he would personally command. He set his staff to scan the ground with telescopes to find a possible route up the mountain. At the same time, he kept his men out of enemy sight. Roberts's mantra was to mislead and surprise. He would rely on his infantry and cavalry—all well-trained regular troops—to assault where the enemy least expected.

The obstacle that faced Roberts was later described by him as follows:

> 'The Peiwar Kotal is a narrow depression in the ridge, commanded on each side by high pine-clad mountains. The approach to it from the Kuram Valley was up a steep, narrow, zigzag path, commanded throughout its entire length from the adjacent heights, and difficult to ascend on account of the extreme roughness of the road, which was covered with large fragments of rocks and boulders. Every point of the ascent

was exposed to fire from both guns and rifles, securely placed behind breastworks constructed of pine-logs and stones. At the top of the pass was a narrow plateau, which was again commanded from the thickly-wooded heights on each side, rising to an elevation of 500 feet.'[6]

Troops—who were visible to the enemy—spent two days preparing for a frontal attack. Roberts's own men, as well as the enemy on Peiwar Kotal, believed this to be the plan of attack. It was only at dusk on 1 December that commanding officers were assembled by Roberts and shown the real plan. The attackers would advance immediately on the right to reach the foot of the pass, where they would arrive before dawn on 2 December. They would then storm the enemy positions. The British tents remained in place, and camp fires would be kept burning all night to persuade the enemy that the attacking force had not moved.

Roberts's plan involved a serious risk for which he was openly criticized by tactical experts long after the battle had been won. His force was smaller than the enemy's, yet he planned to divide it. Roberts may or may not have known that a similar risk had been taken fifteen years before. At the Battle of Chancellorsville in May 1863, Robert E. Lee divided his force of forty-five thousand and sent twenty-five thousand, under Stonewall Jackson, on a wide flank march that brought him into a position to descend like a wildcat onto the right of the Union position, which was in the air because this flank was uncovered. It was a great victory for the Confederacy but was sadly clouded by the terrible wound that Jackson suffered, which led to his death a month later.[7]

At Peiwar Kotal, Roberts detached one thousand men to make a demonstration from the west to threaten the enemy's right flank, while he took 2,233 men and eight guns to make the main attack from the east onto the enemy's left flank. Roberts's party made the difficult descent into the Kuram Valley and upward to make the main assault, using the inadequate path described earlier. The journey took the troops well to the east before the path bent back towards the enemy positions. As the force began their advance up the mountain at first light, shots came from one of the Indian battalions in the lead. These had been fired by Muslim troops who were attempting to warn the enemy. Roberts, suspecting treachery, redeployed his men and brought forward the Fifth Gurkha Rifles and his half-battalion of the Seventy-Second (Seaforth) Highlanders. (A number of sepoys were subsequently court-martialled.) Roberts's infantry immediately assaulted the first enemy defensive positions, where the Afghans were too surprised to resist.

The attackers then found themselves on a large plateau while Roberts brought up the remainder of the force. Roberts's men had not been reorganized when the forward units were advancing through a dense forest. The main enemy position was on the far side of this. It took some time before all the troops were assembled, as some of them had lost their way in the forest. However, Roberts's guns soon repelled enemy counter-attacks. Roberts's men attacked so ferociously that they carried all before them. The enemy fled and left their guns behind, and then British cavalry followed and pursued the retreating men. The battle had cost fewer than a hundred casualties for the attacking force; enemy casualties were far greater. It was a striking victory. The Afghan defenders were approximately equal to eight infantry battalions plus irregular forces of tribesmen. Reinforcements had been on the way, but they were only due to arrive as the battle was being lost. If they had reached the battle in time, they would have made a difference. Roberts's drive and his will to maintain the initiative had saved the day.

Time was now needed to bring up supplies because Roberts's column was short of transport animals. The force then proceeded towards Kabul, but it made only slow progress because they had to pass through country where there was grumbling resentment of the foreigners. But by the end of the year, the war was clearly coming to its end. The amir decamped and left for Russia, in the hope of rallying support from that country. However, he died on the way. His successor was his son, whom he had kept in jail for five years. The new amir wanted the war to end, and this accorded with the wishes of the viceroy. The viceroy dispatched Cavagnari (now Sir Louis) to Kabul to negotiate the peace process. This was difficult because the British required some Afghan frontier provinces as protectorates, for which they would pay an annual subsidy. Negotiations finished in May 1879, and Cavagnari himself prepared to become the British ambassador in Kabul. He established his delegation in the Bala Hissar, the large walled citadel south-east of Kabul that overlooked the city.

Roberts was rewarded for his services despite unfortunate press reports in Britain that his troops had treated the Afghan population with unbending discipline. Roberts received the thanks of both Houses of Parliament, and he was granted a knighthood. The main award given to service officers during the nineteenth century was the Order of the Bath, and its origin dated from the Middle Ages. The first grade of the order was Companion of the Bath (CB), for lieutenant colonels, colonels, and brigadier generals. Roberts had already received this. Major generals (two-star in today's army) and lieutenant generals (three-star) received the next step, Knight Commander (KCB). The ultimate award, given to (four-star) generals and field marshals, was the Grand Cross (GCB). Before long, Roberts also received this. The British honours system is complicated but demands little from the public purse. The insignia— the stars, medals, and ribbons—are inexpensive to produce. But they are granted sparingly. Since they carry the direct authority of the Sovereign, they are highly valued by the recipients; and to the ambitious, they act as a spur to exceptional effort.

Mayhem in Kabul

Roberts happily spent the summer of 1879 in Simla with his family. He had a congenial job as a member of a commission examining military expenditure, in which his main concern was how to simplify the organization of the army: a difficult task that Roberts continued to address in future years.

However, early on 2 September, shattering news arrived that Cavagnari and his entire mission in Kabul had been murdered.[8] The assassins were disaffected Afghan soldiers who had not been paid for some time and had rioted to get their money. Cavagnari could not help them, shots were fired, and the Afghan government was totally unable to pacify the rioters. The viceroy immediately decided to send as strong a force as possible to Kabul to come to the assistance of the amir and punish the criminals. The three columns that had fought earlier in Afghanistan had been mostly dispersed. However, Roberts's relatively small column was still mobilized and could be reinforced. He was given command of the expedition.

The strength of Roberts's force was 192 British officers, 2,558 British other ranks, and 3,867 sepoys: a total of 6,617 men, more than twice the number that had triumphed at Peiwar Kotal. Roberts had artillery, cavalry, infantry, and engineers. The infantry included three British battalions: Sixty-Seventh Foot, Seventy-Second (Seaforth) Highlanders, and Ninety-Second (Gordon) Highlanders. One of the young officers in the Gordons was Ian Hamilton, whom Roberts met for the first time and who was later to join Roberts's personal staff. He would greatly improve the musketry of the Indian army. Hamilton built an impressive career, although it ended in failure at Gallipoli.

With no delay, the column began to march on Kabul. They soon came across a force of two thousand Afghans, and these were fought off in a sharp engagement in which another soldier in the Gordons, an NCO in one of the rifle companies, distinguished himself for his bravery and power of command. He was Colour Sergeant Hector Macdonald, the son of a crofter in the Highlands:

> 'Macdonald's men immediately responded to him, with one man's cry echoing through the ranks: "We'll make ye an officer for this day's work, Sergeant!" and another soldier shouting: "Aye, and a general too!"'[9]

There was considerable doubt about whether the Afghan government was totally innocent of the murders. The amir, Yakub Khan, joined Roberts on his march. Roberts thought that he looked very shifty and suspected that he was passing secret messages to Kabul to warn the defenders to prepare for an attack.

Progress was slow because of the rough terrain and streams that had to be waded. When the force reached the Charasia Plain, Roberts halted to enable units that were straggling at the rear of the column to catch up. The plain was cultivated, and at the far side was the last barrier before the large crowded city of Kabul: a range of high volcanic hills with some lower hills in front of them. The direct route to Kabul was through a gorge in these hills. The enemy was concentrated on their left, on both sides of the gorge. Roberts planned to attack the enemy flank with infantry and clear the gorge with cavalry. The infantry went in at 11:30 AM on 6 October 1879. The low hills were soon cleared, but the higher hills (some seven thousand feet high) were occupied by enemy troops in good tactical positions.

The Highlanders and Gurkhas stormed the heights, and by nightfall, the enemy had been ejected. The battle became known as Charasia. Major White of the Gordon Highlanders was awarded the Victoria Cross. He was later to command the Ladysmith garrison that was besieged during the Second Boer War. Colour Sergeant Macdonald received the rare distinction of a battlefield commission. This was the battle in which British units communicated over long distances with the flashing mirror of the heliograph. This was soon one of the most important pieces of technology used by the Victorian army in the tropics.

Roberts's force advanced towards Kabul and, on 7 October 1879, camped short of the city. Kabul, at that time, had a population of fifty thousand and was constructed of low mud-covered buildings that were spread over a wide area, overlooked by the Bala Hissar. The enemy force that had fled from Roberts's troops had reached the west of the city, and he sent out large detachments of cavalry and infantry to chase and attack them. However, the enemy melted away, leaving behind eighty-seven guns and much transport. The Afghan tribesmen lived to fight another day.

Yakub Khan was still with Roberts and had his quarters in the British headquarters camp. Before long, he decided to abdicate, and Roberts formally took over the government of the country but made it quite clear that this was a temporary arrangement. Yakub Khan was sent to India, where he lived in retirement for more than forty years. He had a substantial fortune in his possession, which Roberts took over and subsequently returned to the Afghan government.

The Anglo-Indian force made a spectacular show of their entry into Kabul. This included large concentrations of troops in the Bala Hissar, a flag-raising, military bands, the reading of a formal proclamation, and a thirty-one-gun salute. It was important for the new rulers to establish their absolute authority. Martial law was imposed and the population disarmed. A number of buildings (including the Bala Hissar) were razed, and a substantial fine was levied on the city. Roberts then dealt with the murderers of Cavagnari and the members of his embassy staff. Courts-martial were set up and formal evidence taken. The death warrants were personally signed by Roberts, and almost one hundred criminals were publicly hanged. (Roberts was harshly criticized in the British press, as he had been for his supposedly cavalier treatment of the Afghans after the Battle of Peiwar Kotal.) Kabul held vast piles of arms and ammunition, and on 16 October, there was a massive explosion as a magazine of gunpowder was detonated accidentally.

Roberts received further recognitions. Telegrams of thanks and best wishes arrived from the Queen and from the viceroy. He was also promoted lieutenant general (a three-star rank in the army today). Roberts's main task now was to bring peace to the country by encouraging the unruly tribes to accept British military authority and put away their weapons. But Afghanistan is never quiet for long, and the following months witnessed shots fired in anger in many places as groups of tribesmen attempted to attack British camps.

Ian Hamilton—who has already been mentioned as a young officer with promise—was brought to Roberts's attention in October 1879. Hamilton, a twenty-six-year-old subaltern in the Gordon Highlanders, was slowly recovering from fever while his battalion was fighting through the hills to reach Kabul. Hamilton and his friend 'Polly' Forbes were mounted on ponies and slowly making their way to catch up with their battalion.

They reached the battlefield of Peiwar Kotal and found it full of debris from the fight that had taken place the previous December. The young officers soon afterwards came across an outlying picket on a hill, and they were shocked to see a party of soldiers running away helter-skelter. They had abandoned their rifles, which meant that they

had committed a serious military offence. A single soldier kept his
rifle and was hanging back. The two young officers quickly occupied
the picket and sent for help. They then used the rifles to open fire on
a tribal raiding party that had attacked the British position. A British
infantry company arrived, and Hamilton and Forbes descended the hill
in search of the enemy. An indecisive battle took place in which one of
the tribesmen used an ancient blunderbuss and the two officers used
their pistols. They were too groggy to shoot straight, but the tribesman
disappeared.

News of this minor brush with the enemy reached Roberts, and the
result was described by Hamilton:

> 'Lord Roberts, or Sir Fred Roberts as he then was, sent for
> me to his tent and made me tell it to him. He then gave me
> a glass of sherry and said he would write home and tell my
> father what had happened, and so he did—longhand and
> at length. The indirect sequel was Sir Fred's offer to me two
> and a half years later to come on his staff, and the sherry and
> the letter give a useful glimpse of the secret of his popularity.'

Hamilton, who was still not fully fit, was appointed ADC to the
commander of the cavalry brigade that was part of Roberts's force: an
unusual job for an infantry officer, and one full of excitement.[10]

After Roberts had taken Kabul, a serious uprising took place in
December 1879. It was driven by religious frenzy, stoked by charismatic
mullahs. Roberts's intelligence officers detected Afghan forces advancing
on Kabul from three different directions, the most dangerous coming
from the west. Roberts sent two columns to meet the threat. He specified
precisely the time at which the two formations should come together
and then make a concentrated attack. However, the two brigadiers
coordinated their timing badly, and the two formations came close to
defeat in detail. Roberts rode out to take personal command.

The number of Afghan attackers was thought to be a hundred
thousand (but was more likely to have been half that number). On 11
December, Roberts concentrated his men in the entrenched camp at

Sherpur, two miles north of Kabul. They were besieged there, and the enemy forces briefly entered Kabul and looted quantities of arms and ammunition. The Afghans soon turned north to attack Sherpur, where Roberts had seven thousand men under command. By now, he had telegraphed army headquarters in India to request reinforcements; these eventually arrived after the siege had been lifted. In the snow, Afghan tribesmen made attack after attack, but these were mowed down by the musketry of the defenders. It was all over on 23 December, and the tribesmen melted away. The next few weeks were peaceful, and Kabul was the scene of sports and Christmas festivities.

Roberts's March from Kabul to Kandahar

In April 1880, the Kabul Field Force totaled 14,000 men and 12,500 followers, plus thirty-eight guns. While Roberts was carrying out his job successfully in Kabul, a division had occupied Kandahar. This was commanded by Sir Donald Stewart, who had been one of the three original column commanders during the invasion in November 1878. Roberts and Stewart were good friends.

In May 1880, there was a change of government in London, and the Liberal Party under Gladstone took office. One of their objectives was to withdraw Anglo-Indian troops from Afghanistan, reversing what was known at the time as a 'forward policy'. Stewart, who was senior to Roberts, was ordered north to Kabul, leaving behind a small occupying force. He was given the task of withdrawing all Anglo-Indian forces from Afghanistan as soon as he was sure that peace would be maintained. Earlier in the year, a new amir, Abdur Rahman, had been identified and sponsored by the British government. His appointment was announced at the end of July. He was not to receive regular subsidies like his predecessors, which meant that his position was weaker than theirs.

Because Stewart was senior to Roberts, Roberts was now free to return to India to take some leave. (Roberts may have felt piqued, but he never admitted it.) He rode to Jalalabad, where he was greatly interested

in the scene of the battle that had taken place in April 1842. Then, as
he rode on towards the Khyber Pass, he had a strange premonition:

> 'My intention, when I left Kabul, was to ride as far as the
> Khyber Pass, but suddenly a presentiment, which I have
> never been able to explain to myself, made me retrace my
> steps and hurry back towards Kabul—a presentiment of
> coming trouble which I can only characterize as instinctive.'[11]

Roberts was quite right. Well before he reached Kabul, he was
met by Stewart, who gave him the shocking news that the forces left
in Kandahar had been defeated at the Battle of Maiwand and suffered
1,109 casualties. The remaining Anglo-Indian troops were now besieged
in Kandahar.[12]

The relief of Kandahar had to be made by a force from Kabul
since it would have taken an unacceptably long time for men to march
from India. Stewart made his decision and cleared it with Indian army
headquarters in Simla. Roberts and his men set off on 9 August 1880.
They had to march 320 miles in heat that sometimes reached 110 °F,
covering rough territory occupied by hostile tribes. The force had no
base of operations; they lacked communications, so if there was a serious
enemy attack, there was no way of sending for reinforcements; and there
were no engineers to clear the way if the enemy placed obstacles. It was
the same route that Alexander the Great had taken from Kandahar to
Kabul in 320 BC. (The name Kandahar is a corruption of the name
Alexandria.)

Roberts's force comprised 9,986 men in three infantry brigades and
one brigade of cavalry—in the normal way, each infantry brigade had
one British and three Indian units. There were, however, only eighteen
guns, all mountain artillery because heavy wheeled guns would have
slowed the progress of the force. There were eight thousand camp
followers. More than eight thousand horses and mules left Kabul, but a
few died *en route*. The march took twenty-three days, and the maximum
distance covered in a day by the whole force was nineteen miles. What
slowed the pace was not just the ability of troops and followers to

march long distances. Even more onerous was the need to transport ammunition (e.g. 540 rounds per mountain battery and 200 small-arms rounds per soldier). Some food was carried, but vegetables and fodder were purchased during the journey. Eight thousand animals needed a massive quantity of fodder. The logistics of the march demonstrated mastery on the part of Roberts and his staff, but the difficulties they faced dramatically demonstrate the improvement made by the introduction of motor transport (MT) in the twentieth century.

Some of the roads were so inadequate that men had to march in single file. The march was physically gruelling, but there was not much interference from Afghan tribes, although they often looted the rear of the column:

> 'The wretched followers were so weary and footsore that they hid themselves in ravines, making up their minds to die, and entreating, when discovered and urged to make an effort, to be left were they were. Every baggage animal that could possibly be spared was used to carry the worn-out followers; but, notwithstanding this and the care taken by officers and men that none should be left behind, twenty of these poor creatures were lost, besides four native soldiers.'[13]

On the longest days of marching, the force was on the road from dawn to dusk. Roberts did not ride all the time in his place in the column: he would ride up and down and spend part of his time with the infantry and part with the cavalry. He also made a point of welcoming every battalion, regiment, and battery into camp in the evening, to show the men that he refused to relax until the men had been settled and fed. Some were badly sunburned and others were sick. During the final days of the march, Roberts was himself ill. He had suffered a similarly debilitating sickness on a number of past occasions, and a diagnosis based on modern pathology points to a duodenal ulcer.

The column reached Kandahar at the end of August, but Roberts and his staff had known for some time that the enemy commander, Ayub Khan—with a substantial body of men and some artillery—was in a strong position outside the city. They would have to be evicted. Roberts faced a line of three mountains, with the Baba Wali Kotal Pass between the second and third of these. Roberts sent out a regiment of cavalry and a battalion of infantry to make a full reconnaissance to try and find the details of the enemy position. He formulated his plan on the basis of this information.

By next morning, 1 September, Roberts was refreshed after a peaceful night, and at 6:00 AM, he gave his personal orders to his senior commanders. His plan was to make a strong feint towards the Baba Wali Kotal (the enemy left), and then sweep around the mountain and assault the enemy right. This strategy was successful, and the infantry— Gurkhas, Sikhs, and two battalions of Highlanders—assaulted the enemy position with great dash. The enemy fled the field, abandoning their guns. Roberts's force suffered 248 casualties (thirty-five fatal), while the enemy lost more than one thousand men killed.

The relief of Kandahar was the greatest success of Roberts's career to date. He was awarded the GCB, the highest grade of the Order of the Bath. Among many letters of congratulations, he received a handwritten letter from the Queen. Within a few days of the relief of Kandahar, Roberts had to attend a medical board, and he was immediately sent on extended sick leave. He had not been to England for twelve years and was delighted to return there. His wife was, at the time, living in Somerset.

Roberts was surprised that his arrival in England at the end of 1880 was nothing short of triumphant. The long march in distant Afghanistan to rescue an isolated British garrison struck a resonant chord with the British public. Roberts himself was astonished at this public perception because he regarded the march a much less arduous military operation than his advance on Kabul in September and October 1879. This had been a shorter distance, but he had faced and overcome much more enemy opposition. In addition to his GCB, he was invited to Windsor Castle to stay with the Queen. He received the thanks of both Houses of Parliament. He was offered a baronetcy, which he accepted. Oxford University gave him an honorary degree. He also received a grant of £12,500 (about £1,250,000 in today's money). Wolseley had been given twice as much. This difference was probably a reflection of the unfavourable press reports about the strict discipline that Roberts had imposed on Kabul and the number of murderers he had sent to trial and subsequently hanged.

The Second Anglo-Afghan War, like the First, ended up with a return to the *status quo*. This was inevitable in view of the decision by the British government on both occasions to withdraw the Indian army. This meant that Roberts's four memorable victories did not bring peace to Afghanistan in the long term; but with Afghanistan as a buffer state, the Russian Bear was kept within its frontiers.

Roberts was now in his late forties. He was highly experienced and, as a legacy of his years on the staff, he was a clear thinker and writer. As a commander, he had demonstrated two important talents. The first was his mastery of battlefield strategy: his ability to 'think big'. He prepared for battle by deploying his men on the ground in such a way that when the opposing forces met, he was strong where the enemy was weak. His most effective tool was deception, luring the enemy away from where his attack was going to take place. He won four battles—battles important enough to be emblazoned on regimental colours—Peiwar Kotal, Charasia, Kabul, and Kandahar. Only the battle of Kabul, which took place after the capture of the city, was touch-and-go. This was because of the tactical failings of Roberts's subordinates; but when he took direct control, he quickly regained his balance and seized the initiative again. Roberts's second talent was the remarkable way he understood the men under his command and was very popular with them. He was never isolated in a distant headquarters; his soldiers were invariably aware of his presence.

Few generals possess these two talents in combination. During the First World War, no leader on either side had them. However, Montgomery—the most highly regarded British military commander of the Second World War—had much in common with Roberts. He had the same flair for battlefield strategy. He also managed to get 'under the skin' of his soldiers and made himself known to every one of the large number of individual units in his command. He always greeted them with 'Break ranks and close in on me'. Both Roberts and Montgomery were small in stature, but they made up for this by their honed strategic skills and their instinctive power of leadership: something that came from their understanding of their men, who were the real battle-winners.

Endnotes

1. Jones, John Philip, *Battles of a Gunner Officer* (Barnsley, South Yorkshire: Pen & Sword, 2014), 205.

2. The phrase was coined by an intrepid officer of the East India Company Army called Arthur Conolly, who was murdered at the age of thirty-five. He had travelled north to Bokhara, to try and secure the release of Russian and British prisoners who had been held there. But he was killed on the orders of the emir of Bokhara. The Russians soon afterwards occupied that country.

3. The First Afghan War is described in: Farwell, Byron, *Queen Victoria's Little Wars* (New York: W. W. Norton, 1972); Hopkirk, Peter, *The Great Game* (New York: Kodansha International, 1992); Meyer, Karl E. & Brysac, Shareen Blair, *Tournament of Shadows* (Washington DC: Counterpoint, 1999); Yorke, Edmund, *Playing the Great Game* (London: Robert Hale, 2012).

4. Roberts of Kandahar, Field Marshal Lord, *Forty-One Years in India* (London: Michael Bentley, 1897), *Volume II*, 102–126.

5. Ibid., 127–167.

6. Ibid., 148.

7. Barney, William L. *The Oxford Encyclopedia of the Civil War* (Oxford: Oxford University Press, 2011), 66–68.

8. Roberts of Kandahar, *Forty-One Years in India, Volume II*, 168–320; James, David, *Lord Roberts* (London: Hollis & Carter, 1954), 102–149; Farwell, *Queen Victoria's Little Wars*, 200–217.

9. Jones, John Philip, *Johnny. The Legend and Tragedy of General Sir Ian Hamilton* (Barnsley, South Yorkshire: Pen & Sword, 2012), 44.

10. Ibid., 43–46.

11. Roberts of Kandahar, *Forty-One Years in India, Volume II*, 330.

12. Ibid., 321–379; James, *Lord Roberts*, 150–166; Farwell, *Queen Victoria's Little Wars*, 211–217.

13. Roberts of Kandahar, *Forty-One Years in India, Volume II*, 349.

CHAPTER 11

WOLSELEY'S GROWING REPUTATION: AT THE WAR OFFICE AND OVERSEAS, 1871–1882

Wolseley had been posted to the War Office in May 1871, where he worked for the dynamic Secretary of State for War, Edward Cardwell. (See chapter 8.) During his period in office, Cardwell followed a menu of six army reforms that he planned to implement. In this, Wolseley provided energetic support. Visible progress was made on four of these: the introduction of breech-loading rifles; the abolition of the purchase of commissions; the reduction in the size of overseas garrisons, apart from India; and the introduction of short service for the soldiers in the ranks. The remaining reforms would take longer: establishing linked battalions for the regular army and the rationalization of the auxiliary (i.e. part-time) forces of militia, volunteers, and yeomanry. Reforming the auxiliary forces had to wait until the twentieth century, after the Second Boer War of 1899–1902. This war cast doubts on the long-term value of traditional cavalry, including the yeomanry, and there was also much indecisive discussion about horse soldiers becoming mounted infantry rather than maintaining their traditional roles as lancers, hussars, and dragoons.

During Wolseley's period at the War Office under Cardwell, he was a colonel and assistant adjutant general. When he returned from

West Africa in March 1874, he was a major general with an impressive fighting reputation. During his absence in West Africa, a general election had taken place, and Gladstone's Liberal government had been replaced by Disraeli's Conservative administration. The new Secretary of State for War and Wolseley's chief was Gathorne Hardy. He and the prime minister were less single-minded about army reform than their predecessors. However, this did not deter Wolseley.[1]

Wolseley's first thought was to work towards applying the Cardwell Reforms to the Indian army, and he would have a chance of doing this at a later date. In the meantime, he accepted the position of Inspector General of the Auxiliary Forces, the heterogeneous collection of part-time infantry and cavalry regiments. Wolseley was only in this job for eight months, and he made limited progress. Cardwell's plan was to devote attention first to the infantry and use each military district as a centre for regular, militia, and volunteer elements of the county regiment. Each would have a depot, which would be a large headquarters covering a regular regiment of two linked battalions, two militia battalions, and a variable number of volunteer units. The auxiliary units would therefore cluster around the regular ones, with the same names, uniforms, and regimental traditions. The system worked well, and it was developed later by the Haldane Reforms of 1908. The Haldane plan would have made it possible to expand the army to a far larger size in the event of a major war. However, in 1914, Field Marshal Lord Kitchener, the newly appointed Secretary of State for War, had very different ideas and decided to create his own new army from scratch. There was a large opportunity cost in this because what was sacrificed was the simpler and more economical expansion planned by Haldane.

At this time, Wolseley also spoke publicly about two issues connected with army recruitment. The first was whether auxiliary forces should be required, if they were mobilized, to serve abroad rather than exclusively for home defence. Wolseley disagreed with this because he believed—correctly—that it would depress recruiting into the auxiliaries. The second problem that had emerged was that the introduction of short service had not (as expected) boosted recruitment into the regular army. Wolseley thought that the most effective solution to this would be to increase private soldiers' pay, from one shilling to two shillings a day. However, the increase in the size of the army estimate that this would cause was enough to discourage any action by the government.

Army reform, like any other government reform, is a subject that takes a long time to resolve. It is inevitably debated in Parliament, committees are set up, they report, and these reports are also debated. A good deal was in the air when Wolseley left England for his next appointment overseas. He had been offered an unusual opportunity that meant his attachment to the Colonial Office, which paid his salary. His job was in Natal, and it was different from anything he had ever done before. An important benefit for Wolseley was that it broadened his understanding of politico-military cooperation because the appointment he received was as military governor of Natal.[2]

Wolseley in Natal and the Evolution of the British Empire

At this time, the old colonies settled by British immigrants—Canada, Australia, and New Zealand—were prosperous and politically stable and well on the way to becoming self-governing dominions. Other smaller colonies—in the Far East, the Caribbean, and Africa—were economically not so well developed and were run by colonial administrators born and educated in Britain. The largest of these colonies was South Africa.

The British colony in South Africa comprised three British provinces—Cape Province (by far the largest), Natal, and the new Crown Colony of Griqualand West. There were also the two Boer provinces of Orange Free State (OFS) and Transvaal. These had been formed by the Boer settlers who, in 1835–1837, had made the Great Trek north across the Orange River and then in smaller numbers across the Vaal. One of the reasons for their departure was Britain's abolition of slavery. Both Boer provinces were independent and, therefore, not really within the British sphere; but they were not capable of administering their affairs efficiently and were often close to bankruptcy. In 1877, they accepted British rule reluctantly (and, in the event, temporarily). Finally, there were a number of black African kingdoms, the most powerful of which were the Zulus under their charismatic leader Cetewayo. The Zulus had an organized and highly disciplined army. They were armed with a number of rifles, and every man also had his *assegai*: a short deadly weapon, half-sword and half-spear. Natal is to the east, on the shore of the Indian Ocean. It has a frontier with Transvaal. The black kingdoms were also all adjacent to Natal. Wolseley always sensed potential trouble with the Zulus, and before he left Natal, he wrote:

> '. . . took notes in preparation for an invasion of Cetewayo's territory. Thinking that I should have a command when the war, which everyone in South Africa knew and felt must come off sooner or later, did take place. With his 40,000 men armed with firearms, he would be no mean enemy.'[3]

The five most important provinces—three British and two Boer—were ruled by the white population, which accounted for only 20 percent of the colony's total population of twenty million men, women, and children. (See **Map 12**.) There was no slavery, but the whites were the employers, and the blacks were the labourers and servants who worked for food and lodging and a small wage. There was a rigid social and economic dividing line between the whites and the blacks, and when war broke out between the British and the Boers—in 1881 and again in 1899—the blacks did not fight on either side. The economy of all the provinces was based on farming: growing crops and rearing livestock. (*Boer* is the Dutch word for farmer.) It was a number of years before the discovery of gold on the Witwatersrand in the Transvaal and diamonds at Kimberly in the OFS, and this totally transformed the economy of the Boer provinces. It also led eventually to the Second Boer War.

Wolseley was appointed lieutenant governor of Natal, and he arrived in Durban on 26 March 1875. His job was to transform the government of the province, and this was by no means an easy task. The driving force behind the reforms was Lord Carnarvon, who held the top government appointment, Secretary of State for the Colonies.

Before Wolseley's arrival, the province was self-contained and ruled by a lieutenant governor and a small legislative council of mostly elected representatives.[4] Carnarvon's plan, which was similar to one he had implemented in Canada, was that the South African colony should form a large confederation of all the white provinces, including the two independent Boer ones. As part of this plan, the Natal government would be subservient to the central government, which would levy the taxes and be responsible for defence. This was an important consideration because of the possibility of an attack by hostile black tribes. In 1873, some of the Zulus had rebelled, but their uprising was crushed. In 1879, there was a much more serious rebellion, which led to an initial disaster for British arms before peace was re-established.

Wolseley did not have a high opinion of the Natal politicians, including Theophilous Shepstone, who had the unusual job of living with the Zulus and keeping an eye on them. Wolseley described the legislative council in the following words:

> 'Held a legislative council: no unofficial member present; a poor weak lot. Shepstone excepted, and I am afraid that whether owing to natural disposition or to the effects of age, that able as he evidently is, he is also lazy.'[5]

He also had an unfavourable opinion of many of the settlers, although not all of them:

> 'Sunday 4 July, lunched at an English farmer's house; he was from Gloucestershire, where he had had a farm of thirty acres: now he rents a farm on 8,000 acres and says that if he had a farm of his own, he could do well: anything and everything grows well, but he says that the people here are so lazy that they don't work to try and raise good crops: he gave us some cider that he had made himself. I wish we had a few thousands of such men here; if we had, Natal would soon be a prosperous place.'[6]

Wolseley argued that the Natal colonists should be prepared to lose some of their authority in exchange for British regiments on the spot, ready to protect the colony from trouble from the Zulus. The only defence force in the colony itself was some untrained regiments of part-time volunteers. Wolseley was permitted to appoint four British officers to join his staff, all of whom had fought with him in the Ashanti expedition. They were Captain Lord Gifford and three members of the 'Wolseley Ring': Colonel George Colley, Major Henry Brackenbury, and Major William Butler. These trusted men travelled over the country, including the Boer provinces, everywhere representing the views of their chief. Wolseley himself also travelled widely and took steps to arrange an independent military command made up of troops from the Cape and Mauritius, which would be quickly available to meet any native uprising.

During most of Wolseley's time in Natal, he met apathy and opposition. He quickly realized that any constitutional change had to be passed by the legislative council, which meant that he had to engineer the appointment of more non-elected members. He had to bring this about with some delicacy. His solution involved some bribery in a good cause: lavish spending on entertainment to try and sweeten the atmosphere. His life became a round of dinners and balls, which were very popular with the Natal ladies. He introduced the new game of lawn tennis, a less strenuous version of real (or royal) tennis, a game that dated from the sixteenth century. He arranged for the British government to underwrite a loan to build railways. He also persuaded the leading newspapers to give their support.

Although Wolseley's task was difficult, he eventually managed to enact a constitutional change by which the governor would gain substantial—although not total—control and was thus able to give effect to Carnarvon's policies. The legislative council was increased to twenty-eight members, of whom thirteen would be appointed and fifteen elected. Of the latter, one would be chosen as the impartial speaker, making the relative numbers thirteen and fourteen. As a result, 'the governor has only to obtain one elected member on his side to pass another bill on the Constitution question'.[7]

Wolseley's job was now complete, and he could return to England. He handed over to his successor, Sir Henry Bulwer, in August 1875 and returned to the War Office shortly afterwards. He had spent less than a year there, and he found it rather frustrating. Unacceptably slow progress was being made to link the battalions of the regular army. In the background was Wolseley's feeling that the Indian army had to be pressed to adopt the Cardwell Reforms. Short service, in particular, was unpopular with Indian army officers. As late as the 1880s, Roberts—when commander-in-chief in Madras—expressed his opposition, and this was typical of the views of his contemporaries. Short service was, however, eventually confirmed—although in India, it was slightly modified, allowing soldiers to prolong their service to spend eight years in the subcontinent.

From Commander-in-Chief to Military Governor

In 1876, the Duke of Cambridge and Gathorne Hardy were also concerned about India and supported the proposal that Wolseley should transfer temporarily to the India Council, the branch of government that supervised all aspects of the administration of the subcontinent. The problem that was being confronted at the time was the perennial trouble with Russia: the *Great Game*. Russia was building railways in her Muslim provinces in the south, and this would obviously make it easy to transfer troops nearer to India. At the same time, Russia was on bad terms with Turkey, which ruled the miscellaneous territories in the Balkans and had brutally suppressed a revolt in three Slav provinces in the north. The Slavs were under the general protection of Russia (a continued protection that was one of the triggers that started the First World War).

War broke out between Russia and Turkey in 1877, and Britain came very close in joining Turkey with the intention of weakening Russia's threat to India. A British expeditionary force was prepared, to be commanded by General Sir Robert Napier, with Wolseley as second in command. However, the Congress of Berlin, engineered by

Prince Bismarck, the German chancellor, brought an end to the crisis in the Balkans. As a part of the settlement, Britain received the island of Cyprus, for which Britain paid Turkey annual sums of money. The population of Cyprus is three-quarters Greek and one-quarter Turkish: an uncomfortable combination.[8]

At this time, Wolseley was hoping for a senior appointment in India, as commander-in-chief of the army of the Bombay Presidency. Instead, the Foreign Office appointed Wolseley as British high commissioner in Cyprus. (The Duke of Cambridge was not consulted. He was displeased: something that did not improve his relationship with Wolseley.) Wolseley left for the island and arrived in July 1878, and he appointed his staff from members of the Wolseley 'Ring'. There was no fighting, and Wolseley's main task was administration, and he was also expected to decide whether or not Cyprus would be a suitable base in the eastern Mediterranean for the British army and navy.[9]

The island was run down because of decades of Turkish neglect:

> 'The wells are few, and scarcely a river or rather what is marked on the map as a river, has more than a pool here and there of stagnant water in it. Where are the forests we thought Cyprus was covered with? This is in everyone's mouth, yet no one can give a very satisfactory answer. Like everything else that made this country a splendid one in ancient times, the forests have disappeared under the influence, the blighting influence, of the Turk.'[10]

It was also uncomfortably hot in the summer, and a quarter of the British troops suffered from fever. The winter was cold enough to force guests in Government House to wear fur coats when they sat down to dinner.

Wolseley's administration soon began to show benefits. He sorted out the public finances, and he levied taxes and customs duties large enough to balance the public books. He carefully evaluated the merits of Cyprus as a military base and decided against it. The climate was too unhealthy for the troops, and there was no good harbour for the navy.

Alexandria was a much more suitable base, although Cyprus would be able to provide animals to supply any future British expedition in the Middle East.

Within a very short time, Wolseley had transformed the administration of the island, although the divided population remained a permanent problem because of the mutual antagonism between the Greeks and Turks. Over the years, the economy improved, and many farmers began to make a good living.

One important military task was successfully launched during Wolseley's time in office. Cyprus was professionally surveyed by the Royal Engineers. There were some delays because of expense, but in 1885, a fifteen-sheet map of the island, based on professional triangulation, was published. It was a work of very high quality and bore the name of one of the officers who had done the job: Lieutenant Herbert Horatio Kitchener, Royal Engineers. By the end of the nineteenth century, Kitchener would be a household name in Britain.[11]

In April 1879, nine months after Wolseley's arrival in Cyprus, a serious problem in South Africa demanded a solution, and Wolseley was considered to be the man to carry out the task. He was soon in London, to participate officially in the committee that was discussing short service. But in reality, the government wanted him back in London to tell him that he would be sent to South Africa as high commissioner and commander-in-chief for the Transvaal, Natal, and the native states, including the most important: Zululand. Zululand is on the coast and is shaped roughly like a triangle, with Natal to the south-west and Transvaal to the north-west. (See **Map 12**.) Wolseley was briefed by a number of people, including the prime minister, and soon afterwards, he sailed to South Africa, returning to the colony from which he had departed four years before.

Before Wolseley's arrival, the civil and military commands had been split. The high commissioner for South Africa was Sir Bartle Frere, and the commander-in-chief was General Lord Chelmsford. They had both believed that the Zulus posed a threat to the white colonies, and Chelmsford invaded Zululand in January 1879. He bit off more than he could chew. The British camp on the conical hill of Isandhlwana was attacked by a large force of Zulus. The 950 British troops on the spot did not occupy the hill itself but were strung out in a circle on the ground around the base. There was no depth in the British position, and when the Zulus advanced in their tactical formation that resembled the horns of a bull, they surrounded the British force and wiped it out. The subsequent stubborn defence of Rorke's Drift, seven miles away, demonstrated the bravery of the British infantry and earned the respect of the Zulus. However, these two encounters with native enemies were remembered for the British army's tactical ineptitude, the large number of casualties, and the loss of face.

Chelmsford was demoted and remained in South Africa as the army second in command. Before Wolseley sailed from England, he put together his staff, most of whom (like his staff in Natal in 1875) were members of the Wolseley 'Ring'. His discussion with the prime minister was described by Disraeli in a letter to the Queen:

> 'In favour of Confederation, but until Zululand is tranquil and settled, it is impossible, as Cape would not combine with Natal, with a Zulu war always impending. Induced him with great difficulty to speak about the conduct of the war, but ultimately and with pressure, he said it had been carried out on a wrong principle: the base should have been the sea, not 200 miles up the interior . . . should employ human beings as porters.'[12]

Wolseley's task was ultimately to arrange a political settlement in South Africa, but military operations were needed first. He was therefore promoted to the local rank of full (i.e. four-star) general. He was only in his early fifties, and his career had been outstanding. As an experienced army officer accustomed to command, he was decisive, with clear and strongly expressed opinions. But he was developing a reputation for being a little too self-confident, which did not endear him to people as important as the Duke of Cambridge, Disraeli, and the Queen. In words he confided to his diary, he also felt occasionally under siege because of people in the War Office he imagined were his enemies.

When Wolseley arrived at Cape Town on 23 June 1879, he learned that Chelmsford was, on his own initiative, marching into Zululand in two independent columns to attack Cetewayo. This was a slow process because supplies had to be hauled in ox-drawn wagons. Wolseley did not like this idea at all and attempted unsuccessfully to halt the advance. But at Ulundi, Chelmsford defeated twenty thousand Zulus with his army of five thousand (of whom four thousand were British). However, Cetewayo got away.

Many British soldiers were now exhausted and had to be repatriated to England. They included two members of the Wolseley 'Ring', Major Redvers Buller and Brigadier General Evelyn Wood. Nevertheless, Wolseley pursued the war energetically and met and pacified a number of Zulu chiefs. On 28 August, Lord Gifford captured Cetewayo: 'He has a very wise countenance and is quite the king in his bearing and deportment. He is very fat, but as he is tall, he carries it off; he is very black and wore round him a coloured tablecloth.'[13] He was taken to England and presented to Queen Victoria, who was impressed with him but thought that he needed watching. Her advice was taken when he was returned to Zululand. Relations between the Zulus and the British were never satisfactory, and the province was annexed in 1900.

Although the Battle of Ulundi had been a victory over the Zulus, there was soon a fresh uprising by the Pedi tribe, led by a native chief called Sekhukhuni. He commanded six thousand native warriors, two thirds armed with rifles. He occupied a town and an adjacent steep hill called the Fighting Kopje, which was honeycombed with caves and was a strong defensive position. This time, Wolseley took personal command of the expedition and had a force of 1,400 British infantry, 400 Colonial cavalry, and 10,000 native mercenaries. He made a careful reconnaissance of possible routes to advance to the enemy position and even employed the Royal Engineers to construct roads. Wolseley's men stormed the Fighting Kopje, and he watched their progress, impressed not only by his own troops but also by the Pedi tribesmen who fought bravely to the last. Sekhukhuni was captured and was given into the hands of the Boers in Pretoria.[14]

The British had defeated two native uprisings, and Wolseley now turned to his main tasks, which were to centralize control over all the provinces in South Africa: the three British colonies, the two Boer republics, and the native homelands. In November 1879, he proclaimed a confederation, on the lines of the system he had earlier instituted in Natal. Each of the provinces would be ruled by a governor and legislative council, with most members appointed, not elected. There would be central control of taxation and—most importantly—defence. Wolseley was particularly anxious to extend confederation to the two Boer republics because of their economic potential. It was already clear that gold was being mined in the Transvaal.

The Boer republics had accepted confederation with some reluctance, but they badly needed military support against the natives. However since the Zulus and Pedi had been defeated in battle, the Boers were becoming more determined to return to complete independence.

This question was to be resolved after Wolseley's departure. When he left South Africa in May 1880, he handed over command to his friend and a prominent member of the Wolseley 'Ring', Major General Sir George Colley (whose name would soon be changed to Pomeroy-Colley). The weight of Colley's command was to prove onerous. The First Boer War broke out almost immediately, and it would lead to the Boers achieving a substantial degree of independence. On the top of Majuba Hill—which the Boers successfully stormed on 27 February 1881—Pomeroy-Colley was killed by a Boer marksman. Wolseley considered him the most able man he had ever met.

Wolseley, with his main task apparently completed, prepared for his next appointment. On 8 March 1880, he had accepted, after a deliberate delay, the important appointment of quartermaster general (QMG) in the War Office.[15] He would become one of a triumvirate of officers who directed the central affairs of the army: the commander-in-chief, the adjutant general (AG), and the quartermaster general. Although generals who exercised commands overseas had great operational freedom, they had to work within parameters dictated by London. In particular, the adjutant general directed all aspects of manpower, and the quartermaster general controlled the huge range of supplies needed by an overseas army in peace and war.

Nevertheless the job in London was a disappointment to Wolseley, who had set his heart on the plum appointment of commander-in-chief of the Indian army. This was shortly to become vacant, and it was in the event given to Sir Donald Stewart, the victor of the Second Afghan War. It was because Wolseley had hopes of the position in India he delayed accepting the job of quartermaster general. Because he was disappointed about failing to get the Indian command, he suspected—with little justification—a conspiracy against him in London:

> 'However I have all the Royalties against me, including the Queen. I shall win in the end, and their Royal Highnesses will regret having made an enemy of one whom I believe could do more for them if they were in trouble than any of the poor courtiers whose advice they now listen to.'[16]

One consideration that made Wolseley happier about his appointment in London was that there was a change of government. The Conservatives had been defeated in a general election, and Gladstone and his Liberal Party formed a new administration. The new Secretary of State for War, Hugh Childers, was to continue Cardwell's pioneering reforms, and Wolseley would be in London to assist him. However, Wolseley would in due course develop a considerable dislike of Gladstone, and this would be expressed in the diary he kept during the Nile expedition to rescue Gordon. (See chapter 13.) As a reward for his military and political services in South Africa, Wolseley received the GCB, the highest grade of the Order of the Bath. But his rank of full general was not yet confirmed. He took up his new appointment in the War Office on 1 July 1880.

During Wolseley's time as QMG, a number of policy issues emerged; and although they were only peripherally his concern, Wolseley was deeply involved. The first matter was the treaty ending the First Boer War, which granted the Boer republics a substantial degree of independence. This was unpopular in Britain. Many people, including the Queen, regarded it as a humiliation. Tempers eventually cooled, partly as a result of a substantial increase in the size of the British garrison in South Africa. But a grumbling problem remained, and the Second (and larger) Boer War broke out in 1899.

The second and third issues were the important army reforms of short service and linked battalions. In both of these, the Cardwell Reforms had been passed into law but were still debated after more than a decade. They were firmly supported by the new Liberal government, in particular by Hugh Childers. These reforms were intensely important to Wolseley, and he needed no urging to express his views. Much of his work as QMG was routine, and army reform was intellectually and personally engaging. His support of reform was not welcomed by the commander-in-chief, the Duke of Cambridge, who was Queen Victoria's cousin and a deeply rooted conservative. In contrast to Wolseley, Roberts spoke openly in favour of long service and against linked battalions. His views differed from official government policy, but they found favour with the duke. These differences now entered the public domain, with much thoughtful comment in journals read by the educated classes.

On this stage crowded with squabbling actors—Gladstone, Childers, Wolseley, the Duke of Cambridge, Roberts, and many well-informed journalists—a *deus ex machina* now descended. Gladstone decided that he needed support for government policy in the House of Lords, and he proposed raising Wolseley to the peerage. This was too much for the Queen and the Duke of Cambridge, whose alliance was as strong as ever. Gladstone's proposal was considered and discussed and dragged on, especially because the duke could never accept a newly elevated peer as quartermaster general. Although Gladstone retreated, Wolseley received a significant consolation prize.[17] He was moved up the hierarchy and appointed adjutant general—in effect, the commander-in-chief's deputy. (He was eventually to succeed the duke as commander-in-chief.) Wolseley was appointed on 1 April 1882 and held the job of AG for eight years, during which time he changed the nature of the position. While he was AG, he was given two active service commands; at the end of each, he returned to his position in the War Office. Roberts, meanwhile, had been offered the position of QMG in succession to Wolseley, but he had declined because he chose instead to be commander-in-chief in Madras.

During Wolseley's first months as adjutant general, the subject that dominated his attention was a plan to drive a tunnel under the English Channel. A private member's bill had been proposed in Parliament in 1875, and preliminary engineering work was already under way. Wolseley opposed the idea, and for once, the commander-in-chief was behind him, and so was the Secretary of State for War. Wolseley's argument was that a tunnel would make Britain vulnerable to invasion. And since the country no longer had the protection of the water that separated the country from France, Britain would have to create a conscript army as large as those of the major continental powers. The public supported Wolseley and the other opponents to the tunnel. An official committee was convened but was divided. However, over time, the proposed tunnel declined in importance, and interest died out in the 1890s. The project was, of course, revived during the second half of the twentieth century, with a different outcome.

Another matter of direct importance to Wolseley in his capacity as adjutant general was the Army Reserve, which was growing in size as a result of short service, since increasing numbers of men were completing their regular service and joining the reserve. Wolseley was particularly concerned with the continued training of these men and the need to monitor annually their physical fitness. The physical fitness of the army as a whole was, of course, a matter of first importance; and during Wolseley's first years as AG, the low level of recruitment led to a reduction in the physical standards demanded for regular recruits, e.g. the army had to reduce the height requirement below the traditional five feet seven inches.[18]

However, Wolseley's attention to all manpower questions was unexpectedly put on hold. In July 1882, his services were called for to command an expedition to Egypt.

Insurrection in Egypt and Wolseley's Greatest Victory

In 1875, Disraeli, as prime minister, used British government funds to purchase a controlling interest in the Suez Canal Company. This was a decision of great strategic importance. Since the canal was the shortest route for ships sailing between Britain and India, it was much easier than before to garrison the subcontinent and to conduct the increasing volume of export and import business. Around 80 percent of the Suez Canal traffic was British.

The Suez Canal had to be politically secure if shipping was able to use it freely. As a result, Egypt—which had formerly been relatively unimportant for Britain—now became a major concern. A politically stable Egyptian government called for a British military presence in the country. No attempt was made to annex Egypt and force it into membership of the British Empire, but there was a continuous military presence that could play an active role if trouble started. (During the First and Second World Wars, the Egyptian army played no part, and all battles were fought against the Germans and Italians by the British and their colonies and allies.) The policy of keeping the Suez Canal free by the presence of British troops in the background was extremely successful. No attempt was made by the Egyptians to take over the Suez Canal until 1956: a long period of peace that was the result of Wolseley's victory in 1882.

Egypt in the nineteenth century was part of the Ottoman Empire. Constantinople is distant from Cairo, so that the ultimate control by the Turkish sultan was relaxed although not apathetic. The ruler of Egypt, the Khedive, was an appointed official, but the government was characterized by inefficiency and corruption. During the 1870s, the country became bankrupt, with tax receipts below what was needed to fund government spending. This situation had forced the Khedive to sell his shares in the Suez Canal Company to the British government.

The French and British governments stepped in to control Egyptian finances. (The French were involved because the canal had been built by them.) At the same time, the sultan of Turkey replaced the Khedive. But public unrest over misgovernment was so great that an army colonel, Ahmed Urabi, led a revolt that threatened the Egyptian government and the Suez Canal. In May 1880, with Urabi now in power. British and French warships sailed into Alexandria Bay and began a futile bombardment. This angered the Egyptians even more, and this was the last of any French cooperation in Egypt since they had a good deal on their hands pacifying Tunisia.

Gladstone, who was now prime minister, dragged his heels over British military intervention. But at last, on 20 July 1882, Hugh Childers, Secretary of State for War, announced the appointment of Wolseley as commander of an expedition to suppress the Egyptian insurrection. The Duke of Cambridge and the Queen gave their rather grudging approval. Wolseley went to war with his substantive rank of lieutenant general (three-star), since his temporary promotion to full general had not been confirmed when he returned from South Africa. Gladstone proposed and got agreement to a vote of £2,300,000. (Finance was always a matter of great importance to him.)

The expeditionary force was thrown together hurriedly in a way that Wolseley did not like. Around 16,400 men came from the home army, and 14,400 from India and the Mediterranean. The force totalled two under-strength fighting divisions, although the men were all experienced regulars.[19] The total strength of the force, including men in the line of communications, was forty thousand. There was also strong artillery support. One unusual addition was a detachment of volunteers—part-time infantry. The volunteers had been organized in 1859, and the Egyptian expedition was the first occasion any of them had been mobilized. They were men of the Post Office Rifles, a London regiment, who went to Egypt to organize and man the army's telegraph services.

Wolseley found jobs for a number of his friends in the Wolseley 'Ring'. Many senior officers also clamoured to go to Egypt; they included the Duke of Connaught, Queen Victoria's third son, who commanded a brigade of Foot Guards. A total of eighteen generals joined the expedition, and Wolseley had to find sinecures for a number of them.[20] The British soldiers wore uniforms unsuitable for the tropics: scarlet-and-blue serge, green uniforms for the Rifle regiments, and thick pleated tartan kilts for the Highlanders. (The Indian army troops had more comfortable clothing.) Many men were quickly exhausted by marching in the sun. They all wore round sun helmets made of cork covered in white canvas, with a short rim over the face and a longer rim over the neck.

During the war, the fighting took place in an inverted triangle of territory. The top runs along a 150-mile stretch of the Mediterranean coast from Aboukir and Alexandria in the west to Port Said and the Suez Canal in the east. The other two sides of the triangle stretch south-east from Alexandria and south-west from Port Said, and meet in Cairo. (See **Map 10**.)

The main enemy camp was at Tel-el-Kebir, north-east of Cairo. When his forces were in place, Wolseley planned to assault Tel-el-Kebir, a name that would eventually be added to the battle honours of a number of British regiments. Wolseley's first objective was to maintain total secrecy. He ordered a detailed plan to be drawn up to seize Aboukir in the west. This was intended to mislead the enemy, and he assumed that newspaper correspondents and Egyptian spies in Alexandria would let the cat out of the bag. Just before this deception plan was put into operation, Wolseley drove ahead with his real plan, which was to concentrate on the east by holding and defending the Suez Canal. This involved repairing the damaged railway between Suez and Ismailia, from where the line turned west towards Tel-el-Kebir. The Suez Canal pilots were no longer at work, and Wolseley had to make new arrangements. He selected a sailor to whom he delegated the task of steering the ships through the Canal. He chose well and found a man with a future. He was Captain John (Jackie) Fisher of the Royal Navy, who, in the early twentieth century, became a great naval reformer who prepared the service for the forthcoming conflict with Germany.

On the railway running west from Ismailia, there is a chain of stations: Magfar, Tel-el-Mahuta, Kassassin, and Tel-el-Kebir (from where the Sweetwater Canal runs south-west to Cairo). Wolseley needed to capture the first three of these places before he could assault the enemy's main camp at Tel-el-Kebir.

Wolseley reached Ismailia on 21 August 1882, and the Suez Canal was in British hands the next day. Repairs were made to the railway between Suez and Ismailia, and the job was completed on 27 August. The stations between Ismailia and Tel-el-Kebir were taken with little fighting. The Egyptian army had a good deal of artillery, but it was substantially ineffective. The British troops' main problem was the heat, which was debilitating. On occasions, the water ration was reduced to a pint a day per man. After the capture of these three stations, Wolseley had to reorganize his troops in preparation for the final assault, and large supplies had to be brought up by rail. The enemy anticipated the British assault and launched a counter-attack. This was defeated by a dramatic charge by the Household Cavalry, the 'Donkey Wallopers', who were more often associated with their ceremonial duties in London. On 8 September, the British army was concentrated at Kassassin, and Wolseley deployed his troops for battle.

The enemy position was entrenched and ran for four miles north into the desert. The enemy force—eighteen thousand regular troops and seven thousand irregulars—was larger than Wolseley's. The Egyptians were armed with excellent American breech-loading rifles, and although their seventy guns were not very effective, they had a few new Krupps pieces. Wolseley commanded 17,400 men—a mixed division of infantry and cavalry. Since he was outnumbered by the enemy, he decided to take a risk in his plan of attack. The army was ordered to advance in total silence during the night, despite the danger of losing direction, and then assault the Egyptian lines at first light on 13 September. Wolseley hoped that the infantry would get within three hundred yards of the enemy before they were detected.

The plan succeeded. The weight of the attack was carried by the Highland Brigade. It was a soldiers' battle, with hand-to-hand fighting and the use of cold steel. Although the Sudanese and some other enemy troops fought well, the Highlanders charged with terrifying *panache*.

> 'Thinking of the slaughter, eight inches of a blood-stained sword protruding from his broken scabbard, Captain Andy Wauchope of the Black Watch remarked: "What brutes we men are!" The sights were pitiful indeed. An NCO recalled the wounded Highlanders "burying their heads in the sand to cool them and all who were able crying for water," though men who made it to the banks of the Sweetwater gulped a

foul liquid "you would not wash the doorstep with, as it was thick with blood and mud.""[21]

Wauchope was probably the wealthiest man in Scotland because of the size of his estates, which included rich coalfields. During the Second Boer War, he was a major general commanding the Highland Brigade. In December 1899, he fought the brutal battle of Magersfontein, where the brigade lost a quarter of its men. The Highlanders who were killed included Wauchope.

The Tel-el-Kebir position was in British hands by 07:00 on 13 September, and Wolseley ordered his cavalry to pursue the retreating enemy towards Cairo. The city surrendered on the evening of 14 September. Wolseley had won a considerable victory. His army had suffered 476 casualties, of whom fifty-eight were killed, but the enemy lost thousands of men. The Khedive was immediately restored to power. He rode in a carriage in a ceremonial parade, and the Duke of Connaught was by his side. This was at Queen Victoria's request. Wolseley was not best pleased. Urabi was court-martialed and exiled, but he was eventually allowed to return to Egypt.

On 21 October 1882, Wolseley and the majority of his troops left Egypt. In December, after a few days in Paris, he resumed his work as adjutant general at the War Office. He was well rewarded for his remarkable achievement during the two-month campaign. He was granted a peerage as Baron Wolseley of Cairo. He was awarded £30,000, and—at last—he was given the substantive rank of (four-star) general. However, Wolseley was not unreservedly grateful. He thought that he deserved to be made a viscount; receive a £35,000 award; and be promoted to field marshal.

Before he retired, he became a viscount and field marshal. But in the meantime, he felt a degree of resentment, especially since a letter he received from the Queen was full of praise for his soldiers but said nothing about him. This all reinforced his feeling that there was a conspiracy against him among people in high places.[22]

Endnotes

1. Kochanski, Halik, *Sir Garnet Wolseley. Victorian Hero* (London: The Hambledon Press, 1999), 75–78.
2. Ibid., 78–83.
3. Cavendish, Anne (ed.), *Cyprus 1878. The Journal of Sir Garnet Wolseley* (Nicosia, Cyprus: Cyprus Popular Bank Cultural Centre, 1991), 164.
4. Preston, Adrian (ed.), *The South African Diaries of Sir Garnet Wolseley, 1875* (Cape Town: A. A. Balkema, 1971), 114–134.
5. Ibid., 158.
6. Ibid., 207.
7. Ibid., 191.
8. Kochanski, Halik, *Sir Garnet Wolseley. Victorian Hero*, 85–90.
9. Ibid., 91–95.
10. Cavendish, *Cyprus 1878. The Journal of Sir Garnet Wolseley*, 22.
11. Ibid., 184–197.
12. Preston, Adrian (ed.) *The South African Journal of Sir Garnet Wolseley, 1879–1880.* (Cape Town: A. A. Balkema, 1973), 299.
13. Kochanski, *Sir Garnet Wolseley: Victorian Hero,* 101.
14. Ibid., 103–105.
15. Preston (ed.) *The South African Journal of Sir Garnet Wolseley, 1879–1880,* 347.
16. Ibid., 357.
17. Kochanski, *Sir Garnet Wolseley: Victorian Hero,* 110–122.
18. Ibid., 123–131.
19. Ibid., 133–136.
20. Farwell, Byron, *Queen Victoria's Little Wars* (New York: W. W. Norton, 1972), 256–258.
21. Wright, William, *A Tidy Little War. The British Invasion of Egypt, 1882* (Stroud, Gloucestershire: Spellmount, 2009), 254–255.
22. Kochanski, *Sir Garnet Wolseley: Victorian Hero,* 136–150.

CHAPTER 12

ROBERTS'S RETURN TO THE LAND OF HIS ADOPTION: HIGH COMMAND IN MADRAS AND CALCUTTA

Roberts returned to India at the end of 1881. He had been away for two years, mainly on leave, but also on a fruitless journey to South Africa and a brief visit to Germany. In the spring of 1881, the First Boer War had come to a sudden end at the Battle of Majuba Hill in February of that year. The British commander during this battle was Major General Pomeroy-Colley, a member of the Wolseley 'Ring'. (In 1880, he double-barrelled his original name of Colley.) He had badly miscalculated the strength of the British position on Majuba Hill, and the Boers ejected the British force. Pomeroy-Colley was killed. Control of the Transvaal reverted to the Boers, but before the consequences of this defeat had been appreciated in London, Roberts was appointed governor of the provinces of Natal and Transvaal. However, this job ceased to exist when the Boers took control. Roberts therefore returned after spending only twenty-four hours in Cape Town.[1]

After his return from South Africa, he paid a visit to Germany and learned something that proved of great professional value. He spent three weeks attending army manoeuvres in Hanover and Schleswig-Holstein.

He was a guest of the German emperor, and he had instructive meetings with a number of distinguished figures, including Field Marshal von Moltke, the victor of the Franco-Prussian War and the man who was widely considered to be the creator of the most powerful army in the world.

When Roberts sailed to India later in 1881, he was forty-nine; and although this was a relatively young age for a very senior appointment, he was well qualified because of his outstanding record as a commander in battle and his long years as a staff officer, which gave him a sound grounding in logistics. The military pyramid—described earlier in this book—shows that as an officer rises in rank, he has progressively fewer jobs available to him. Roberts was a lieutenant general, which in the twenty-first century is a three-star rank. During the two world wars, when Britain deployed large armies, a lieutenant general was a corps commander, with a force made up of at least three divisions and sixty thousand men.

In the nineteenth century, a lieutenant general often had to go into temporary retirement on half pay until an appropriate job became vacant. If this did not happen within a reasonable time, the retirement became permanent. Roberts was lucky. The army command of the Madras Presidency opened up, and the job seemed entirely appropriate for Roberts, who was a highly experienced officer in the Indian army. He and his wife sailed to India accompanied by their two daughters, although their nine-year-old son remained in school in England. Roberts's formal title was now Lieutenant General Sir Frederick Sleigh Roberts, Bt., VC, GCB, CIE. (This last award made him Companion of the Order of the Indian Empire: a decoration introduced when Queen Victoria became Empress of India.)[2]

The territory of India during the nineteenth century was made up of the countries that are today India, Pakistan, Bangladesh, and Sri Lanka. Britain governed this enormous country in a rather cumbrous way—by splitting it up into three presidencies based in Calcutta, Bombay, and Madras. Each had its own lieutenant governor and its army commander-in-chief, who was assisted by a full staff. Of the three presidencies, Calcutta was the most important. It was the seat of the viceroy. The Bengal army, which accounted for more than half the number of troops in the country, reported to the commander-in-chief of the Calcutta Presidency. He was *de facto* head of the Indian army as a whole and dictated all important matters of policy.

After the mutiny, the Indian army was changed in two important ways, and Roberts had a good deal to do with this. Comparing the army at the time of the mutiny and the army fifty years later:

- Although the total size remained approximately the same, the number of British troops rose from 39,800 to 74,300, and the number of Indian troops was reduced. The universal rule was that a handful of the most senior officers in a native regiment were British. (The promotion prospects made Indian regiments popular with young British officers.)
- The artillery became stronger, from batteries employing 10,600 men to batteries employing 22,000 men.[3]

Before the First World War, half the British army was training in the United Kingdom and the other half serving in overseas colonies. The latter included the British troops in India, and the addition of these to the Indian army made the Indian army bigger than the British army. The balance changed at the outbreak of war in 1914, which began a massive growth in the size of the British army. By the end of the war, the British army was ten times the size of what it had been at the beginning; and during the conflict, it had also suffered hundreds of thousands of casualties. In the Second World War, because of the threat from the Japanese army in South-East Asia, the Indian army grew to 2,500,000 men, the largest all-volunteer army in the world.

The Madras Presidency

When Roberts assumed command in Madras, the number of soldiers who reported to him was fifty thousand in garrisons over all parts of southern India. A third of the officers and men were in British units, which normally spent about ten years in the subcontinent. The Indian units were quite different. In each of these, the senior officers—nine in each cavalry regiment and eight in each infantry battalion—were British and spent their whole careers in the country. The army of the Madras Presidency was a formidable force, more than four times the size of the one that Roberts had led on the march from Kabul to Kandahar. Roberts had great affection for the Indian soldiers he commanded, but as he made the acquaintance of more and more units under his command, he began to have doubts about their fighting qualities:

> 'Long years of peace, and the security and prosperity attending it, had evidently had upon them, as they always seem to have on Asiatics, a softening and deteriorating effect; and I was forced to the conclusion that the ancient military spirit had died in them... they could no longer with safety be pitted against warlike races, or employed outside the limits of southern India.'[4]

There was a limit to what could be done about recruitment in an army whose soldiers came from southern India, but when Roberts assumed command in Calcutta, he began a process of encouraging potential recruits from the martial races in the north: a policy on which he placed greater and greater emphasis.

As early as February 1883, Roberts was a member of a military commission that recommended replacing the presidency system with four corps of equal size (approximately two divisions each). The commission also recommended a reorganization of the Indian staff system and—most importantly—reducing the number of native regiments. These recommendations were supported by the viceroy and the government in India, but they were rejected in London. The Duke of Cambridge and the War Office considered them dangerously radical.[5]

In Madras, Roberts saw the need to inject new life into his large command, and the challenge honed his powers of leadership. Before he had settled into his new job, he had been offered a major appointment in London, as quartermaster general in succession to Wolseley. But he had declined this offer because of his keenness to command soldiers. Training was the first priority—in particular, training infantry in the field and on the rifle range. Ian Hamilton, who joined Roberts as an aide-de-camp (ADC) in June 1882, had great talent for musketry training. Hamilton was the young officer whom Roberts had met in Afghanistan in October 1879. As described earlier, Lieutenant Hamilton of 2/Gordon Highlanders was recovering from fever and travelling by pony in the hope of catching up with his battalion, which was already marching to Kabul. Hamilton and another young officer had come across a picket that had been abandoned by a party of soldiers because of an attack by Afghan tribesmen. The two young officers rapidly turned the tables, the tribesmen melted away, and Hamilton was invited to meet Roberts, who gave him a glass of sherry and later wrote a letter to his father. Roberts did not forget the young man.

Ian Hamilton subsequently fought on Majuba Hill and was badly wounded in the arm. He was recommended for the Victoria Cross. This is always granted sparingly: even more sparingly in battles lost than in battles won. Hamilton was therefore disappointed. But when he returned to England, he was honoured by an invitation to dine with the Royal Household in Windsor and have an audience with the Queen. He then began to study diligently for the examination for entry into the Staff College. However, he received an invitation to join Roberts as an ADC. He did not hesitate to accept, which meant that as one avenue to advancement closed, another opened. He got rid of his textbooks and was soon sailing to India and joined Roberts in June 1882.

At 5:30 AM on the day of his arrival, Hamilton's train steamed into the railway station at Bangalore, one of the largest cantonments in the Madras army. He was greeted by Roberts himself, and this gave him an immediate insight into the secret of Roberts's popularity with his troops. They were his number one priority. At 11:30 AM that same morning, Hamilton had begun his duties. In an immaculate uniform and mounted on an obstreperous charger, he followed Roberts along the long line of soldiers in a grand parade of the whole garrison.[6]

Although the general had a number of senior officers carrying out administrative jobs in army headquarters, his personal staff comprised only three officers. The most senior was Colonel Pretyman (nicknamed Pretyboy), the military secretary, whose job was to provide his chief with informed advice about all the officers' appointments in the command. There were also two ADCs. One was Lieutenant Neville Chamberlain (no relation to the twentieth-century English politician), who invented the game of snooker and was later inspector general of the Royal Irish Constabulary. The other ADC was the newly promoted Captain Ian Hamilton (who was soon nicknamed Johnny). The job of the ADCs was to accompany their chief the whole time and act as 'gallopers', to carry out a multiplicity of tasks both military and social. In the same way that Wolseley, during the Ashanti expedition, gathered around him a cluster of officers who were carrying out staff assignments—a group who became known as the Wolseley 'Ring'—Roberts's close working companions became known as the Roberts 'Ring'. Pretyman, Chamberlain, and Hamilton formed the nucleus.

Roberts's tenure at Madras was tranquil in that the army was not engaged in any active operations.[7] He could therefore devote much attention to army reform. One specific concern was short versus long service. These alternatives applied originally to British troops, but during the 1880s, they also applied to native troops in the Indian army. The plan that was being implemented in London was that soldiers would enlist for short service: seven years with the Colours followed by five years in the reserve, for which they received a modest quarterly bonus. This system was introduced in order to boost recruiting and reduce the average age of the men in the ranks and, at the same time, rapidly build up a reserve force.

Roberts was not happy with short service because it deprived the army of men who were prepared to devote many years of their lives to the service: old soldiers whose experience strengthened the *morale* of their younger comrades. Roberts offered two alternatives. The first was three years with the Colours followed by reserve service (a plan that would be favoured by men who wanted to give the army a trial before committing themselves further); the second was a twelve-year enlistment.

These proposals did not impress either the Duke of Cambridge or the officers and civil servants in the War Office, including Wolseley. Roberts therefore published his views in the London press. However, he got nowhere. After he had retired, he devoted his life to another issue regarding enlistment, the highly controversial matter of compulsory service. This was a controversy with serious political implications and has to be discussed in some detail. (See chapter 16.)

Roberts did much to improve the lives of the young British soldiers in India. He not only aimed to better the lot of the men in the ranks but he also wanted to encourage new recruits, to open up careers that offered promotion prospects for the best soldiers. He engineered greater leniency for soldiers convicted of military crimes, and he lifted some of the petty restrictions in barrack life. He also gradually improved food, clothing, education, barracks, and canteens. When he became commander-in-chief of the Indian army, he introduced a number of regimental clubs for the lower ranks:

> '... good-sized, well-lighted rooms, where soldiers can amuse themselves in a rational manner, and where they can have supper and a glass of beer with comfort and decency.'[8]

Roberts embarked on a long-term programme to improve the musketry of the infantry. As mentioned, he had much help from Hamilton, who had been dedicated to the cause of musketry since his earliest days in the army. He had attended the course at the School of Musketry at Hythe and passed with top honours. He was appointed musketry instructor of 2/Gordon Highlanders and tackled the job with enormous enthusiasm. He was not popular with the officers and NCOs whose main interest was the barracks square, but the field officers were 'astonished, and not altogether displeased'. The Gordons crept up the rankings and became the best shooting regiment in India.[9]

The Martini-Henry rifle, introduced in the 1870s, was breech-loading but only fed one round at a time. In the late 1880s, the new Lee-Metford rifle had a bolt action and an eight-round magazine that enabled rapid fire.[10] Hamilton's ambitious objective was to wean British infantry away from crudely aimed volley firing and teach the men to use their rifles as precise instruments to kill the enemy. In 1914, the British infantry had achieved worldwide pre-eminence in the speed and accuracy of their fire: 'fifteen aimed shots a minute'. The soldiers in the ranks produced an enviable volume of accurate fire although, at that time, a British battalion had only two Vickers medium machine guns. The infantry soldiers were all either marksmen or first-class shots. The army pay scale offered a slight increment in pay for a first-class shot and an additional increase for a marksman.

Roberts also realized the potential of machine guns. Wolseley possessed a single Gatling gun during his successful campaign against the Ashanti in early 1874. Ten years later, Roberts obtained two Nordenfeldt guns which, like the Gatling, produced repeat fire from a cluster of rotating barrels. One of Roberts's guns had ten barrels, and the other had five. Roberts had them tested on the rifle range at Bangalore. When they were used by unskilled men, they secured 777 hits in two minutes on a target at 1,200 yards: about the same as the fire of fifty first-class shots from a British infantry battalion. This was an impressive performance, and Roberts fully appreciated its importance. However, he concluded that this type of machine gun—because of its weight and the fact that it had to move on wheels—was a weapon strictly for defence and not to support attacking troops. All subsequent experience of machine guns—in particular the Maxim/Vickers medium machine guns used universally during the First World War—confirmed that Roberts's judgment was correct.[11]

Roberts spent his time during the long months of moderate heat (India is never cool except in the foothills of the Himalayas) inspecting the many and variegated units of the Madras Command. It was something supremely important because of his contact with his men in the ranks:

> 'If, after an exhausting march, Lord Roberts reached camp
> with a sharp go of fever in him—do you suppose he would
> go to his tent and lie down? Not much! There he would sit,
> half-dead, his staff simply writhing in their saddles with

fatigue, while he watched the long column march in for four long hours and exchanged kindly greetings with any of the extra exhausted.'[12]

Roberts, with his constant focus on the men he commanded, was invariably thoughtful in saving them time and trouble by always issuing simple written instructions: 'It only takes one minute, my dear Johnny, and it is so much more satisfactory.'[13]

During the months of extremely hot weather, Roberts and his staff moved to the pleasant hill station of Ootacamund (Ooty), which is seven thousand feet above sea level. The long periods spent there repaired Roberts's health, and he had no more outbreaks of fever. At Ooty, Hamilton's duties were primarily social: greeting guests, arranging receptions and dinner parties, amateur theatricals, and—not least— arranging musketry competitions for the team from Roberts's own headquarters. Shooting would take an increasingly important share of Roberts's life in India.

After rather more than two years with Roberts, Hamilton was due for six months of home leave, and he embarked for Britain in October 1884. When he reached Egypt, he learned that an important expedition was being mounted to rescue General Gordon, who in May had become isolated in Khartoum, besieged by a powerful Muslim force commanded by the legendary Mahdi. The commander of the relief expedition was Wolseley, who had to lead his force in a very difficult journey of a thousand miles up the Nile to reach Khartoum. Wolseley did not leave England until September, and his relief force was being put together when Hamilton found himself in Egypt. This force included 1/Gordon Highlanders, the battalion linked to Hamilton's own 2/Gordons. As a result of acting swiftly and pulling strings, Hamilton managed a transfer to the battalion that was going to march with Wolseley. To an enthusiastic young soldier like Hamilton, the opportunity of taking part in active service was professionally and personally more attractive than a tranquil leave in Britain. Hamilton had an adventurous experience, although Wolseley was intensely disappointed that he did not arrive in time to rescue Gordon. (See chapter 13.) Khartoum remained unfinished business for the British army, and it was not until 1898 that a successful expedition was mounted to reach the Sudan in strength and capture the province. It was commanded by Kitchener, a very different type of commander from Wolseley.

While Wolseley's advance was in its planning stage, an important event took place in India: an event that had a serendipitous influence on Roberts's career. The appointment of a new commander-in-chief of the Indian army—one of the greatest positions in Queen Victoria's army—was due to be made in 1885 when the present incumbent retired. He was Sir Donald Stewart, Roberts's old comrade from the Second Afghan War. The most suitable candidate to succeed Stewart was Wolseley; but Roberts was also a keen contender, and he was strongly supported by Stewart.

After Hamilton had left India *en route* to Egypt, Lord Randolph Churchill (Winston Churchill's father) visited India. He was a leading politician but was not in office at the time since his party was in opposition. He met Roberts, and they went to a camp and inspected an Indian army brigade that was scheduled to join the Nile expedition. This brigade was not under Roberts's command. The men looked smart and capable, and Lord Randolph—an intelligent and observant amateur—was very impressed by their appearance. But Roberts—an experienced professional—did not think much of them since he judged that the battalions had been softened by too much peacetime soldiering. Lord Randolph was incredulous, but Roberts was correct. The brigade performed inadequately in the field. In one Bengal battalion, 'the men quite lost their heads and fired wildly, being more dangerous to their friends than their foes'.[14] Churchill never forgot his conversation with Roberts.

When the time came some months later to appoint the new commander-in-chief of the Indian army, Lord Randolph's party had formed a government, and he was personally made Secretary of State for India, the member of the government who decided all top appointments in India. This is the way in which Roberts was selected in 1885 as commander-in-chief of the Indian army and commander of the Bengal army, based in Calcutta. Winston Churchill wrote subsequently that nothing gave his father more pleasure than to give Roberts his greatest professional opportunity.[15]

Commander-in-Chief of the Indian Army

Roberts's appointment was announced in July 1885. He was granted a brief leave in England, and he returned to take over his new responsibility in Calcutta at the end of the year. The number of men in the Bengal army accounted for almost 60 percent of the strength of the Indian army as a whole.[16] Roberts commanded the Bengal army directly and had *de facto* authority also over the armies of the Bombay and Calcutta Presidencies. He was promoted acting general (four-star).

Roberts had two large responsibilities as commander-in-chief. They were equally important, and both demanded a similar solution, which was armed preparedness. One responsibility was to maintain the integrity of the Indian frontiers, especially the North-West Frontier because of the *Great Game,* and the North-East Frontier at Assam, where Burma was badly governed and largely in the hands of dacoit bandits. In both places, the Indian army had to maintain a strategic defence, but at the same time carrying out tactical offensives to demonstrate that the Indian government was on the *qui vive* and would scotch any trouble before it became serious. The second responsibility was internal security—detecting and suppressing any sign of public unrest and, most importantly, maintaining the loyalty of the sepoys. India was not a powder keg. Law and order were maintained by strong but not aggressive control by the army, which worked closely with the military and civil police. Ultimately, maintaining the frontiers and monitoring an essentially peaceful population depended on a well-trained and disciplined army, with strong *morale.* This is something that Roberts fully understood.

The Indian army fought outside the frontiers on only rare occasions during the nineteenth century, the two Afghan wars being the most important exceptions. However, as mentioned, during the twentieth century, the Indian army made a major contribution to the Allied victories during both world wars—in particular the second, where the Indians fought successfully against the Germans and the Japanese.

When Roberts had taken over in Calcutta, the first problem he faced was continuous disturbances in Burma, a country plagued by dacoit bandits. Burma is three times the size of the United Kingdom. It is difficult to fight over because of the jungle and the mountains and rivers; and it has a hot, steamy pestilential climate. The Indian government wanted a peaceful and stable neighbour, where British businesses could carry out their trading without disturbance. This did not need continuous military action, just some form of stable government.

The Indian army had invaded Burma in 1824 and 1852 (where Wolseley fought as a junior officer and did well). At this stage, Britain annexed a substantial strip of territory along the Burmese coast. In 1878, King Thebaw came to the throne. He was a monarch whose wild and unstable behaviour gave him a worldwide notoriety. The viceroy unsuccessfully attempted to negotiate with Thebaw to allow British businesses to conduct trade in exports and imports. Thebaw was, in the meantime, negotiating with France to invite French businesses to operate in Burma. The situation was totally unsatisfactory to the Indian government, and ten thousand troops were dispatched to occupy Mandalay, which they did without difficulty. However, the problems continued. The viceroy visited Burma, accompanied by Roberts. The occupying force was increased to twenty-five thousand, and Thebaw's kingdom in northern Burma was annexed.

Roberts then visited the country for a second time and travelled widely to study the difficulties on the ground. He realized what was needed was a 'bottom-up' and not a 'top-down' approach. To implement this, he drew up a sensible plan to divide the country into six large provinces, each commanded by a brigade of the Indian army. Control was decentralized and put in professional hands. Roberts also made a point of establishing good relations with the Buddhist priesthood and with the local population, whom he thought were a happy and contented people. He provided instructions comprising eighteen points to guide the work of his brigade commanders. Here is a single example, with its precision and lack of circumlocution:

> '#2. Where two or more columns are acting in concert, the details of time and place of movement should be settled beforehand with the greatest nicety, and the Commanding Officers of all such columns should be provided with the same maps, or tracings from them, so that subsequent changes of plan, rendered necessary by later information, may be understood and conformed to by all. Officers commanding columns must do their utmost to get into, and keep up with, communication with one another. This can be effected by visual signalling, spies and scouts, and patrolling.'[17]

The North-West Frontier continued to be potentially dangerous because of the aggressive frontier tribes—and in the background, the Russian menace. Small expeditions continued to be mounted, to pacify the unruly frontier tribes. More seriously, a force was sent to Kashmir in 1891 to counter a Russian move to garner the support of a frontier tribe.[18] Roberts, taking the long view, concentrated on communications rather than building fortifications. He made his point in a note to the Indian government:

> 'I would push on our communications with all possible speed; we must have roads, we must have railways; they cannot be made on short notice, and every rupee spent upon them now will repay us tenfold hereafter. Nothing will tend to secure the safety of the frontier so much as the power of rapidly concentrating troops on any threatened point, and nothing will strengthen our military position more than to open out the country and improve our relations with the frontier tribes.'[19]

As he had done in the Madras Presidency, Roberts travelled widely. What he learned about the regiments recruited from different races reinforced the impression he had received in Madras. He believed that, by far, the best soldiers were those from the martial races; and he was now in a position to boost the recruiting from these.

> 'The same courage and military instinct are inherent in English, Scotch, and Irish alike, but no comparison can be made between the martial value of a regiment recruited among the Gurkhas of Nepal or the warlike races of northern India, and of one recruited from the effeminate peoples of the south.'[20]

Politicians who did not know India found it difficult to understand Roberts's trenchant feelings. However, he was able to put his opinions into practice when he received authority to recruit additional regiments to handle the annexation of northern Burma. He formed five new regiments from the Gurkhas and three from the Sikhs. He also gradually disbanded a number of Indian regiments and companies of 'doubtful material'.

The long-standing feeling that the officers of the old India army were the poor relations of their comrades in the regular British army had changed radically by the end of the nineteenth century, mainly as a result of Roberts's reforms when he was commander-in-chief in Calcutta. The best evidence of this change was the emergence of Indian army officers who, in the final stages of their careers, commanded large British forces in the field as well as Indian troops. The First World War saw the rise of Birdwood, and the Second World War made Auchinleck and Slim national figures.

The *leitmotiv* echoing through all the years of Roberts's command in India was training. His emphasis was on the infantry because he increasingly believed that cavalry would give way to mounted infantry—a belief that would be amply confirmed during his experience as commander-in-chief of the British army during the Second Boer War.[21] Roberts concentrated his military training on musketry, to teach soldiers new skills beyond volley firing. In improving the shooting ability of the Indian army, his right-hand man was Ian Hamilton. Hamilton was back in India in 1886. His participation in the Nile expedition had been recognized by the award of the Distinguished Service Order (DSO), a decoration normally granted to majors and lieutenant colonels and only given to more junior officers for exceptional service. Wolseley had been defeated by time and distance. Hamilton was convinced that if the Nile expedition had been commanded by Roberts, it would have succeeded. Hamilton was fully aware of the fierce sense of urgency that Roberts had displayed in the Second Afghan War. Roberts was critical of how Wolseley had divided his force: a mistake he himself would not have made.[22]

After accompanying Roberts to Burma, Hamilton was soon given the key appointment of Assistant Adjutant General for Musketry at Army Headquarters, and promoted brevet major and then brevet lieutenant colonel.[23] Here he came into his own. With the enthusiastic support of his chief, Hamilton's main aim was to prepare the infantry realistically for wartime conditions. He rewrote the whole of the Native Musketry Regulations; targets were painted with human figures, not bullseyes; and the quantity of live ammunition for firing practice was increased. As a result, field firing improved dramatically:

> 'Markers hidden in deep trenches worked running or disappearing targets under a hail of bullets and, when the attack closed in to 250 yards, tossed out balls three feet in diameter made of canvas stretched over strips of bamboo, which bounded down the steep *glacis* upon the firing lines faster than even charging Ghazis would have rushed. Units possessing fire discipline shot them to bits—others missed them clean.'[24]

After Hamilton had spent two and a half years in the job, the musketry efficiency of the Indian army had been transformed, and his personal contribution to this had been widely recognized. Hamilton was not yet forty, and after Roberts had left India, Hamilton's career continued to prosper. And he was not forgotten by his old chief. The Second Boer War began badly for the British, and Roberts was sent to South Africa to impose his customary 'grip' on an army that had, until then, not performed well. Hamilton was appointed to command a division that he would lead north into Boer territory. The fortunes of the British army immediately improved, although it took a comparatively long time before the Boers were finally defeated. The British generals, including Roberts and Hamilton, had not anticipated the transformation of the conflict into guerrilla warfare.

Farewell to India

Roberts's five-year appointment as commander-in-chief of the Indian army came to an end in 1890. Although the position was extremely attractive to talented younger officers, the authorities in London and Calcutta decided to extend Roberts's term by another two years. This was a practical demonstration that he had done well. But in agreeing to this, Roberts sacrificed the possibility of succeeding Wolseley in the coveted post of adjutant general in the War Office. This was a job he had earlier been promised. He finally left India in 1893 and received a peerage, becoming Baron Roberts of Kandahar, and further decorations with stars to wear on the breast of his uniform. He received another appointment in 1895, as commander-in-chief of the British army in Ireland. The title of his autobiography, published in 1897, was *Forty-One Years in India*. It fills two large volumes and is well written and full of exciting events. Roberts did not follow the example of many public figures and employ a ghostwriter.

It is not easy to judge Roberts's eleven years in high command in India. He took over the army of the Madras Presidency when he was forty-nine, and he finished his term as commander-in-chief of the Indian army when he was fifty-nine. It was during these ten years that he was at the peak of his ability, enthusiasm, and energy. The job of a general is to win battles, and Roberts did not have the opportunity of leading men into battle during this decade of his life. His active service commanding relatively small forces in Afghanistan in 1878 demonstrated great strategic and tactical strengths. However, during his years of high command in India, Roberts's objectives were to protect the integrity of India's frontiers and to maintain internal security. The country was at peace during the whole of his time in command, and the tasks of the army were carried out effectively but without fuss. For this, Roberts deserves great credit.

However, judgment of Roberts's ability as a commander depends ultimately on how he would have handled a situation when fire dominated the battlefield. A great commander has to demonstrate strategic ability: the skill to deploy his forces in such a way that he is concentrated where his enemy is dispersed. He also has to possess tactical ability, practiced knowledge of how to conduct the four phases of war: advance to contact, attack, defence, and withdrawal. And his personality must have the strength to stiffen the sinews of his men and to give them the will to win. The big unknown is how Roberts would have conducted a major twentieth-century war. What would have happened if Roberts—like Slim during the Second World War—had led a great Indian army against a militarily sophisticated opponent?

The reason why this question should be addressed is that many of Roberts's juniors who commanded large armies during the First World War all behaved inadequately, or at least fought futile and expensive battles until they learned the tactics needed for the new conditions of warfare. Like Roberts, they had learned their lessons in small wars. Chapter 15 describes Roberts's successes during the Second Boer War, which—literally and figuratively—was the last nineteenth-century war and the first twentieth-century one. Roberts's performance during this war throws a good deal of light on his generalship.

Endnotes

1. Roberts of Kandahar, Field Marshal Lord, *Forty-One Years in India, Volume II* (London: Richard Bentley, 1897), 379.
2. James, David, *Lord Roberts* (London: Hollis & Carter, 1954), 181–198.
3. Heathcote, T. A., *The Indian Army* (London: David & Charles, 1974), 201–202. The figures describing the comparative sizes of the Indian army in 1857 and 1906 are accurate, but they omit certain troops who were not strictly in the regular Indian army. For this reason, there are some discrepancies with the figures in chapters 2 and 4.
4. Roberts of Kandahar, *Forty-One Years in India, Volume II*, 383.
5. Robson, Brian (ed.), *Roberts in India. The Military Papers of Field Marshal Lord Roberts, 1876–1893* (Stroud, Gloucestershire: Army Records Society, 1993), 242–245.
6. Hamilton, General Sir Ian, *Listening for the Drums* (London: Faber & Faber, 1944), 150–171.
7. James, *Lord Roberts*, 181–197.
8. Robson (ed.), *Roberts in India*, 273.
9. Jones, John Philip, *Johnny. The Legend and Tragedy of General Sir Ian Hamilton* (Barnsley, South Yorkshire: 2012), 28.
10. Duckers, Peter, *British Military Rifles, 1800–2000* (Princes Risborough, Buckinghamshire: Shire Publications, 2005), 21–25.
11. Robson (ed.), *Roberts in India*, 314–315.
12. Hamilton, *Listening for the Drums*, 157–158.
13. Ibid.
14. Robson (ed.) *Roberts in India*, 317.
15. Jones, *Johnny*. 41–42.
16. Mollo, Boris, *The Indian Army* (Poole, Dorset: New Orchard Editions, 1981), 87.
17. Robson (ed.), *Roberts in India*, 357–362.
18. Roberts of Kandahar, *Forty-One Years in India, Volume II*, 445–447.
19. Ibid., 407–408.
20. Ibid., 442.
21. Robson (ed.), *Roberts in India*, 332.
22. Ibid., 316.
23. Jones, *Johnny*, 78–80.
24. Hamilton, *Listening for the Drums*, 211.

CHAPTER 13

WOLSELEY, GORDON, AND THE MAHDI

Charles Gordon was a British military hero who became a household name when he was in his thirties. His career took him from hard campaigning in the Crimea and then in China to becoming governor general of the large, barren, and unstable province of the Sudan.

He was the son of a major in the Royal Engineers who later became a lieutenant general. The younger Gordon, after his education at the Royal Military Academy, Woolwich, followed his father into the same regiment. Since the Engineers are the most scientific and intellectual branch of the service, they take the pick of the graduating Woolwich cadets. Gordon, like Wolseley, had been born in 1833, and the two met in the Crimean War in the trenches before Sebastopol (as described in chapter 3). He had piercing blue eyes and a natural air of command together with brains and energy. In his youth, he became an Evangelical Christian, and his Christian belief was to be the dominant force throughout his life.

After the Crimea, Gordon volunteered for an assignment in China. When he was thirty, he was a brevet major and given command of a multinational force of 2,100 men formed to crush the Taipings, a large group of violent rebels who terrorized a province inhabited by twenty million people. The Taipings were led by a highly unstable commander who eventually committed suicide after they had been defeated by Gordon. Since Gordon was an officer in the Chinese army, he wore and was photographed in a mandarin's costume. He displayed great energy and tactical skill, and it was not long before he smashed the rebels. He was, by now, a colonel in the British army. And was made a field marshal in the Chinese army—a force he trained assiduously. When he returned to Britain in 1867, he was already famous and became known everywhere as Chinese Gordon. Before Gordon had been appointed to quell the Taiping rebellion, Wolseley had been considered for the job. In 1865, the two men discussed their experiences in China (see chapter 6), and it is interesting to speculate whether Wolseley would have done as well as Gordon.

When Gordon was in Britain, the first thing he did was to establish a school for waifs and paupers in Gravesend and personally spent many hours teaching there. Gordon's personality was a strange mixture of attributes, and some influential people thought he was mentally unstable, and others suspected that he took to the bottle. Wolseley thought Gordon 'the most remarkable man I ever knew'. However, Redvers Buller—a leading member of the Wolseley 'Ring' and Wolseley's chief of staff in the expedition to save Gordon—believed that 'Gordon was not worth the camels needed to rescue him'. The opinions of senior officers and politicians were evenly divided between Wolseley and Buller. Nevertheless, to the British public, he was a hero.

It is not entirely fanciful to compare Gordon with another soldier of distinction—Stonewall Jackson, who had been born a decade before Gordon. Jackson had also received a military education, at the United States Military Academy, West Point. As a newly commissioned officer, he fought in the war between the United States and Mexico, where a number of reputations were made. Like Gordon, he had a scientific bent and became, for a time, a professor of mathematics at the centre of military studies in the Southern states, the Virginia Military Institute. Jackson, like Gordon, was a devout Christian warrior; and when Wolseley met him during the American Civil War, he thought he resembled an Ironside of Cromwell's army. Both Jackson and Gordon were skilled tacticians and had enormous drive. They both died as a result of enemy action—Jackson was in his early forties and Gordon in his early fifties. Gordon's untimely death in early 1885 was a personal tragedy to Wolseley, who had commanded the British army column sent to rescue him in Khartoum. Gordon was besieged there as a result of a number of difficult and generally unwise decisions.

In 1869, Gordon had become frustrated because there was no job open to him. He volunteered to serve in Abyssinia and in Ashanti, but his offers came to nothing. Then in 1874, when Gordon was forty-one, he accepted a job from the Khedive of Egypt to become governor of the large equatorial province of the Sudan, south of Egypt, in the upper reaches of the Nile. It was not unusual for a British officer to receive such an appointment. With the Suez Canal in operation, the British government was anxious to establish a presence in Egypt. The Khedive, in his turn, welcomed British help, especially after the 1883 Battle of Tel-el-Kebir. The British consul general in Cairo, Sir Evelyn Baring, was extremely influential, and the Khedive invariably took his advice. Many British officers were serving in Egypt, filling a large number of the higher ranks of the Egyptian army.

Gordon spent five unhappy years (1874–1879) as governor of the Sudan. There were many problems in that province, not least the slave trade which the British government intended to stamp out: Gordon estimated that more than three-quarters of the Sudanese population were slaves. He travelled widely by camel over the barren countryside, in conditions of extreme heat during the day and freezing cold at night. Overworked and constantly frustrated by the difficulties he had to face, he attempted to resign on a number of occasions; but he stayed on, with great reluctance. In 1878, his appointment was upgraded to governor general. When he left the Sudan in 1879, he returned to England and took his time to arrange a new appointment—to stamp out the slave trade in the Belgian Congo, a colony that was under the tyrannical rule of King Leopold of the Belgians.

In 1881, when Gordon was still in England, the Sudan was threatened by a greater problem than had ever occurred before. A charismatic leader had gathered around him a substantial army of Muslim tribesmen called dervishes, who intended to overthrow the Egyptian government of the

Sudan. (British troops, in the era before political correctness, called the dervishes 'fuzzy-wuzzies'.)

The leader of the insurrection was an ill-educated apprentice boatbuilder and itinerant preacher. His name was Mohamed Ahmed, and he was soon universally known as the Mahdi, 'the Expected One':

> 'The tall, broad-shouldered, majestic man, with the dark face and black beard and great eyes—who could doubt that he was the embodiment of a superhuman power? Fascination dwelt in every movement, every glance. The eyes, painted with antimony, flashed extraordinary fires; the exquisite smile revealed, beneath the vigorous lips, white upper teeth with a V-shaped space between them—the certain sign of fortune.'[1]

The Mahdi had the mysterious ability to inflame the religious passions of primitive people. Fanaticism and belief in *Shariah* law spread like wildfire.

Two British expeditions to quell the uprising had been defeated with great bloodshed. The situation soon became even worse. The warlike tribes captured twenty thousand rifles, ten artillery pieces, and large quantities of ammunition. They surrounded Khartoum, and Gordon was called back to defeat them. However, there were different points of view about whether Gordon should return to the Sudan and take arms against the rebels because of the quite reasonable view that a Christian should not be sent to battle a Muslim army. However, the influential London press supported the proposal that Gordon should command the army against the rebels, and this decided the issue.

Defeating the rebellion had now become the responsibility of the British government. Even more seriously, the situation was growing urgent. Lord Hartington, Secretary of State for War, operated at a slow and deliberate pace; but by the end of July 1884, he was convinced that an expedition had to be mounted to save Gordon. Gladstone, the prime minister, hesitated because of the cost of the expedition (likely to be £20,000,000), although Parliament would be able to vote the money in instalments. But at last, the decision was made.

Wolseley and other senior officers in the War Office started making early preparations to arrange transport in Egypt for the British expeditionary force. This was a very complex matter. They had to find and ship to Egypt eight hundred boats to carry troops up the Nile, together with experienced men to steer them through difficult water. And they had to find 1,200 camels to cross the desert and the saddles and equipment needed by the troops perched on top. Boats were purchased in Canada with boatmen to steer them, and other boats were constructed in Britain in forty-seven different boatyards. The vessels were thirty feet long, with twelve oars and two masts. Many of the camels came from India, although it was soon found that demand from the British army pushed up the price.

Gordon was a serving officer in the British army although, for some years, he had worked in colonial administration. He had been promoted major general in 1882. He returned to the Sudan in January 1884 to an uncertain future. When he left Charing Cross Station, he had an impressive send-off from many leading figures, including the Duke of Cambridge. However—and perhaps not unexpectedly—his mission was by no means clear. The Duke of Cambridge thought that Gordon was going to Suakim to report on the situation there. Hartington believed that Gordon was on a mission of peace to evacuate the Khartoum garrison. But when Gordon reached Egypt, he was given contradictory instructions by Consul General Baring. Gordon was ordered to take control of the Sudan as governor general and supervise an orderly evacuation. He then had to find a local governor general who would establish a strong government under the *aegis* of Egypt. Gordon had an extremely difficult job to perform.

Before long, Gordon was himself in Khartoum, a city of forty thousand people. The city was soon isolated by the dervishes, although for some time, Gordon was able to send messages to Cairo. When it was eventually decided to send a column to relieve Gordon, no one could tell how long it would take to get through, but it would be months rather than weeks.[2] Gladstone, Hartington, and the Duke of Cambridge soon agreed that the expedition should be commanded by Wolseley (now Lord Wolseley), and he received the appointment on 26 August 1884.[3]

He was, at the time, still adjutant general—the post he had returned to when he came back from Egypt in December 1882. The Sudan was at the top of his mind in January 1884 because he had been asked to prepare a paper on the possible withdrawal of the British garrison in the Sudan. In this report, the name of Charles Gordon appeared.

Wolseley Divides His Force

Wolseley left London in early September 1884, and because of the difficulties of organizing the expedition, the troops began their movement up the Nile in mid-October. By this time, any organized expedition would have been very hard-pressed to reach Gordon in time. The initial delay was simply too long. The first cause of the delay was Gladstone's indecision, but the second was the enormous logistical challenge of mounting the operation. Wolseley felt that he had got off to a bad start. His journal of the expedition was introspective and pessimistic, and he complained sourly about everybody and everything he encountered. He was constantly aware of the difficulties he would be facing: the pressing shortage of time and the number of dervish rebels he would have to engage in battle.

> 'Now I have to fight the whole of the Mahdi's army—not only six or eight times larger than mine, but with at least seven times as many guns as I have. I confess this is no pleasing prospect, and if compelled to do so, I shall embark upon it with the greatest reluctance.'[4]

Gladstone was particularly favoured by the general's unrelenting wrath. On 25 November 1884, Wolseley wrote in his journal:

> 'Had this wretched Mr. Gladstone only had the grasp of a statesman he would have begun this business two or three months earlier and we might now have had in this case ample supplies here by this date for all the force. May God grant me success: without His aid, I can do nothing.'[5]

On 5 February 1885, Wolseley found Gladstone's colleagues in the cabinet equally culpable. Wolseley praised the heroism of his soldiers:

> 'It is not their fault they were not here two months ago, nor is it mine: that fault lies at Mr. Gladstone's door, shared by that great self-important lump of flesh Sir William Harcourt and perhaps one or two others of this curiously-composed Cabinet that has, for years, been steering the National ship upon every rock they could discover.'[6]

Wolseley's staff was made up of his friends in the Wolseley 'Ring'. He was, however, increasingly disenchanted by Buller:

> 'What an odd man is Buller. I should never again have him as Chief of the Staff. He always raises objections to every proposal, although in the end he comes round to it. He loves to build up imaginary difficulties with one hand to have the pleasure of demolishing them with the other . . . In fact, all the world are fools and he alone is wise.'[7]

Wolseley thought, or at least hoped, that Buller would have made a better field commander than chief of staff. After the commander of the desert force had been killed, Wolseley sent Buller to take over, but he was too late to get to Khartoum in time. Buller also did very badly during the Second Boer War. In Natal in 1899, Buller's weaknesses finally led to his undoing.

Some of Wolseley's sourness may have been due to the size, remoteness, and isolation of the enemy territory where his soldiers would have to fight. Khartoum lies in the middle of the desert, a thousand miles as the crow flies from the mouth of the Nile, but involved a 1,650-mile journey by water because of the way the river meanders. Two routes to Khartoum were possible. (See **Map 11**.) The route favoured by the people who knew the country best was via Suakim, a small port on the Red Sea that was easy to reach from the Suez Canal. Khartoum lies an apparently manageable distance west of Suakim. But as Wolseley soon realized, he could not lay his hands on nearly enough camels to transport his army 250 miles across the waterless desert to Berber on the Nile, and from there upstream to Khartoum. A railway from Suakim would have taken too much time to build and would have been vulnerable to marauding tribes. This left the route up the Nile. This was immensely long and fraught with difficulties, the greatest of which were the six cataracts. These are extremely rough patches of water with rocks and rapids; some were several miles in length. In most cases, the cataracts were impassable by boat unless the men disembarked and manhandled the vessels upstream.

Wolseley's force was very small, though he judged that its quality would prove decisive against the large numbers of undisciplined dervish tribesmen. He had a total of 7,200 men from well-trained British regular battalions, plus some Egyptian units. However, although the total numbers were so small, Wolseley took the controversial step of dividing his army. Wolseley's plan was that 5,400 men were to be transported up the river in large rowing boats called whalers, which could be emptied and pulled upstream on the cataracts. The remaining 1,800 men were organized into a desert force mounted on camels: an extraordinary hotchpotch drawn from subunits of elite British regiments with aristocratic officers. The officers and men in these regiments were considered to be the most robust in the army, and all men selected for the desert force were aged at least twenty-three. This desert force, in theory, would be able to charge forward during the last stage of the advance and relieve Khartoum. The Duke of Cambridge was very uneasy about Wolseley's plan to form his desert force from separate subunits of different regiments. But Wolseley considered it a matter of principle that the commander should make his own decisions on the spot:

> 'As I have often said before, an English general under existing conditions when detailed for any military operation has to begin his campaign by fighting the Duke of Cambridge.'[8]

When Wolseley decided to divide his small army, he disregarded the basic strategic principle of concentration of force. What made the situation even worse was that the distances to be travelled were very long, communications were poor, and Wolseley himself would be isolated for much of the time. The expedition was at all stages impeded by the problems of logistics. It was impossible to estimate accurately how many days the troops would take to reach Khartoum. But Wolseley personally estimated the speed of the average loaded camel to be two-and-half miles an hour. By pressing the camel column, Wolseley thought that twenty-five miles a day would be possible.[9] With a total of 1,650 miles to cover—not to speak of military action *en route*—the only conclusion that Wolseley could reach was that it was touch-and-go.

One of the soldiers among the 5,400 who would be travelling up the Nile was Captain Ian Hamilton.[10] He was a junior member of the Roberts staff in India and was later to earn a considerable reputation for improving the musketry of the Indian army. In 1884, he was on his way to Britain, where he intended to enjoy a long leave. When he reached the Suez Canal, he learned that 1/Gordon Highlanders was one of the battalions that would participate in the relief expedition. Hamilton's own battalion was 2/Gordons, and he used a good deal of ingenuity and persuasion to arrange a temporary transfer between battalions. Before long, he was attached to 1/Gordons and commanding a company of one hundred Highlanders. They were to go to war in boats up the Nile.

There were serious problems with the command of the expedition. Wolseley himself was with neither of the columns but was stuck in a headquarters on the river far to the rear, with only tenuous telegraph communications to the two advancing formations. He was therefore not able to command 'from the saddle', as he had done in previous campaigns. He had to rely on telegraphic messages to communicate his orders and was therefore not certain that they had been understood and acted on. Wolseley, isolated in his headquarters, was forced to remain idle for much of the day. He was hot and uncomfortable in his uniform:

> '. . . flannel shirt, linen or a sort of mole-skin, khaki-coloured breeches and untanned boots: during the day I wear a sort of Norfolk jacket of the same material as my breeches, a good kummerbund and a huge solar topee on my head. When

the sun goes down, I put on trousers and Norfolk jacket of serge—the latter being scarlet, being in fact the identical one I wore in the 1882 campaign. It is very necessary to have a padded protection to the backbone when exposed to the sun.'[11]

Illustrations of Wolseley's troops—mainly drawings that appeared in the London press—show that many were dressed in scarlet or blue serge tunics. The uniform worn was obviously uncomfortable since it was an article of faith that soldiers needed thick woollen pads underneath their tunics to protect them from heatstroke.

Heat, Delays, the Desert, and the Nile

Hamilton had his staff officer's uniform with him, and he had to get equipped for regimental service. The quartermaster of 1/Gordon Highlanders issued him with a private soldier's scarlet tunic, which he wore with his own pleated woollen kilt in the Gordon tartan. Because of the time taken to order and deliver the whalers, the large force of troops travelling by boat did not set off until 1 November 1884, two weeks after the desert force. However, although they covered one thousand miles against little enemy opposition, their journey up the Nile was not quite as rapid as they hoped.

Hamilton and his company moved upstream against the current. They were loaded in eleven whalers. They carried personal ammunition, supplies to repair the boats, and a four-month supply of rather miserable food: tins of bully beef, hard tack biscuits that were soon inhabited by weevils, and tea, which they had to make with canned condensed milk. The desert column of officers and men from 'crack' regiments was much better fed with a variety of canned delicacies. Permitting such a difference in the rations provided to the two columns was a dereliction of duty on the part of Wolseley. Each of Hamilton's boats was more or less independent and followed its own route; the whole company got together every ten days. The feelings of the men, as described by

Hamilton, were 'as nearly as possible those of a party of Boy Scouts dressed up like Red Indians and let loose in a flotilla of canoes'. At the cataracts, the men had to wade waist-deep in water to haul the boats, but the soldiers treated the whole affair as a great adventure.[12]

There were serious problems with the command of the expedition. While Wolseley himself was isolated at his headquarters on the Nile in the rear of the advancing columns, the two column commanders ran their own wars. Tragically and unexpectedly, the original two column commanders were both killed. Major General Earle lost his life in action in the Battle of Kirbekan, in which Hamilton took part. The officer who then took command on the river column was an administrator and a weak leader. The original commander of the desert column, Brigadier General Stewart, a highly promising soldier, also later lost his life, and his successor was an intelligence officer with no command experience. He was Major General Henry Wilson, who lacked drive to such a degree that Wolseley had to replace him. Buller was sent forward to take over, but by then, it was too late.

The river column had taken more than three months and advanced almost one thousand miles when they reached the fourth cataract. Here they found and attacked a large party of dervishes. This took place on 10 February 1885, at Kirbekan, about three hundred miles north of Khartoum. The soldiers did not know it at the time, but the city had already fallen.

Kirbekan lies upriver in the great bend of the Nile that loops to the east then south and west to reach Khartoum. (See **Map 11**.) Not far from the eastern bank of the river, the Kirbekan Ridge runs for about half a mile to the east. Eight hundred dervish warriors were on top of this ridge, and with small-arms fire, they were blocking the advance of the whalers of the river column. Major General Earle was on the spot and was not the type of leader to go on the defensive. He was determined to take the fight to the enemy. He quickly detached Hamilton's company and some Egyptian artillery as a fire group to keep the enemy's heads down. He then led his remaining infantry on a right-hand encircling sweep, with the soldiers in open order and using their rifles to good effect. He managed to attack the enemy from the rear and caught them unawares. They were soon wiped out, but the brave and resourceful Earle was killed by the last bullet fired on the battlefield.

Earle's tactics were based on those inculcated into British riflemen at Shorncliffe by Sir John Moore, in the years before the Peninsular War. These tactics were diametrically opposed to the defensive use of the 'infantry square': a drill that was still practiced by the British army at the end of the nineteenth century. Hamilton's company buried the general under a palm tree. Hamilton, who wrote much poetry, composed an elegiac verse, expressing (in Wordsworth's phrase) 'emotion recollected in tranquility'. Earle's tactical flair and leadership from the front made an indelible impression on Hamilton, and his own style of leadership was based on it. Hamilton was a natural tactician. However, as he demonstrated in Gallipoli in 1915, he was a less-than-adequate strategist.

Before the end of December 1884, six weeks before the Battle of Kirbekan, the desert column had branched off. After the camels started moving across the desert from Kori, the river column traversed the fourth cataract and moved fifty-five miles north-east to reach Kirbekan. The task of the desert column was to bound directly across the desert to Khartoum, a distance of less than two hundred miles, in contrast to the five hundred miles of the river route. The desert column encountered nothing but difficulties. Inevitably, water was in short supply. The soldiers were forced to survive on one pint in the morning and another pint in the evening. Stewart, the commander of the desert column, was anxious about his rear and diverted a number of men from his small force back to the Nile to keep away any hostile dervishes. Before long, the detached party returned, and they rejoined the main column in the middle of January.

The Mahdi, showing admirable tactical sense, now deployed substantial forces to block the British advance. The result was the bloody and indecisive battle at Abu Klea, fought on 17 January, in which the British used the tactics of defensive infantry squares. Stewart himself was wounded and died shortly afterwards.

There was now great confusion. As mentioned above, Stewart's successor, Wilson, had never before commanded troops. Wolseley was only intermittently in touch with the headquarters of the desert force, but he soon realized that Wilson was flaccid and missed many opportunities. He therefore sent Buller forward to take over. It was too late. On 26 January, the dervishes took Khartoum, and Gordon was killed by a number of natives wielding spears. This was a disaster for Wolseley. He grieved for his friend Gordon, and at the same time, he did not easily recover from the failure of his mission.[13]

However, Wolseley always had plentiful resilience. He was soon convinced that the failure to relieve Gordon did not spell the end of the campaign. But he could not move without instructions, so he telegraphed London to clarify what he should do next. Again the government prevaricated but eventually agreed to continue the fight so long as Wolseley did not demand further reinforcements.

After Abu Klea, the desert column was in no condition to continue to fight, and on 20 February 1885, he ordered them back to join the rest of the army, which was still making progress up the Nile. Wolseley also halted the river advance, and all his troops were soon together. As things worked out, the Gordon Relief Expedition never got to Khartoum, and the British had to wait for thirteen years before they finally reached the city where Gordon had been defeated. This followed the Battle of Omdurman in 1898. But by then, the Mahdi was no longer alive. He had died of typhus a few months after he had taken Khartoum and killed Gordon.

After Wolseley halted his troops in February 1885, he did not take too seriously the government's statement that there would be no further reinforcements, and he dispatched to London a substantial menu listing the numbers of additional troops he needed to continue to campaign. The size of his demands, which came at the same time as a call for troops for another purpose—to build up strength to counter Russian threats against India, part of the *Great Game*—marked the end of the Nile campaign. The river column found that going down the cataracts was much easier than going up them.

Unaccountably, the British government, in February 1885, ordered work to begin on the railway from Suakim. This was abandoned after eighteen miles of track had been laid, confirming Wolseley's earlier scepticism about the Suakim route. There was no further advance up the

Nile to Khartoum until 1898, when a new expedition was commanded by a very powerful and single-minded leader, General Kitchener.

Wolseley's campaign ended on an unpleasant note for the Gordon Highlanders, although their performance had been exemplary throughout. The London press was still full of stories about the expedition, and some were very uncomplimentary. Wolseley suspected that officers of the Gordons had been the source of some of the unfavourable rumours, and he therefore summoned the commanding officer to vent his displeasure. Wolseley threatened that none of the officers of the battalion could expect any decorations or promotions as a result of the campaign. This may have been due to a fit of ill temper because Wolseley, by now, was a very disappointed man. However, Hamilton was spared; and as a reward for his services at Kirbekan, he received the Distinguished Service Order (DSO), a decoration awarded to officers for action or good work in the field that ranked immediately below the Victoria Cross. It is normally given to field officers (majors, lieutenant colonels, and colonels), and it was a special distinction for Hamilton, who was only a captain.[14] Wolseley himself received no reward for his services.

Why Did the Expedition Fail?

War always demands a price—often a very high price—in lives and money. Victory at a minimum cost demands disciplined planning. This should be carried out at three levels: grand strategy, battlefield strategy, and tactics. These are conceptually separate, although the lines between them are often blurred. They are described in chapter 1, but in view of their importance, a brief reminder is useful:

- *Grand strategy* defines the way in which a military operation will achieve (or contribute to the achievement of) national objectives. Such objectives are usually political rather than strictly military. Grand strategy is therefore a concern of the most senior politicians and soldiers. An important element of grand strategy is the need to relate ends to means. Have enough resources been mobilized?

- *Battlefield strategy* is the concern of the commander of a military operation. He will understand the grand strategy, but his battlefield strategy defines how he will deploy on the battlefield his resources in men and firepower. His guiding principle is normally to concentrate his strength in places where the enemy is weak.

- *Tactics* defines an army's operations when battle is joined. It is the concern of subordinate leaders: commanders of divisions, brigades, and units and then in stages down to the private soldier in his foxhole.

In the past, it was unusual for the grand strategy of a major conflict to be clearly defined and efficiently executed. This is because of the deep-seated antipathy between the politicians and the soldiers (often referred to in the First World War as the 'frocks' and the 'brass hats'). In the First World War, British military operations were biased towards the Western Front, certainly after the failure of the Gallipoli expedition in 1915. The prime minister, Lloyd George, was refreshingly unorthodox, but he was confronted by a phalanx made up of the Chief of the Imperial General Staff (CIGS), Robertson, and the generals in France led by their chief, Haig. To the 'Westerners' (as they became known), the only field of operations was France and Flanders, where five British armies were in the line. The situation in the Second World War was different, and the grand strategy of that conflict was the constant concern of the decision makers, who exhibited great skill. Churchill combined the offices of prime minister and Minister of Defence, and he and the CIGS, Brooke, had a close, abrasive, but highly productive relationship. An added complication was the alliance between Britain and the United States, with the political chiefs (Churchill and Roosevelt) and the military chiefs (Brooke and Marshall) all working together with a similar degree of abrasiveness and productivity. The synergy that developed between these four individuals was a war-winner.

The grand strategy of the Gordon Relief Expedition left many questions unanswered. Formulating it was the responsibility of the prime minister, the Secretary of State for War, and the commander-in-chief of the army. Gladstone was a peacetime prime minister who was uncomfortable leading the country to war. Hartington was a talented Secretary of State for War but worked very slowly. There was no general staff, and the Duke of Cambridge, the commander-in-chief, was old and a profound conservative who distrusted officers who were less conservative than he.

The lack of detailed discussion between these three men meant that when the Gordon Relief Expedition was being planned, there was no consideration of ends and means. To fight an army of tens of thousands of Muslim fanatics, Wolseley would muster a force equivalent to only half a division, made up of a patchwork of units and subunits who had never operated or even trained together. Wolseley would be compelled to move his men over a distance of 1,650 miles of river and desert before he confronted the main enemy. Most important of all, he was subjected to great time pressure. No one had estimated how long Gordon would be able to hold out in Khartoum, and this meant that uncertainty would be added to the urgency under which Wolseley was already operating. As a result of the pressing problems he faced throughout the expedition, it is not surprising that his journal should contain so many complaints about other people—in particular, the politicians in London. When Gladstone died shortly before the end of the century, Wolseley refused to go to his funeral.

Wolseley's battlefield strategy has been criticized because he divided his small force. This was not a capricious decision: it was influenced by the arrangements that had been made to transport the troops, with the use of 800 boats and 1,200 camels. Nevertheless, it was a mistake. The desert force was only about two battalions in strength, and they were greatly outnumbered by the dervishes at Abu Klea. This battle was not, surprisingly, a defeat—but an important contributory factor was the regrettable loss of Brigadier General Stewart. At the Battle of Kirbekan (a great success for the river column), Major General Earle also lost his life, but this only took place at the moment of victory. At a later time, Roberts thought it was wrong to divide the force. His disciple, Ian Hamilton, believed that Roberts would have had a much greater sense of urgency than Wolseley; and with an undivided force, he would have stormed his way to Khartoum and got there in time. This was, of course, total speculation.

Britain's response to Gordon's plight in Khartoum was a matter of national importance, and the decisions had to be made at the highest level: the prime minister and cabinet had to issue the orders. This process took time—in the event, too much time—but underlying it, two alternative courses of action were possible.

The first was to maintain the *status quo*, with Gordon remaining in Khartoum for as long as he was able to hold out. But inevitably, the city would fall, and Gordon's body would eventually be in the ruins. If this happened, the ambition to colonize the Sudan and introduce a stable government in the province would be sacrificed. The prestige of Great Britain among Muslims would also be seriously diminished: a matter of considerable importance because the number of Muslims in the world is much larger than the number of Christians. (This was true in the nineteenth century, as it is today.) But the most serious effect would be on the British population. The sacrifice of Gordon would never be forgotten by the public, to whom he had, for a long time, been a hero. The second course that Gladstone could follow was to mount a relief expedition. This was always a gamble, and it became more so the longer it took for him to issue orders to proceed. By the time the expedition was under way, it had little chance of success. The strength of Wolseley's command was inadequate, and the methods of sending the troops into battle in boats and mounted on camels were full of uncertainties. There was also a pressing shortage of time, and what made this worse was the reliance on guesswork about how long Gordon would be able to hold off the besieging dervish hordes.

The two alternatives that Gladstone faced were not one bad and one good. They were both bad, and he chose the second one as the less bad. But to make matters worse, he delayed for so long that it virtually guaranteed the failure of the expedition. This must be laid at the door of Gladstone, hence the repeated references to this delay in Wolseley's journal. The failure of the expedition had all the expected consequences: the death of Gordon, the loss of the Sudan, the diminution of British prestige, and the disappointment of the British public. After news reached Britain that Gordon had died, memorial services were held in churches all over the country, including St. Paul's Cathedral and Westminster Abbey.

Gordon was not the only man who died during the expedition. Large numbers of British and Egyptian troops were killed and wounded: these included two generals, the column commanders. The expedition also cost a great deal of money, which is something that Gladstone took very seriously. There was also an effect on Gladstone's own career. In June 1885, the Liberal government fell, mainly because it could not pass a budget, but this defeat also had Gordon's name written all over it. When Gladstone was in his eighties, the Liberals eventually returned to power, and he became prime minister for the fourth time. He was a figure who dominated British politics during the last decades of the nineteenth century, but he was never a successful wartime leader.

Endnotes

1. Strachey, Lytton, *Eminent Victorians. General Gordon* (London: Folio Society, 2000), 218.
2. Kochanski, Halik, *Sir Garnet Wolseley. Victorian Hero* (London: The Hambledon Press, 1999), 151–159.
3. Wright, William, *Warriors of the Queen. Fighting Generals of the Victorian Army* (Stroud, Gloucestershire: Spellmount, 2014), 110–112.
4. Preston, Adrian (ed.), *In Relief of Gordon. Lord Wolseley's Campaign Journal of the Khartoum Relief Expedition* (London: Hutchinson, 1967), 139.
5. Ibid., 72.
6. Ibid., 137.
7. Ibid., 112.
8. Ibid., 41.
9. Ibid., 55.
10. Jones, John Philip, *Johnny. The Legend and Tragedy of General Sir Ian Hamilton* (Barnsley, South Yorkshire: Penn & Sword, 2012), 71–78.
11. Preston, *In Relief of Gordon. Lord Wolseley's Campaign Journal of the Khartoum Relief Expedition*, 35.
12. Jones, *Johnny. The Legend and Tragedy of General Sir Ian Hamilton*, 75.
13. Ibid., 75–77.
14. Ibid., 77–78.

CHAPTER 14

ENGLAND'S ONLY GENERAL AND ENGLAND'S ONLY OTHER GENERAL

Wolseley's name had for years been familiar to the officers of the British army because of his bestselling manual *The Soldier's Pocket-Book for Field Service*, which was full of practical advice. His fame had also spread beyond the army: his contribution to military reform had received a good deal of publicity, and he had become a hero to the public on his return in 1874 from his successful campaign against the Ashanti. It was at this time that he had become known (at least half-seriously) as 'England's only general'. The victory of Tel-el-Kebir had added to his public esteem, and although the unsuccessful expedition to rescue Gordon did not enhance his reputation, most of the odium had—with justification—damaged Gladstone's and not Wolseley's standing with the public. On his return from Egypt, Wolseley returned to the War Office, where he had much work to do. His term as adjutant general was due to expire in 1887, but it was extended to 1890 at the request of Lord Hartington, Secretary of State for War, and with the agreement of the Duke of Cambridge.

A factor that kept Wolseley's name in the public eye was that he was now a peer and was able to contribute to debates about the country's defences in the House of Lords. Meanwhile, Roberts was being a highly effective commander-in-chief of the Indian army, and he was engaged in a dispute with Wolseley because he needed an additional eighteen thousand men of the British army to reinforce the garrison in the subcontinent. Wolseley resisted this since the British army was particularly under-strength, with a recent shortage of recruits. This was because British agriculture was in bad shape, and many farm labourers—traditional army recruits—were taking better-paid jobs in factories. As Roberts's name became more widely recognized in Britain, he was being called (also half-seriously) 'England's only other general'. Roberts remained very popular with the rank and file, both British and Indian. However, Wolseley, having reached high rank and the House of Lords, was growing more distant from the men in the ranks. (Ian Hamilton was very struck by this during the Gordon Relief Expedition.)

During Wolseley's five years at the War Office after his return from Egypt, there were no wars or even war scares. However, there was no shortage of squabbles among the various important figures in Whitehall and the Horse Guards—the senior politicians, the generals, and the Duke of Cambridge—which meant tiresome disagreements over sometimes important matters of policy. Wolseley published his views in articles in widely read journals until the Queen herself asked him to stop. This seemed to be a reprise of what happened in 1880, when Wolseley was disappointed not to be made commander-in-chief of the Indian army, and he suspected that the Queen and the Duke of Cambridge were conspiring against him. They had also discouraged him from publishing favourable views on the army reforms of Cardwell and Childers, although they were, by now, official government policy.

In the late 1880s, home defence became an important element in British military plans in view of a possible (if unlikely) invasion by the French army, which was four times the size of the British. Home defence required cooperation between the army and the navy, but the navy was unenthusiastic. To the Royal Navy, the defence of the island was its responsibility and nobody else's. The army plan for home defence— formulated in 1886—was based on a reorganization of the home army into three corps, mainly of regular units but including a few battalions of volunteers. The plan was for the individual formations and units in these corps to train together, but large-scale military exercises were not possible because of a shortage of funds.

Wolseley, having fought in recent wars, laid great emphasis on training troops for the most important military manoeuvres: advance to contact, attack, defence, and withdrawal. This meant that soldiers spent more time in the field and less on the parade ground. He also wanted new uniforms: more comfortable than existing kit and more suitable to wear in the field. It was not long before the British army was clothed in khaki. And by the end of the century, the army's round solar topee with a short brim was being replaced by the much better Wolseley helmet with its wide brim. Wolseley and the Duke of Cambridge did not see eye to eye on either field training or new uniforms. However, two important improvements were made in the equipment of the army.

The first was the Lee-Metford rifle, with a magazine of eight (later ten) rounds fed by bolt action, which meant a much more rapid rate of fire. The second took place after a lengthy experimentation with different types of machine guns, which led to the introduction in 1887 of the Maxim gun—a medium machine gun that, in a modified form, would be used by the British army for eighty years. These guns were initially supplied two to a brigade, six to a division. By 1914, there were two to every battalion; and during the First World War, these numbers were greatly increased. Eventually, a separate Machine Gun Corps was established. This was disbanded after the end of the First World War, and the impressive memorial to the corps still stands at Hyde Park Corner.

During Wolseley's tenure, two matters arose which were of direct concern to him as adjutant general. One of these came from his strong feeling that the selection processes for promotion to senior ranks had to be improved. This was in direct opposition to the Duke of Cambridge, who never changed his view that promotion had to be governed solely by seniority. In 1890, a Promotion Board was set up, charged with scrutinizing the records of officers eligible for specific promotions and giving advice to the commander-in-chief, who continued to make the final decisions. Wolseley was frustrated because he realized that promotion would continue to be based on seniority, at least while the

Duke of Cambridge remained commander-in-chief. However, Wolseley won a minor victory by slightly reducing the total number of general officers in the army.

The second matter was even more problematical. Wolseley knew perfectly well that every one of the most important continental armies had a general staff. A major committee was convened in 1889 under the experienced and talented Lord Hartington. This became known as the Hartington Commission. It recommended an Army Board comprising political and military members. Their responsibility would be grand strategy and all major matters of army organization. Under the Army Board, the commander-in-chief would be head of a structure made up of a chief of staff and a number of staff officers with specific functions, who would work closely together. The adjutant general would become the chief of staff, although the job would not go to Wolseley, whose time as adjutant general was coming to an end.[1]

The Hartington Commission was a forward-looking body, but it was, unfortunately, twenty years ahead of its time. As things worked out, two leading members of the commission disagreed with the majority findings, and the government was not prepared to accept major innovations. The Hartington recommendations were rejected. The lack of a general staff in London meant that expeditionary forces in the field also suffered from the same deficiency. Buller—the commander-in-chief of the force in South Africa in 1899—did not have a fully functioning staff since the system had fallen into decay in Britain. One of the results was the agonizingly slow advance of his army to the relief of Ladysmith:

> '. . . the absence of a definite system of staff duties, leading sometimes to waste of time, and sometimes to a neglect of indispensable precautions, was undoubtedly prejudicial to the smooth running of the military machine.'[2]

When Roberts arrived in South Africa to assume overall command in January 1900, he took immediate steps to form a general staff, with the powerful figure of Lord Kitchener as its chief. Roberts had been accustomed to a fully effective staff during his years commanding the Indian army.

After the end of the Second Boer War, with army reform now a matter of pressing urgency, a new committee was set up in London under the influential figure of Lord Esher. This concluded that the many failures of the British army during that war had to be addressed, and it made specific recommendations. These included a general staff, essentially on the lines of the findings of the Hartington Commission. At the same time, the anachronistic post of commander-in-chief was finally abolished. The last two officers to hold this post had been Wolseley and then Roberts.

Wolseley's Climb to the Top of the Pyramid

When Wolseley left the War Office in 1890, he was fifty-seven years of age. However, his path to becoming commander-in-chief was firmly blocked because the Duke of Cambridge had no intention of retiring, although his last active command had been in the Crimea. In 1890, he was seventy-one, a direct contemporary of his cousin, the Queen.

However, the post of commander-in-chief would open up sooner rather than later, and Wolseley was keen to take an appointment in Britain so that he would be available at short notice. Proximity was important because there was another officer who was a keen contender and had a good deal of 'pull'. He was the Queen's third son, the Duke of Connaught, who had commanded a brigade of Foot Guards in Egypt in 1882 and served under Wolseley. Wolseley was offered jobs in Australia and India, Finally, he accepted the post of commander-in-chief of the army in Ireland. This was a job which was as much diplomatic as military, and it involved large-scale official entertaining as well as command of thirty thousand men in garrisons spread across the country. Ireland provided many recruits for the British army: more than twice as many per one thousand eligible men as England, Scotland, and Wales.[3]

Wolseley had been born in Ireland and was a member of the Anglo-Irish Protestant ruling class. Like other members of this establishment, he had little respect or affection for the Irish people, who were Catholics and mostly subsistence farmers or farm labourers. At the time, Irish agriculture was not as depressed as it often was, but a political issue was becoming extremely important. This was home rule, which was being hotly debated in Westminster, where Gladstone—prime minister for the fourth time—was determined to grant it. In 1892, the House of Commons passed a Home Rule Bill, but this was, predictably, rejected by the House of Lords. Wolseley opposed home rule, but he quite properly took no part in the debate in the Lords. Home rule was not to be enacted for another thirty years, after a world war in which large numbers of Irish soldiers were killed, and there had been a bloody uprising in Dublin in 1916.

During the 1890s, the Irish Command slumbered. Wolseley spent much time inspecting army garrisons in all parts of the country. He concluded that the number of troops stationed in Ireland could be reduced, which would have eased the financial burden (and pleased Gladstone). However, the Duke of Cambridge disregarded his advice and nothing was done. The duke reprimanded Wolseley for not sending him regular reports on the military activity in Ireland, to which Wolseley replied that there was none. With time on his hands, Wolseley started writing, as he had done earlier in his career. He published a biography of the Duke of Marlborough, and then one of Napoleon. Wolseley's private life was not easy at this time. Although he had a reasonable income, some members of his family needed financial support, and he acted generously.

Wolseley occasionally made the long journey to London. He continued his membership of the Promotion Board and was also closely concerned with the size and organization of the army. The issue of short versus long service continued to be debated, but although Roberts in India argued in favour of long service, there was no chance that it would be adopted. Other matters important to Wolseley were the size and training of the Army Reserve, the physical fitness and maturity of the soldiers sent abroad from their home battalions, and—most importantly—the total number of infantry battalions and their strength. Wolseley would return to these issues when he became commander-in-chief in 1895, when the Duke of Cambridge finally retired.

The duke was seventy-six and in failing health (although he was to outlive his cousin the Queen). There was no clear successor, although there were three tough and ambitious candidates: Redvers Buller, the Duke of Connaught, and Wolseley. Buller, adjutant general, was on an inside track and jockeyed for the job, although his record in the Gordon Relief Expedition had been little better than mediocre. The Duke of Connaught lacked experience, and even the Queen eventually had to accept this. Wolseley was the best qualified, but he was far distant in Ireland. The Queen wanted Wolseley to be the British ambassador in Berlin, where her grandson, Kaiser Wilhelm II, reigned over a militaristic nation. This possibility had been mentioned to Wolseley, and this appointment would have been an interesting piece of casting; it would certainly have pleased the kaiser.

However, according to the (unwritten) British Constitution, the decision had to be made by the government. This was the newly elected Conservative administration under Lord Salisbury. The Secretary of State for War was a heavyweight who was accustomed to making decisions and issuing orders: Lord Lansdowne, who had been governor general of Canada and viceroy of India. Wolseley was a known quantity; he was sixty-two, mature but not too old, and had recently been promoted to the rank of field marshal. He succeeded the Duke of Cambridge and finally reached the top of the pyramid.

During the period of uncertainty before Wolseley's appointment, he felt, as he had done before, that people in high places were conspiring against him. Indeed, the Queen was not at all pleased, and she wrote to the prime minister on 11 August 1895. She deplored the fact that Wolseley had been offered the choice of ambassador or commander-in-chief and said that nobody had asked her permission for these offers to be made:

'I dislike the appointment of Lord Wolseley as Commander-in-Chief, as he is very imprudent, full of new fancies, and has a clique of his own.'[4]

The Queen was, of course, referring to the members of the Wolseley 'Ring', whose careers had prospered in parallel with Wolseley's. The ten men discussed briefly in chapter 9 all became generals.[5] Most—but not all—fulfilled their promise, although some were promoted above their ceiling. There was also the unquantifiable measure of opportunity cost: the value of the services of the men who had not been promoted, some of whom might have done better than those who were.

Of the ten, Evelyn Wood eventually reached a higher rank than any of the others: field marshal. In the Gordon Relief Expedition, he was the director of the line of communications. He then held the Aldershot command, and although Wolseley made him adjutant general in 1897, he never became commander-in-chief.

Four men became generals (four-star): Henry Brackenbury, Redvers Buller, George Greaves, and Baker Russell. Brackenbury had a reputation for intellectual ability. In the Gordon Relief Expedition, he took over the river column after the death of Earle; and when news came through that Gordon had lost his life, Brackenbury supervised the withdrawal of that column. He was a well-known administrator, and some people thought he was qualified to be commander-in-chief. However, there was too much competition in 1895. Buller was (as earlier explained) in the running to succeed the Duke of Cambridge, but he did not make the cut. Immediately before the Second Boer War, he held the important Aldershot command, which was the basis of any expeditionary force ordered overseas. In 1899, Buller went to South Africa. His army was in Natal, and they were immediately in trouble. The Boers were agile, but the British were lethargic, and the decision was soon made to appoint Roberts to overall command. Roberts's difficult job was to snatch victory from the jaws of defeat, which he managed to do. Greaves eventually commanded the Bombay army but was not promoted commander-in-chief in India. People regarded him as pompous and volcanic, and most unusually for a Victorian general, he lived in a *ménage à trois*. Russell was a fearless commander of the cavalry division at the Battle of Tel-el-Kebir. He afterwards held peacetime commands but did not again go to war. This was because he was not a favourite of the Duke of Cambridge, who generally disliked members of the Wolseley 'Ring'.

One officer, William Butler, became a lieutenant general (three-star). He organized the river column for the advance up the Nile to rescue Gordon. However, he had a difference with Wolseley, which was eventually resolved. Butler also had a serious quarrel in South Africa in 1898, where he commanded the British army. He fell out with Milner, the British high commissioner, and also Rhodes, the prime minister of the Cape Province. Butler lost his job and returned to London, where he made it widely known that the war that was shortly to break out would be long and difficult. No one believed him until the first shots were fired and it became obvious that the Boers were a formidable enemy.

Four members of the 'Ring' became major generals (two-star): George Colley, John Frederick Maurice, Hugh McCalmont, and John McNeill. Colley (later Pomeroy-Colley) commanded the British troops who were defeated on Majuba Hill in 1881, and Colley himself was killed at the age of forty-five. Maurice made his name as a highly respected instructor at the Staff College and became well known as a military biographer. McCalmont, like Russell, was a fighting cavalryman. He served with Wolseley in a junior capacity in many campaigns but never reached high command. His last job was command of a division in Ireland based in Cork. McNeill, who won the Victoria Cross early in his career, became famous (and also infamous) for his action at Tofrek in March 1885. This was an incident in a minor campaign against the dervishes in Suakim on the Red Sea. The battle was a bloody victory, but McNeill was criticized in London because he allowed his infantry brigade to be unsupported. He was one of Queen Victoria's favourite generals, and she resented the way he had been criticized. He received a number of decorations from the Queen and ended his career as an equerry to King Edward VII.

All the members of the Wolseley 'Ring', except Colley, were still serving in 1895, and a number of them were still close to Wolseley. One thing that was immediately obvious was that the new commander-in-chief would be very different from his predecessor. The army would be receiving greater doses of ideas and energy from the top. Worldwide, there was much unfinished business. The army's main function was still to provide overseas garrisons, and problems in the Sudan and South Africa needed to be addressed. Five years after Wolseley became commander-in-chief, the unfinished business in South Africa brought together, virtually for the first time, the careers of the two senior men in the army: Wolseley and Roberts.[6]

Roberts's Return to Europe

Roberts was sixty-one when, in early May 1893, he finally left India. After a restful voyage, Roberts—with his wife and younger daughter—disembarked in southern Italy. They then travelled to Rome, where they were received by the Pope. When they got to England, they were greeted by impressive welcoming parties and were the guests at many banquets. Roberts was invited to Windsor, where the Queen thought that he 'looked extremely well, and not a day older'. He had not been in England since 1881, and people he met noticed his manner and appearance: 'his "authority", that self-assurance that comes only to those who have reached the very top of their profession'. And surprisingly, he had not, at the same time, lost any of his youthful enthusiasm.[7]

It was clear to the government that Roberts's experience and energy qualified him for further employment, although no one then guessed that as an active commander, he would be called at the age of sixty-eight to take on the most important fighting command in the British army. This was in 1900. In 1893, the appointment that interested Roberts most was to be viceroy of India. At the time, this was not considered possible because he had so recently been commander-in-chief of the Indian army, although Field Marshal Wavell succeeded in making the switch in 1943, when India was in danger of invasion.

The most suitable command for Roberts in 1893 would have been Aldershot, the main training ground of the British army. But this went to the Duke of Connaught. Roberts was more pleased than disappointed because he had such a genuine loyalty to the Royal Family. He remained on leave during the winter of 1893–1894. He took his seat in the House of Lords. He rode to hounds in Ireland. He received the freedom of many cities and inspected a number of volunteer regiments. The public got to know him as 'Bobs'—a result of a long poem by Rudyard Kipling in the style of a music hall song. He bought a house in the outer suburbs of London. He also started writing: in a series of articles which earned him a few guineas, he demonstrated that he could write engagingly and clearly. In one, he made a perceptive judgment on Napoleon and Wellington, and his view of the Iron Duke almost certainly guided him personally during his military career.

> '. . . the schemes of the French Emperor were more comprehensive, his genius more dazzling, and his imagination more vivid than Wellington's. On the other hand, the latter excelled in that coolness of judgment which Napoleon himself described as "the foremost quality in a general"'.[8]

His journal articles were turned into a book, which was well received. He then devoted two years to a larger project, a memoir of his service in the subcontinent, *Forty-One Years in India*. When it is read today, 120 years after its publication, the two large volumes are still reader-friendly; they are graphic and strongly paced. Roberts wrote it himself, although he consulted many of his former comrades to check that he got the details right. The style has been described as 'vivid simplicity', a reflection of Roberts's own character.[9] The work was greeted by reviewers in leading publications with universal warmth, and it quickly went through thirty-five (*sic*) printings and was also translated into German and Urdu.

In 1895, Roberts received his field marshal's baton. Shortly afterwards, Wolseley became commander-in-chief, and this created an opportunity for Roberts to succeed him in Ireland. This was a much more limited job than commander-in-chief in India, but there were more opportunities for what Roberts liked to do best: spend time with troops, who in Ireland (unlike India) were all British. He developed a dialogue with Lord Lansdowne, the Secretary of State for War, and one result was that Roberts was permitted to make an unusual reform, one typical of his focus on the soldiers in the ranks. Young soldiers who had committed crimes (but not felonies) had their records expunged after they had spent a period of exemplary conduct. Roberts was by now a well-known figure, and he received letters from many important people outside the army. He responded to these punctiliously. One idea that emerged from this correspondence was his belief that all fit young men should be required to serve a brief period of military training. When Roberts retired, he devoted much of his time to this proposal (a subject discussed in chapter 16).

Ireland—as it had been in Wolseley's time—was a tranquil command. Roberts enjoyed his fox hunting in the winter. And as part of his job, there was a great deal of official entertaining: dinners and balls to which large numbers of people were invited. Roberts was, however, still devoted to his calling; and in 1897, when he was sixty-five, he told Lansdowne that he yearned for real work.

The Roberts 'Ring' had never been as large or cohesive as the Wolseley 'Ring'. Wolseley's followers—the 'clique' as Queen Victoria called them—were not popular with many other officers in the army. The Roberts 'Ring' did not have this problem. At this time, some of the members were George White, a Gordon Highlander who eventually became a field marshal; Ian Hamilton, also a Gordon, who became a (four-star) general; William Penn Symons, an infantryman who, in 1899, died of wounds as a major general; and Henry Rawlinson, a Green Jacket who transferred to the Coldstream Guards, who also became a (four-star) general and commander-in-chief in India. In 1898, it was becoming increasingly likely that war was going to break out in South Africa. Rawlinson had been on Kitchener's staff in the army that had advanced up the Nile, earlier in 1898, to defeat the dervishes at Omdurman and recapture Khartoum. Rawlinson thought that it would be a productive idea for Kitchener to meet Roberts. Kitchener therefore spent a few days with Roberts in Ireland. Rawlinson was correct. Kitchener was greatly impressed by Roberts, who reciprocated the warm feelings. It is fortunate that Kitchener, in this way, became a *de facto* member of the Roberts 'Ring' because, in rather more than a year, they became comrades in arms. It was also fortunate that Roberts had had a quiet time in Ireland, so that he could lie fallow to prepare him for command in South Africa, the most important assignment he had ever been given.

Wolseley in the Horse Guards

Wolseley's years as commander-in-chief did not begin happily. He resented Buller's attempts to lobby for the appointment and never forgave him. Buller had become another figure whom Wolseley accused of conspiring against him. Wolseley even quarreled with Lansdowne, the powerful politician whose cooperation was vital to the efficiency of any commander-in-chief. Some people felt that although Wolseley had reached the apex of his career, his age was becoming a problem, and his physical health and energy were flagging.[10]

Lansdowne outraged Wolseley because of a restructuring of the War Office, which the government had ordered without any debate in Parliament. This reorganization had been started by Lansdowne's Liberal predecessor, Henry Campbell-Bannerman, and this indicated broad Parliamentary support despite the lack of debate. In the new organization, four department heads in the War Office would now report to the Secretary of State for War. The commander-in-chief would still be the main military adviser to the government, but his control over his subordinates was weakened. Wolseley tried his best to undermine the new system, although it had been set up specifically to lighten his personal workload. The Lansdowne plan was the beginning of a general staff system. Wolseley was in favour of such a system, but not in the way it was set up by Lansdowne.

During Wolseley's period as commander-in-chief, the issue that took most of his efforts was his attempts to boost the size of the army, something that was very difficult because of the opposition of the politicians who held the purse strings. Wolseley's argument for a larger army came from a review of the specific demands on the army to garrison a world empire, which also meant having enough men in the linked battalions at home to feed the overseas battalions. There was a lack of balance, with seventy-six battalions abroad and sixty-five at home. In 1895, Wolseley proposed fifteen new battalions. Lansdowne was receptive to the idea but was reluctant to add an additional £2,000,000 to the army estimates to pay for them. This was the beginning of a lengthy process of negotiation, which was interrupted for seven months in 1897 when Wolseley had to be treated for glandular fever and jaundice. One of Wolseley's proposals, for more powerful guns for some of the artillery, was rejected on the grounds of cost. The final number of troops was finally agreed upon in 1898 with the cabinet's agreement to increase the size of the army by nine thousand men, adding six new battalions and increasing slightly the size of every battalion in the army. These modest increases meant that the army had to accept many recruits whose physical standards should have disqualified them, but some months of plentiful food and physical exercise were often enough to improve their strength and well-being. Wolseley remained convinced that it would need an increase in army pay to bring in a better type of recruit; but this was, of course, never acceptable to the politicians, who were the guardians of public finance.

Although Wolseley had fought his corner conscientiously, and although a modified version of his plan had been accepted, this outcome shows a narrowness of vision on the part of Britain's military and political leadership. A war in South Africa was already on the horizon. The fighting ability of the Boers had been clearly demonstrated in the Battle of Majuba Hill in 1881. Even more seriously, the devastating effect of modern firepower had been shown in the American Civil War and in the conflicts between Prussia and Austria and Prussia and France. Armies had developed a far greater 'punch' over the course of fifty years, and this was certainly true of the British army with its new breech-loading rifles and its machine guns. What was not generally realized was that a large increase in firepower strengthened defences, and this made attacking more difficult and costly in human life. What was lacking in the Horse Guards and War Office in 1898 was someone with the vision and force of personality possessed by Kitchener at the beginning of the

First World War. Wolseley's modest plans were soon shown to be totally inadequate when the British army faced the Boers in 1899.

A British military victory in Africa provided an unusual prelude to the war against the Boers. This victory was the result of a well-planned expedition up the Nile that defeated the dervishes and recaptured Khartoum. This was also an enterprise that demonstrated the anomalous position of the commander-in-chief, who was barely consulted. Planning had begun in March 1986 on the initiative of Herbert Kitchener, commander-in-chief of the Egyptian army, and Lord Cromer (formerly Sir Evelyn Baring), British consul general in Cairo who effectively governed the country. In 1896, Wolseley learned that Kitchener had been purchasing large numbers of boats and camels, and this was his first news that something was going on. A military plan was in progress that was (in Cromer's words) 'a Foreign Office war'. One of the underlying triggers of the expedition was a tentative French move towards the Upper Nile, the region south of Khartoum.

Wolseley was asked by the Foreign Office to contribute eight infantry battalions and a cavalry regiment. (Winston Churchill accompanied the expedition as a war correspondent, and he managed to join this regiment when it made a dramatic charge at the Battle of Omdurman.) Apart from these British troops, Kitchener's men were from the Egyptian army. The expedition moved inexorably forward, untroubled by the time pressure that had made life so difficult for Wolseley as he advanced up the Nile in 1884 and 1885.

The Battle of Omdurman in early September 1898 was a devastating defeat for the dervishes, who lost an estimated twelve thousand men. Kitchener's casualties totalled less than five hundred. Khartoum was quickly recaptured. Kitchener immediately travelled upriver, unaccompanied by his army, and held an amicable meeting with the French army detachment that had reached the Upper Nile. (Kitchener spoke French well.) In this way, he defused the problems with the French. After Kitchener left Egypt, he visited Ireland (as earlier described) and met Roberts for the first time.

Storm Clouds in South Africa

The Second Boer War was a delayed continuation of the conflict fought between 1880 and 1881 that had ended in the political *status quo*, with the two Boer republics remaining independent. Much had happened during the eighteen years between the two wars. The Boers in the Transvaal and the Orange Free State remained as obdurately conservative as ever, although the Transvaal had been transformed by the discovery of gold in 1886. Towards the end of the century in the Cape Colony, two uncompromising Englishmen faced the Boer republics with hostility. The first man was Rhodes, the prime minister of the Cape and a multimillionaire. He controlled virtually the world supply of diamonds from his headquarters in Kimberley, where the stones had been discovered in large quantities in 1870. The second was Milner, who had been appointed in 1897 as British high commissioner in Cape Town.[11]

Rhodes and Milner were determined to form a single colony, which would include the two Boer republics. Rhodes had even greater ambitions—to form a mighty swathe of British territory up the east side of Africa, with a railway that would run from the Cape to Cairo. However, during the twentieth century, strong independence movements among native populations spread all over Africa, and these made Rhodes's grandiose vision totally impossible to realize.

The inflexible attitudes of the two Englishmen were matched by the comparably inflexible attitude of Paul Kruger, president of the Transvaal, and Marthinus Steyn, president of the Orange Free State. In the Transvaal, the discovery of gold attracted large numbers of prospectors, whom the Boers called *uitlanders*: foreigners from Britain, Australia, Canada, Germany, America, and Holland. Their numbers had grown to a hundred thousand by 1896. The gold was in the Witwatersrand (commonly called the Rand), a series of ridges running east to west, sixty miles long and twenty-five miles wide, between Pretoria in the north and the commercial capital Johannesburg in the south. The *uitlanders* were unpopular with the Boers because there were so many of them, and also because they attracted black labourers from the Boer farms and caused wages to rise. The Transvaal government levied high taxes on the *uitlanders,* who also had to live in the Transvaal for fourteen years before they got the vote.

The attitude of the Boers caused increasing fury among the British in South Africa and England. In late 1895, 520 men of British origin in the northern Cape Province, commanded by a physician called Jameson, took up arms and raided the Transvaal. It was hoped that the raid would start an *uitlander* rebellion, but nothing happened, and many of the raiders were killed and wounded; the rest were rounded up and handed over to the authorities in the Cape to be tried. This debacle cost Rhodes his job as prime minister of the Cape because the authorities in London and Cape Town had given a nod to Jameson before he rode into the Transvaal. The raid also persuaded Kruger to purchase thirty-seven thousand Mauser rifles from Germany, plus a good deal of ammunition; twenty-two artillery pieces from France; and a number of pom-pom heavy machine guns from Britain!

In early June 1899, a conference was held in Bloemfontein between the Boers and the British authorities in the Cape. There was no constructive result, although Kruger offered to reduce the number of years the *uitlanders* had to live in the Transvaal before they were given the vote. The British refused the offer, and Kruger became even angrier than before. Steyn now also decided to purchase Mauser rifles from Germany. A year before the Bloemfontein conference, Lieutenant General William Butler—a member of the Wolseley 'Ring' who commanded the British garrison in South Africa—had warned Milner and Rhodes that war would come and it would be prolonged and tough. Butler was immediately sacked as the bearer of ill tidings.

The Director of Intelligence in the War Office estimated that if war was declared, forty-eight thousand Boers would take up arms. Every man could use a rifle and was mounted on a sturdy pony. They were organized in local groups called commandos, whose strength varied; some commandos were the same size as companies and others larger. They were warriors who would soon become known as mounted infantry, and many British infantry battalions (although not cavalry regiments) were converted to this role, although they were more tightly

organized than the commandos. By this time, the relationship between
Wolseley and Lansdowne was so bad that Wolseley's warnings about the
seriousness of the threat were not passed on to the cabinet.[12] Wolseley
encouraged the senior officers in the Cape to draw up plans for action in
case of war. However, he did not provide any detailed guidance because
he believed, quite correctly, that the battlefield strategy was a job for
the man on the spot.

Sending a substantial body of men from England took time, and
the government decided that when war was certain, forty thousand
men organized in a large formation, I Corps, would be mobilized,
concentrated, shipped to South Africa, and deployed there. Mobilization
included calling out the Army Reserve to bring the corps up to strength.
During the early months of 1899, Wolseley prepared to dispatch
the corps, but the government was reluctant to spend the necessary
money until war was a definite prospect. This meant a very serious
delay between the outbreak of war and the arrival of the British army.
When they eventually left Britain, the soldiers were all mature men,
mostly with years of experience. There was, however, a shortage of
equipment—notably artillery. In the meantime, Lansdowne offered
the command in South Africa to Buller, who accepted reluctantly. He
disliked South Africa and was realistic about his own deficiencies as a
commander. Wolseley was considered too old for the appointment,
although age did not seem to be a problem for Roberts when he was
given the job at the end of 1899.

Wolseley was having a difficult time. He did not have a happy
relationship with Lansdowne, the government was reluctant to spend
money, and Wolseley was working in an isolated position. He was not
privy to the Colonial Office communications with South Africa, just
as he had been kept in the dark by the Foreign Office when Kitchener's
expedition against Khartoum was being planned. In view of the delays
involved in sending a force to South Africa, it was important to make
a quick decision to send it. But where should it be deployed? Natal
was the most likely alternative since this would provide a route into
the Transvaal. The other possibility was the northern Cape Colony,

close to the Orange Free State, where the railways and bridges could be protected.

On 8 September 1899, the British government sent a modest force from India, and they sailed across the Indian Ocean to Natal. It was nominally a brigade, but with ten thousand men, it was really two infantry brigades without supporting arms. It was commanded by Lieutenant General George White, a member of the Roberts 'Ring', who would be subordinate to Buller when I Corps eventually arrived. On 7 October, this corps was at last mobilized in preparation for the voyage to South Africa. Kruger immediately issued an ultimatum demanding the withdrawal of the troops that were on their way. Even before this ultimatum expired, Boer commandos were crossing into Natal, and the first shots would soon be fired. The war was (of course) going to be short and cheap, like all British colonial wars of the nineteenth century. This view was shared by everyone in Britain: the public, the press, the government, and the army. But it was the army that had to pay the price for this miscalculation.[13]

The war went through two distinct phases. The first was a period of eight months of conventional and vigorous military action with many casualties, especially among the British. This ended in June 1900 when the British occupied Pretoria. The second phase was longer and had not been anticipated. It lasted for twenty-three months of mobile and indecisive guerrilla warfare. It was only brought to an end by two policies. First, defensive lines were erected across Boer territory, controlled by British blockhouses; and second, farms were burned and camps set up for Boer women and children. These camps were badly run and soon became rife with disease.

In October 1899, during the first days of the war, the Boers took the initiative and made a number of incursions into British territory. They besieged two towns, Mafeking and Kimberley, and made a fruitless invasion of the central Cape Province. They also invaded Natal with the intention of attacking the town of Ladysmith, which was a British garrison and rail junction; the troops who had arrived from India were there. The Boers were formidable antagonists. Early in the war, the number of Boers in the commandos outnumbered the British two to one. They rampaged all over the countryside; the country was their home, and they were more experienced than the British in fighting on the local terrain. The Boers also had excellent weapons. Their Mauser rifles were, if anything, better than the British Lee-Metfords and Lee-Enfields; and the Boer artillery included a few heavy guns that outperformed the British fifteen-pounder and thirteen-pounder field guns. The larger Boer guns were known as 'Long Toms', and these made their presence felt when the British were at the receiving end of their fire in the besieged towns.

The most important scene of action was in Natal. In Ladysmith, White now commanded thirteen thousand men made up of the original garrison and the force from India. There were also five thousand civilians (black and white), three thousand horses, and supplies for three months. White took the opportunity to make sorties out of the town before the Boer ring finally closed. One sortie was against a Boer force on Talana Hill on 20 October. The British advanced against the Boers in close order, and this made them vulnerable to small-arms fire. Although there were heavy casualties, the British got to the top of the hill, where they were met by 'friendly' British gunfire. It was a pyrrhic victory. The British suffered 254 casualties, including their commander, Major General Penn Symons, a member of the Roberts 'Ring'. The Boers slipped away, although some were pursued in vain by the British cavalry. (See **Map 12**.)

The second venture out of Ladysmith was an attack at Elandslaagte, a station on the railway fifteen miles north-east of Ladysmith. This was commanded by the thrusting cavalry leader John French, and Ian Hamilton was his second in command. Hamilton, another member of the Roberts 'Ring', had accompanied White from India as a staff officer, but he was now given an opportunity to command troops. French deployed 3,500 men, more than three times the number of Boers who faced him. Hamilton led two and a half infantry battalions and five squadrons of irregular cavalry, the Imperial Light Horse. Hamilton's men assaulted two ridges and took them. The men advanced in open order to minimize casualties. With the British infantry close to victory,

French unleashed three cavalry regiments that charged with lance and sabre. The Boers suffered 425 casualties, compared with the British 263.

The Boers were also active north of Ladysmith. They drove a British force in Dundee back into the town and also defeated British forces at Rietfontein and Nicholson's Nek, causing heavy casualties in both cases. The British garrison in Ladysmith was now surrounded, and White was well aware of the peril of his position. It was the beginning of November, and the Boers had the upper hand.

Buller arrived in Cape Town on 31 October 1899. His Corps had been boosted to fifty thousand men. Buller decided to dispatch 30,500 men, under Lieutenant General Lord Methuen, to the north to relieve Kimberley and Mafeking. Buller then took 19,500 men to Natal to come to the aid of the British force besieged in Ladysmith. It was difficult to enter Natal from the west because of the Drakensberg Mountains, which meant that he had to approach Natal from the south. He instructed White not to get sealed up in Ladysmith, but by then, it was too late. While Buller was making slow progress, the attitude of White was unusually passive. Except for occasional shelling by the 'Long Toms', the garrison led a peaceful life, with church parades and cricket matches. Some aggressive British officers carried out raids and minor operations, and the British defeated a major Boer assault from the south in early January 1900. The garrison looked to Buller for their rescue.

On 15 December 1899—six weeks after Ladysmith was besieged— Buller made his first major assault at the crossing of the Tugela River at Colenso. The Boers, commanded by a remarkable thirty-seven-year-old leader called Louis Botha, occupied a four-mile entrenched position north of the river. The British assault was badly mishandled, and a dozen fifteen-pounder field guns were pushed too far forward. These were captured by the Boers. A party of volunteers made a heroic effort to recapture the guns, but only two were saved. The volunteers included Freddy Roberts, Lord Roberts's only son, who lost his life and won a posthumous Victoria Cross.

Buller's force was only thirty miles from Ladysmith, and contact with the town was being made by heliograph. By mid-January 1900, Buller's force had been increased to thirty thousand men, and he at last found a crossing over the Tugela. His army then encountered a defile between two large hills. One had to be taken before the army could get through. The 1,500-foot hill that Buller assaulted was the infamous Spion Kop. It was captured with difficulty by the British, but they were forced to withdraw. The number of British casualties was not known precisely, but they were between 1,800 and 2,000 men. (Spion Kop was a reprise of Majuba Hill.) Buller's advance continued, and it was now a little easier because the Boers were transferring men to the middle of the country, where the British were advancing on Kimberley. The final assault began on 21 February 1900, and the relieving force entered Ladysmith on 1 March. There was modest jubilation in the town but enormous celebrations in London.

During the first weeks of the war, the British authorities quickly came to the conclusion that the war in South Africa needed a much more serious commitment by the British army. This meant many more men and an overall commander who had a strong personality, 'grip', and experience of leading a large force. Roberts was appointed, despite his sixty-eight years. He would command a force of 150,000 men in addition to the fifty thousand troops already in the colony. The decision to send Roberts was made by Lansdowne, who still had a difficult relationship with Wolseley. Lansdowne was supported by many members of the cabinet. The prime minister, Lord Salisbury, also agreed—although he stipulated that Kitchener should be Roberts's chief of staff.

Roberts was now in a rush to put together a full complement of staff officers, but he still had time to visit the Queen at Windsor and also address the Chelsea Pensioners assembled in the Royal Hospital. Roberts and the men in his headquarters embarked at Southampton before the end of the year and arrived in Cape Town on 16 January 1900. For a month, he had been carrying the crushing burden of his son's death at Colenso, but he got to work immediately after he arrived.[14]

Endnotes

1. Kochanski, Halik, *Sir Garnet Wolseley. Victorian Hero* (London: The Hambledon Press, 1999), 171–197.

2. James, David, *Lord Roberts* (London: Hollis & Carter, 1954), 352.

3. Kochanski, *Sir Garnet Wolseley. Victorian Hero*, 199–231.

4. Hibbert, Christopher (ed.), *Queen Victoria in Her Letters and Journals* (New York: Viking Penguin, 1985), 331.

5. Wright, William, *Warriors of the Queen. Fighting Generals of the Victorian Age* (Stroud, Gloucestershire: Spellmount, 2014). Biographies of generals in alphabetical order.

6. James, *Lord Roberts*, 237–261.

7. Ibid., 238.

8. Ibid., 244.

9. Ibid., 246.

10. Kochanski, *Sir Garnet Wolseley, Victorian Hero*, 213–231.

11. Jones, John Philip, *Johnny. The Legend and Tragedy of General Sir Ian Hamilton* (Barnsley, South Yorkshire: Pen & Sword, 2012), 86–104.

12. Kochanski, *Sir Garnet Wolseley. Victorian Hero*, 233–243.

13. Jones, *Johnny. The Legend and Tragedy of General Sir Ian Hamilton*, 89–104.

14. James, *Lord Roberts*, 265–267.

CHAPTER 15

'THE QUEEN'S GREATEST SUBJECT': ROBERTS IN SOUTH AFRICA

Roberts intended to take the war to the enemy. This meant advancing north from Cape Town to Pretoria, fighting stiff opposition from the Boers on the way. The battleground was very large. Pretoria is one thousand miles from Cape Town, taking account of the bends in the route the troops would have to travel, partly on foot and partly by rail. (See **Map 12**.) Before Roberts's arrival, the British had advanced from the Cape Province most of the way to Kimberley; but before reaching the town, their progress had been blocked by the Boers. Kimberley remained under siege.[1]

Buller had decided to provide Lord Methuen with 30,500 men for his march north, which began in November 1899. Buller concentrated his own force of 19,500 men in Natal, where it made a painfully slow advance to the relief of Ladysmith (recounted in chapter 14). Methuen advanced north, with no opposition until his troops got to seventy miles short of Kimberley, at Orange River Station. Here there was substantial Boer opposition, which soon got worse. Meanwhile, trouble was brewing in the central Cape Province, where Boers had captured the rail junction of Stormberg, fifty miles south of the Orange River, which separates the Orange Free State from the Cape Province. On 11 December, the local British commander, Lieutenant General Gatacre, mishandled his attack on the Boers. Gatacre's force of three thousand men outnumbered the enemy, but orders were misunderstood, and six hundred men were left on a hill south of the railway junction. Most were captured. The unfortunate battle of Stormberg quickly reached the London newspapers.

To the west of Stormberg, Methuen's advance continued until his spearhead of thirteen thousand men reached a position twenty-five miles south of Kimberley. But here, three thousand Boers—commanded by Piet Cronje and Koos de la Rey—employed tactics that confused the British. Unexpectedly, the Boers avoided the high ground and dug fire trenches on the low ground: on both sides of the Riet River, a tributary of the Modder. Both rivers have steep banks and are thick with mud. (This gives the Modder River its name.) The Boer trenches were strongly manned, and there were also some Boer field guns. On 28 November, the Modder River battle lasted for ten hours and was mainly fought by long-range exchange of fire. Two British brigades advanced, but they made little progress, despite Methuen's decision to go forward to join the leading troops. There were 460 British casualties, compared with eighty Boers. The Boers then withdrew, having won a cheap victory. The British licked their wounds.

The British advance continued, but at Magersfontein on 11/12 December 1899, Methuen's men suffered an even more painful setback. The Boer trench line extended for four miles in front of Magersfontein Hill, which is fifteen miles north-east of where the Modder River battle had been fought. On this hill, the Boers established an observation post (which still exists) that provided a complete view of the battlefield. The celebrated Highland Brigade, under Major General Andrew Wauchope, was to bear the brunt of the assault and also the casualties. It was Wauchope—at the time a company commander in the Black Watch—who had participated in the fierce attack and the hand-to-hand fighting at the battle of Tel-el-Kebir on 13 September 1882 (described in chapter 11).

On the night of 11 December 1899, the Highlanders advanced in large, close formations to avoid straying and getting lost in the darkness. But as dawn was breaking, and as they were opening out into a line to assault the enemy four hundred yards away, they received a torrent of small-arms and artillery fire. There was carnage. The situation became worse during the day when the Highlanders, wounded and unwounded alike, were all pinned down by enemy fire and badly blistered by the sun, especially on their legs below their kilts. Once again, there was a large disparity in the numbers of casualties: 902 dead and wounded British and 236 Boers. Wauchope was among those killed. There was now no question of Methuen continuing his advance against Kimberley. The three disastrous battles—Stormberg, Magersfontein, and Colenso— were fought within days of each other, and it was not surprising that this short period soon became known in Britain as Black Week. During the whole course of the war, Black Week was the nadir of Britain's fortunes.

Roberts Takes Command

Roberts landed at Cape Town on 16 January 1900. The most important appointment he made was his chief of staff (and later successor) Lord Kitchener. The prime minister had insisted on Kitchener, and Roberts was enthusiastic about him. Less than two years before, Kitchener had made his name because of the well-organized expedition up the Nile and his defeat of the dervishes. It was shortly after this expedition that he travelled to Ireland to meet Roberts. Roberts himself had long experience of commanding 'from the saddle' and had a formidable range of military talent, not least the magic gift of leadership. Kitchener had an indomitable will and an outstanding 'feel' for grand strategy. He radiated power, although he was a poor delegator. A few years after he left South Africa, Kitchener became the commander-in-chief in India. He had a bitter dispute with the political authorities about control over the finances of the Indian army. He was opposed by the viceroy, but Kitchener was the stronger man, and the viceroy resigned.

Roberts brought immediate 'grip' to his command. He also brought to South Africa an expeditionary force of unprecedented size. Around 150,000 reinforcements arrived, and these included volunteer units from Britain and irregular (mainly mounted) corps from Britain, South Africa, and other British dominions and colonies. Roberts immediately converted some of his battalions to mounted infantry, to match the best of the Boer commandos in mobility and musketry; in addition, they benefited from the sinewy cohesion of British military discipline. The first thing that had to be done was to teach British infantry how to ride, and this took time.

Roberts's personal impact on his men was graphically described by the young war correspondent Winston Churchill:

> 'The conversation stops abruptly. Everyone looks round. Strolling across the middle of the square, quite alone, was a very small grey-haired gentleman, with extremely broad shoulders and a most unbending back. He wore a stiff cap with a broad red band and a heavy gold-laced peak, brown riding boots, a tightly fastened belt, and no medals, orders, or insignia of any kind. But no one doubted his identity for an instant, and I knew that I was looking at the Queen's greatest subject.'[2]

Roberts and Kitchener took three weeks to formulate their battlefield strategy, which was to seize the initiative and make a powerful drive north. They concentrated on the central route, from Cape Town to Kimberley, then to Bloemfontein, and finally to Pretoria. The railway was going to play a major role and would carry as many troops as possible after local Boer resistance had been suppressed. Further to the north, Mafeking was still under siege, but Roberts did not divide his force by sending men to Mafeking. In addition, Buller was ordered to remain in Natal and make what progress he could. This was an advantage to Roberts because Buller was keeping Boer commandos away from Roberts's field of operations as he moved north from the Cape Province.

By 15 February 1900, Roberts's men were in Magersfontein, having travelled by rail for some of the way. Roberts's attack at Magersfontein took the Boers by surprise. This was because men were brought quickly to the battlefield, and British cavalry was very active. French had by now taken command of a new cavalry division, and he aggressively encircled the Boer positions while the British infantry were attacking. Boer morale began to crumble, and Bloemfontein was soon in British hands. The defenders retreated, but they were slow and were soon assaulted by the British army at Paardeberg.

However, immediately after the relief of Bloemfontein, an enterprising commando leader, Christiaan de Wet, captured the main British supply column south of Kimberley. The British lost 180 ox-drawn wagons packed with supplies. This was a hard lesson for Roberts and Kitchener, who had insisted on centralizing all the supplies needed for the army to free the hands of the fighting soldiers, but the mass of supplies was not protected well enough from marauding parties of Boers. Roberts and Kitchener learned their lesson because they continued to realize the importance of logistics for an army on the move. In future, they ordered supplies to be organized by each unit individually, although this meant a good deal of hard labour for the troops.

After the British success at Magersfontein, the Boers got away because Roberts's infantry needed reorganization and French's cavalry was exhausted, although French managed to shadow the retreating Boers from a distance. The cavalry covered a good deal of ground, and it was not practical for the troopers to dismount and lead their horses to keep them fresh. French was a thruster, with a feel for tactical opportunities, but he was highly strung and was not known for his brain power. His chief of staff was Douglas Haig, a better-educated officer with a growing reputation. In August 1914, French—by now a field marshal—commanded the British Expeditionary Force (BEF) that sailed to France. Haig, who was French's principal subordinate, did not conceal his unfavourable opinion of his commander-in-chief. At the end of 1915, Haig succeeded French, and there has always been speculation about whether Haig engineered his promotion through his personal contacts with the Royal Family.

The Boer force that retreated after Magersfontein totaled four thousand men from the Orange Free State, but they were accompanied by many family members and were supplied from ox-drawn wagons.

This slowed the pace of the Boer retreat, which was commanded by the Free State general Cronje. The Boers moved to the east, along the south of the Modder, then crossed to the north bank at Paardeberg Hill, where they camped. They were twenty-five miles east of Kimberley and seventy-five miles from Bloemfontein.

Roberts, who had been on his horse for days, was stricken with haemorrhoids. On 18 February 1900, he handed over command temporarily to Kitchener, whose 'grip' was less secure than Roberts's. Kitchener looked for ways of crossing the steep banks of the river to the north side. He did this by riding, unaccompanied by his staff, to a feature that became known as Kitchener's Hill, where he inspected the battlefield through his field glasses. He drew up an impromptu plan to attack rather than besiege the Boers. A number of uncoordinated frontal attacks followed, but most of these were repulsed with heavy losses. A single brigade got across. This was commanded by Brigadier General Smith-Dorrien, an officer who did not get on with French. (When Smith-Dorrien was commanding one of the two British armies in France in early 1915, he was abruptly sacked by French.) Kitchener charged around the battlefield south of the Modder and exhausted a number of horses while doing so. However, he remained frustrated. The Boer marksmen were more than a match for any advancing British troops.

Roberts returned the next day and immediately changed Kitchener's tactical plan. He realized that the only way to defeat the enemy was to besiege the Boer position by shelling it with all his guns. He also dispatched French's cavalry to encircle the Boers from the east. At this time, Roberts's army had a six-to-one superiority in numbers. Cronje realized the futility of further resistance. The photograph of the large unkempt Boer surrendering to the diminutive but immaculate British field marshal was quickly circulated throughout the world. The two leaders had breakfast together, and Roberts was complimentary about his opponent's bravery. Before long, Cronje and his wife were sent into exile for the rest of the war. It was 27 February, the anniversary of Majuba Hill.

Roberts's force now moved east towards Bloemfontein, but on 7 March, French's cavalry division was stopped in its tracks by Boer rearguards at Poplar Grove, and the British suffered 213 casualties. Bloemfontein fell on 13 March, but there were recriminations between Roberts and French. French had always been temperamental and volatile. His performance at Poplar Grove increased Roberts's doubts about the value of conventional cavalry and further boosted his growing faith in mounted infantry. French's cavalry played an important role in the next phase of the war: the advance across the veldt. However, the mounted infantry had a greater number of men, and they performed extremely well for a formation that was—to all intents and purposes—an experiment.

Across the Veldt with the Mounted Infantry

Roberts's two battles had transformed the war. As Churchill said at the time, Roberts 'had in the brief space of a month revolutionized the fortunes of war, had turned disaster into victory, and something like despair into almost inordinate triumph'.[3]

Roberts and Kitchener had a clear idea about the next stage of their offensive. They summoned Ian Hamilton from Natal, where he had been a staff officer and, later, a commander under General White in Ladysmith. Hamilton was Roberts's devoted follower and had been largely responsible for transforming the musketry of the Indian army. In Natal, Hamilton suffered the lingering effects of typhoid, but he got to Bloemfontein in mid-March 1900. He was by now a local major general and was shortly promoted local lieutenant general. He was forty-seven. He was given command of the Mounted Infantry Division, made up of the Second Mounted Infantry Brigade, the Second Cavalry Brigade, and the Nineteenth Infantry Brigade, plus a substantial force of artillery: thirty-eight guns and a number of rifle-calibre machine guns. The fighting strength was 11,000 men, with 4,600 horses and 8,000 mules. Hamilton's division was made up of eleven units: four mounted infantry battalions, three cavalry regiments, and four infantry battalions. This was a powerful force, although time was needed for the men to train together and, in particular, for the men in the mounted infantry brigade to be comfortable on horseback.[4]

Hamilton had five weeks to prepare for war. Unfortunately, the division was now hit by a typhoid epidemic, caused by drinking contaminated water from the Modder River. To make matters worse, venereal disease was also prevalent. Large numbers of volunteer doctors, nurses, and medical orderlies were drafted in, and the problems were fairly quickly arrested. The doctors included Dr. Arthur Conan Doyle, better known as the creator of Sherlock Holmes.

Roberts's strategy was to advance on a relatively narrow front from Bloemfontein to Pretoria, using rail transport as much as possible. There are three hundred miles from Bloemfontein to Pretoria, then a further two hundred miles from Pretoria to the frontier between the Transvaal and Portuguese East Africa. Roberts's advancing force was made up of sixty-five thousand men in three columns: French's cavalry division on the western flank, Roberts's main force of two divisions (forty thousand men) in the center, and Hamilton's mounted infantry division thirty miles away to the east. Roberts intended to exercise tight control over these four divisions. He also employed five semi-independent detachments beyond the flanks of the main force. These roamed widely. A column moved off to relieve Mafeking, and various columns were free to pursue marauding Boer commandos. Furthest east was Buller's force in Natal. The total number of men in Roberts's command was two hundred thousand. Although these were not all regulars, they represented the largest force that Britain had ever put in the field, and it was five times the fighting strength of the Boers. This disparity in numbers says a great deal about British respect for the Boers' fighting ability. Roberts's subordinate commanders included many officers whose names became prominent during the First World War: Allenby, Byng, de Lisle, French, Haig, Hamilton, Hunter, Plumer, Rawlinson, Robertson, Smith-Dorrien, and Wilson.

Roberts's thinking was dominated by the well-established military principle of maintenance of the aim. He had already defeated the Free State, although various commandos were still causing trouble, and de Wet would be a thorn in the British side until the end of the war. Roberts intended to go straight for Pretoria, brushing off any Boer attacks on his communications along the way.

Shortly after the fall of Bloemfontein, the presidents of the two Boer republics held a council of war at Kroonstad. They resolved to rally support from a number of European countries. This had very little practical effect, although many Europeans—particularly the Germans and the French—sympathized with the Boers, whom they saw as suffering under the heel of their British oppressors. The press in Germany and France was full of lampoons of British soldiers, generally wearing kilts and heavy boots and with malevolent expressions on their faces. In South Africa, the name used to describe the British soldiers was 'rooi nek' ('red neck'), because of the sunburn on the back of their necks above their high khaki collars.

Before the main British force was ready to move north on 3 May, de Wet's agile force made two daring and successful raids. On 31 March, de Wet's commando of 1,500 men skilfully ambushed two batteries of Royal Horse Artillery at the Bloemfontein waterworks at Sannas Pos. The Boers captured 428 prisoners, 117 wagons, and seven guns. On 3 April, eight hundred Boers, with three field guns, attacked a British garrison at Reddersberg; and after a hot fight, they captured six hundred British troops.

Despite these setbacks, Roberts remained unflustered. The march north began on 3 May, although the Mounted Infantry Division began to lead the way on 22 April. The three brigadiers in this division were seasoned campaigners; the Nineteenth Infantry Brigade was commanded by Smith-Dorrien, who had led the only troops who managed to cross the Modder River at Paardeberg. During the march, Churchill was continuously impressed by Hamilton for both personal and professional reasons. Smith-Dorrien felt the same way and considered Hamilton a delightful leader, 'always ready to go for the enemy and extremely quick at seizing a tactical advantage, and with it all, always in a good temper'.[5]

The British army that advanced from Bloemfontein was not a juggernaut, but it was strong, flexible, confident, and well-led. The Mounted Infantry Division operated aggressively on the right flank, and on occasion during the march, it ranged outwards towards the east in search of the commandos. The first phase of the advance took the force 130 miles to Kroonstad. During this advance, Hamilton 'bumped' the enemy on four occasions. The biggest engagement was at the Sand River on 10 May, where the Boers held a hill in some strength and were attacked frontally by the infantry and encircled by the cavalry around the Boers' right flank. The number of British casualties was very small. The army reached Kroonstad on 16 May and stopped to replenish supplies and wait for damage to the railway line from Bloemfontein to be repaired.

The Mounted Infantry Division moved forward again on 22 May. In the valley town of Heilbron, they found the enemy who were, surprisingly, exhausted and did not strike the British before the British struck them. The Boer force comprised a thousand men, five guns, and sixty wagons. Such a large supply train was unusual for de Wet, and it was extremely vulnerable. Hamilton was in the middle of the attacking troops, and although most of the Boers got away, the British force captured seventeen prisoners and fifteen wagons. There were no British casualties.

The next engagement, at Doornkop, marked an important step on the way to defeating the Boers. Roberts moved the mounted infantry division from the right to the left flank of the British army, and Hamilton now started to work closely with French; this was a reprise of the fruitful cooperation between the two leaders at the battle of Elandslaagte in Natal. The battle of Doornkop came at the end of an eighteen-mile march by the mounted infantry division, which had to transport all its supplies. Hamilton's and French's divisions now entered the Transvaal and were approaching the Rand, where the Boers had built strong defensive works. Eight miles south of Johannesburg, the British troops encountered eight thousand Boers at the town of Florida. Florida is situated on a ridge at the western end of which is the hill called Doornkop. French and Hamilton worked out a plan for an assault on the afternoon of 29 May. This was a cooperative effort. French, the senior, and Hamilton, the junior, were getting used to working together.

By this time, Smith-Dorrien was commanding an infantry division of two brigades. The plan was that this division would make an infantry attack from the south, supported by a substantial artillery bombardment. At the same time, the cavalry would move around the left of Doornkop to encircle the Boer right. The cavalry force was made up of French's cavalry division, plus the Second Cavalry Brigade, which was part of Hamilton's Mounted Infantry. French therefore had an awesome force of four cavalry brigades, made up of twelve crack regular regiments. (It was four times the size of the Light Brigade that had made such an unfortunate name at Balaclava.) The infantry advanced on Doornkop, with the men well spread out (about half a mile per battalion) and making the best use of the broken ground to protect them from enemy fire. Unfortunately, much of the ground in front of the Boer positions was burnt black so that the khaki uniforms stood out to make the soldiers targets. However, it was the British infantry that won the day, despite the loss of 250 men killed and wounded. The cavalry had not played a major part.

The British advance continued into Johannesburg. Capturing the town was a virtual walkover. But when Roberts's men advanced towards Pretoria, they found it a more difficult nut to crack. After two days in Johannesburg to gather a minimal quantity of supplies, the British army marched the fifty miles to Pretoria, where the Boer opposition was in the outskirts of the town. They were subjected to many isolated attacks by the British cavalry and mounted infantry, while the British artillery continued to hammer the Boer lines. This engagement lasted for more than a day, and by the end of 4 June, all resistance stopped. To the frustrated eyes of the British, a Boer train crammed with men and horses steamed to the east to fight another day. Three thousand British prisoners had been held in Pretoria, and they were now released. Roberts held a three-hour grand military procession: something that undoubtedly impressed the inhabitants of the town. Kruger got away and took with him the Transvaal treasury worth £1,000,000 sterling. He established a headquarters 140 miles east of Pretoria, and following a further British advance, the old Boer leader departed for Europe, where he died in 1904.

The British occupation of Pretoria did not mean the surrender of the Boer commandos. Seven thousand men from the Transvaal were still at large, although their leader, Louis Botha, made a tentative approach to discuss peace. But this came to an end when news arrived that de Wet and his men from the Free State were still operating aggressively against the British. Roberts immediately went after the Transvaal commandos and led three divisions east along the railway leading to Portuguese East Africa. These divisions were only at half strength because of sickness and casualties from earlier enemy action. On 11 July 1900, the British met a force of five thousand Boers occupying a range of steep hills straddling the railway. The position, twenty miles from Pretoria, was called Diamond Hill because of a massive gemstone that had been found there years before.

Roberts's plan was to attack the enemy from three directions: encircling the Boer position from the north and south, coinciding with a frontal attack. However, the Boers made a tactical retreat, which left the British in the air. On 13 July, Ian Hamilton, who had commanded the sweep from the south, was more successful. His second attack was helped by Winston Churchill, still a war correspondent, who had managed to get up the hill that Hamilton's men were attacking. From his commanding position, he signaled Hamilton's mounted infantry to attack, using a stick with a handkerchief tied to the end of it. Although the Boers pulled back a second time, the battle was over. It was an inconclusive victory for the British, and they suffered 180 casualties. The initial phase of the war, in which both sides fought in organized armies, had come to an end. The conflict now degenerated into guerrilla warfare.

Considering how badly the war had gone before the arrival of Roberts and Kitchener, the campaign was a great triumph for them. The sharp change of fortune of the army under Roberts was due to three factors. The first was Roberts's 'grip', in particular his resolution to maintain the aim of the campaign. The second factor was the substantial reinforcements that Roberts received. The third was the efficient staff system that Roberts and Kitchener introduced.[6] However, Roberts and Kitchener were experienced enough to realize that after the capture of Pretoria, the war was not yet over. The victory to date had been incomplete.

A Lengthy and Expensive Guerrilla War

Roberts and Kitchener were now facing considerable and unexpected problems. The Free State was exploding with a new surge of Boer activity. Eight thousand men in the Free State commandos—experienced fighters under the leadership of Christiaan de Wet—continued to rampage across the countryside. In such a large territory, with mobility limited to the speed of a horse, the commando raiders were always going to possess an advantage because when the British received news of their actions, the pursuers were always going to be too late to catch their quarry. The danger of this situation was that the Boers would maintain the initiative and the British would become unbalanced. Roberts and Kitchener needed to 'think through' their situation and respond strategically, basing their plans on their considerable superiority in strength. Their battlefield strategy was tough and allowed for no compromise; but in the end, it succeeded.

At the end of May 1900, the British annexed the Free State and renamed it the Orange River Colony. The immediate response of the Free State commandos was three astonishingly successful raids that ambushed and plundered a number of British convoys of troops and supplies, at negligible cost to the raiders. The first part of the British strategy was to organize columns, each made up of two thousand to four thousand men, which swept across the veldt in search of the enemy. One group of columns, under the overall command of Lieutenant General Hunter, surrounded a substantial force of Free State commandos in a saucer of land called the Brandwater Basin. Although 1,800 men escaped, 4,300 laid down their arms in a place later called Surrender Hill. However, this was an isolated success, and during the remainder of the year, de Wet's men continued to be aggressors.

This led the British to respond in a way that made them deeply unpopular. The British troops were instructed to burn the farms, kill the livestock, and dispossess the families of the Boers who were still fighting. This 'scorched earth' policy had been common in the fighting on the North-West Frontier of India. However, some British officers refused to carry it out in South Africa. When the Boer women and children lost their homes, they were moved into what became known as concentration camps. Eventually, there were forty-six such camps, holding ninety-three thousand whites and twenty-four thousand blacks. The camps were supervised by British army doctors and nurses, but they were all badly organized. Disease was rife, and large numbers of inhabitants died prematurely. (The description 'concentration camp' was resurrected in Hitler's Germany, but the German camps were far bigger than the South African ones and were populated by Jews and other 'undesirables'. The inhabitants were starved, worked mercilessly, and most eventually ended in the gas chambers.)

The final element in the strategy to subdue the commandos was the building of blockhouses. These were primitive structures with corrugated iron roofs and held up to a dozen sweating soldiers. These small buildings (many are still standing today) were extended across the veldt at intervals of up to a mile, and they were connected by wire that was strong enough to stop a horse. The blockhouses were mutually supporting, and the ground between them was covered by small-arms fire. What this system managed to achieve was to channel the commandos into areas that divided the open veldt into more limited regions where they could be located and attacked by the British columns of mounted infantry. By the end of the war, there were eight thousand blockhouses guarded by fifty thousand white troops and sixteen thousand African scouts. The blockhouse system was mainly built during the period of Kitchener's command. In his early years, he had been an officer in the Royal Engineers, and he never lost his technical skills and interest in engineering projects.

Wolseley, viewing the campaign from London, was not impressed by Roberts's achievement. There may have been an element of wounded *amour propre* on Wolseley's part, particularly since he had himself been considered too old for the appointment. When Wolseley was in his late fifties and sixties, he was less focused on his profession than he had previously been. Lord Lansdowne, the Secretary of State for War, had no hesitation in selecting Roberts for the command in South Africa. Wolseley probably found it difficult to appreciate that the new strategy devised by Roberts and Kitchener would take some time to pay off.

Roberts handed over command to Kitchener on 30 November 1900 and departed for England. He landed in the New Year and was welcomed officially with a number of grand ceremonies. He received the grateful thanks of the Queen and the government, plus a cash award of £100,000 (equivalent to at least £10,000,000 in twenty-first-century money). Roberts was slated to take over from Wolseley as commander-in-chief of the British army before the end of the year. He was to be the last soldier to hold this post.

Between December 1900 and May 1902, Kitchener was in firm command and carried out with great efficiency the policies of farm-burning, concentration camps, independent mounted columns, and lines of blockhouses. Hamilton had returned with Roberts as his Military Secretary, but before long, he returned to South Africa as Kitchener's chief of staff. Kitchener was an improviser and had unparalleled drive. He was not accustomed to delegating authority and lacked Roberts's experience of using an army staff. As a result, Hamilton had little to do until he was given command of a number of columns: a job he relished and in which he did well.[7]

The conflict in South Africa eventually wound down. The Boers were exhausted but unbroken and agreed to peace terms that offered a promise of self-government in the future. A few years after the end of the war, the Transvaal commando leader Louis Botha became prime minister. His eventual successor as prime minister was Jan Smuts, another (although less successful) commando leader, who also later became Chancellor of Cambridge University, where he had earlier studied law at Christ's College. This was an incidental but practical symbol that the Second Boer War was finally over.

However, the deficiencies of the British army in South Africa led to a sharp shock of radical reform—in particular, the establishment, at long last, of a general staff in London. This reform produced improvements that prepared the British army for the much larger conflicts of the twentieth century, conflicts that were also accompanied by bitter disputes between statesmen and soldiers: powerful men like Lloyd George and Robertson, and Churchill and Brooke. These were mainly concerned with grand strategy, and history has shown that in the Second World War, the British got it right, not least because Churchill and Brooke had the persuasive power to get the agreement of the Americans.

Endnotes

1. Jones, John Philip, *Johnny. The Legend and Tragedy of General Sir Ian Hamilton* (Barnsley, South Yorkshire: Pen & Sword, 2012), 105–111.
2. Churchill, Winston, *The Boer War: Ian Hamilton's March* (Norwalk, CT: The Easton Press, 2007), 26. (Churchill's book was originally published in 1900.)
3. Ibid.
4. Jones, *Johnny. The Legend and Tragedy of General Sir Ian Hamilton*, 111–120.
5. Ballard, Brigadier General C., *Smith-Dorrien* (London: Constable, 1931), ix–x.
6. James, David, *Lord Roberts* (London: Hollis & Carter, 1954), 352.
7. Jones, *Johnny. The Legend and Tragedy of General Sir Ian Hamilton*, 120–125.

CHAPTER 16

THE LAST TWO COMMANDERS-IN-CHIEF OF THE BRITISH ARMY

The Second Boer War was a wake-up call for the British army. It had taken almost three years for the British to defeat a loosely organized army of farmers defending their homeland, and the number of British troops needed for the job was five times the number of their elusive enemy. The initial defeats of the British in 1899—defeats loudly trumpeted in British and European newspapers—occurred when the expeditionary force was commanded by Buller, a prominent member of the Wolseley 'Ring', although Wolseley was by now aware of his failings. Roberts and Kitchener were compelled to develop a new strategy to counter the superior tactics of the Boers, but although this strategy took time to work, it inexorably led to victory. Nevertheless, at the time, Wolseley had doubts about Roberts's abilities.

The inadequate performance of the British army was the result of its profound conservatism. The soldiers were tough, experienced, and highly disciplined, but their rigid tactics had not kept pace with modern warfare, e.g. volley firing was still considered more important than marksmanship. The army was stuck in the past because its experience had been exclusively of small colonial wars against native armies that were brave but untrained and badly armed. Even after the beginning of the Second Boer War, the British were blind to the fighting skill of the

Boers, with their tactics based on their nimbleness as mounted infantry and the accurate firepower of their Mauser rifles and Krupp field artillery. The Duke of Cambridge's thirty-nine years as commander-in-chief can mainly be blamed for the army's stagnation. Wolseley was much less responsible although some of the odium inevitably clung to him. As a peer and a member of the House of Lords, he was free to engage in public debates about his role as commander-in-chief. He spoke specifically about how his responsibilities had been restricted: a major cause of his difficulties.

During the time of Cardwell and Childers, Wolseley had played an active part in army reform: the development of the linked battalion system and other organizational improvements. When he was commander-in-chief during the late 1890s, he made persistent efforts to boost the size of the army, but his ambitions were modest: an increase of only a few thousand men. Wolseley, at the time, was not physically fit. Nevertheless, the scope of his appointment had been limited, and (perhaps more seriously) he was focused on details at a time when conceptual thinking was required. The army needed radical reform, not least a general staff in the War Office. Wolseley—because of his health, the confines of his job, and his own personality—was not the person to bring about such large changes. The tragedy of Wolseley was that he was not personally or politically powerful enough to engineer the changes to the army that he thought so strongly were necessary.

After Wolseley had left office, the Queen invited him to make a written report describing the difficulties of the job of commander-in-chief as he had to carry it out. He wrote a forthright memorandum, to which Lansdowne made an equally forthright response. There was no meeting of minds, although the main problem was the way in which the position had been defined by Lansdowne at the beginning of Wolseley's term. In August 1900, Lansdowne resigned and was succeeded by his undersecretary, Sir John Brodrick. Wolseley, after his long career of notable service to the Crown that ended as head of the army, left active service in 1900. As a field marshal, who remains officially on duty although retired, he transferred to the half-pay list. There was a quiet transition, with no fanfare. He had a happy retirement and died in 1913 at the age of seventy-nine.[1]

When Roberts returned from South Africa at the end of 1900, he had an audience with the Queen. This was an auspicious occasion, and one of the Queen's last audiences. She died in January 1901, after a long reign during which Britain had become the strongest and richest country in the world. Her passing seemed a symbol that big changes were going to take place. When Roberts became commander-in-chief at the end of 1900, army reform became his major responsibility. Immediately after the end of the Second Boer War, a commission was set up under Lord Elgin to examine the conduct of the British army. It took the evidence of 114 witnesses and was critical in its report of the action (and inaction) of the commander-in-chief.

The Elgin Commission led the way to the appointment of an even more important body—the Esher Commission of 1903, which recommended changes in the central control of the army. The members of the commission were Lord Esher himself, who was a high-ranking civil servant and confidential adviser to the Crown, a quintessentially 'Establishment' figure; Sir George Sydenham Clarke, a colonial governor with a strong military background; and Admiral Sir John Fisher, then Second Sea Lord and commander-in-chief at Portsmouth, and in line to be First Sea Lord. Fisher was a dynamo, and within a few years, he had transformed the Royal Navy—and naval warfare—by the introduction of the 'Dreadnought', a warship of revolutionary design.

Roberts, Esher, and Army Reform

At the end of the nineteenth century, the office of commander-in-chief of the British army was not as powerful as that of the Indian army, although the Indian army had a rather lower strength and its operations were restricted to the subcontinent and South Asia. However, the Duke of Cambridge in the Horse Guards was growing so old and increasingly conservative that the importance of his position was gradually eroded. This was accompanied by a growth in the influence of the political head of the army, the Secretary of State for War, who in the 1890s was Lord Lansdowne. (One of Caldwell's reforms in the 1870s was to make the commander-in-chief subordinate to the Secretary of State for War.)

Before Roberts's appointment as commander-in-chief of the British army, a scheme had been set up to divide the country into six separate military districts called Commands, each comprising an army corps of three divisions. These were mostly under-strength so that the organization was nominal rather than real. However, two of these corps eventually formed the foundation of the British Expeditionary Force (BEF) that went to France in August 1914; they had trained together in peacetime. The two corps formed the celebrated first six divisions of the BEF, which were brought up to strength by reservists fresh from civilian life, whose main problem, at first, was marching long distances in new and unyielding ammunition boots.

Further reforms followed immediately after Roberts's arrival, and he showed himself as energetic a reformer as he had been in India decades before. Improved weapons were introduced for the infantry, cavalry, and artillery; more efficient transport; simpler and more serviceable uniforms; and advances in military education and training. Most importantly, the life of the men in the ranks was made more comfortable and rewarding, with better barracks and canteens. While these reforms were in progress, Roberts conducted large-scale military exercises, and he spent as much time as he had always done in inspecting garrisons and making his presence felt by the men in the ranks.

In September 1902, Roberts attended the annual manoeuvres of the German army. Despite the formidable reputation of that army, Roberts was not impressed with its drill, tactics, dress, and equipment. Hamilton, who accompanied him, was critical of the amount of pre-planning on which the Germans insisted. This sterilized the initiative of many German leaders, who became incapable of improvising anything on the spur of the moment. The experience of the First World War improved the performance of the German army. Later in that war, and even more during the Second World War, the German army became celebrated for its 'bottom-up' organization, by which sergeants were trained to command platoons; subalterns, companies; captains, battalions; and majors, regiments (the German equivalent of British brigades). Rommel, who would be a field marshal during the Second World War, won the coveted *Pour le Mérite* at the Battle of Caporetto in 1917, when he was a lieutenant in command of half a battalion. After the First World War, the 100,000-strong *Reichswehr* grew into the formidable *Wehrmacht* of the late 1930s, precisely on the principle of growth from the 'bottom up'.

In Britain, the first step to strengthen and broaden government control of the armed services was taken in 1902. The Conservative prime minister, Arthur Balfour, set up a cabinet committee (later known as the Committee of Imperial Defence) to give advice to the government on grand strategy. This committee was made up of the heads of the navy and army and their intelligence chiefs. Since it was the prime minister's private advisory committee, its importance ebbed and flowed in response to the importance of defence to the prime minister at any time. In contrast, the Esher Committee was charged with establishing a more formal and permanent organization.

The Esher Commission devoted itself to the reorganization of the War Office. It worked rapidly and with clear focus, and its report came out in early 1904. After the appropriate legislation, an army staff was appointed: something that had long been considered necessary by both Wolseley and Roberts. A new Army Council of seven men—three civilians and four senior officers—was appointed in overall control. The civilians were the Secretary of State for War (chair of the council), the Permanent Secretary (i.e. the top civil servant in the department), and a Financial Secretary. Three of the four army officers ran departments: Adjutant General, Quartermaster General, and Master General of the Ordnance. The top army officer—in charge of the 'G' branch (operations and intelligence)—was the chief of staff, later known as the Chief of the Imperial General Staff (CIGS). He was the government's main military adviser and conduit of instructions from the government to the army.[2] By a strange convention, he was the only army officer who had to write in green ink. (This convention also applied to the head of MI6, the Secret Intelligence Service.)

Expeditionary forces overseas came under the general staff in London, with the General Officer Commanding (GOC) the overseas force reporting directly to the CIGS. The Indian army worked independently when it was operating in war and peace in the subcontinent and South Asia. However, during the First and Second World Wars, substantial Indian formations joined British armies in France and the Middle East, and as a result, their operations came under the local British GOC and the CIGS.

Although the officers who were Chiefs of the Imperial General Staff before the First World War were not fully effective, the British army was better prepared for war in 1914 than it had been in 1899. These early chiefs had to spend time feeling their way, and most of them found it very difficult: again because of the conservatism of the army. Even as late as 1915, Lord Kitchener, who was a field marshal as well as Secretary of State for War, virtually ignored the CIGS. In one startling instance, Kitchener gave his instructions to Sir Ian Hamilton, the commander of the expeditionary force to assault the Gallipoli Peninsula, without even informing the CIGS! Things changed later in 1915, when General Sir William Robertson imposed his 'grip' on the job of CIGS. He had an extremely forceful personality, and in 1918, he came into serious conflict with the prime minister, David Lloyd George. Inevitably, Lloyd George sacked him. In the Second World War, Brooke was appointed CIGS in 1941. Although Churchill was a demanding taskmaster who made life very difficult for the CIGS, the two highly talented men—the politician and the soldier—became a war-winning duo.

In 1904, the reorganization and the appointment of the CIGS meant that the ancient position of commander-in-chief became superfluous. This spelt the end of Roberts's military career. After less than three years in office, Roberts no longer had a job: his appointment quietly disappeared.[3] He was, like Wolseley, a field marshal and therefore joined the list of officers on half-pay. While Wolseley's retirement was uneventful, Roberts's certainly was not. He discovered a cause. With burning enthusiasm, he proposed that all young men should be conscripted for a short period of compulsory military service. This issue, which would have meant a very important change in both political and military policy, was to occupy all of Roberts's retirement years. It was, alas, doomed to failure.

Roberts and Compulsory Service

Roberts became the figurehead and driving force of an organization called the National Service League, and this was a body that soon made its presence felt. The league proposed a four-month or six-month period (depending on the branch of service) that would be compulsory for all physically fit young men when they reached the appropriate age. During this short period, these recruits would begin to understand the basics of military discipline and learn something of the theory and practice of musketry. The immediate objective was to generate a large and growing pool of partly trained reserves who could be mobilized if a major war appeared likely. This proposal was different from the conscription imposed in France and Germany, where young men had to serve two (sometimes three) years with the colours, followed by brief training every subsequent year. This system meant that the French and German armies were conscript forces, and the regular officers and NCOs spent their time training the conscripts. In contrast, the British army was a regular force used to garrison a widespread empire.

In 1906, when a Liberal government was elected with a large majority, Lord Haldane became Secretary of State for War. As a result of the reorganization he imposed, he eventually earned the reputation as the best war minister in history. Haldane created a two-tier army: a regular army for service overseas, with linked battalions training men at home before they were shipped abroad, and a large part-time Territorial Force for home defence, constructed by a reorganization of the existing militia, volunteers, and yeomanry. When his reforms were underway, Haldane decided to arrange for the publication of a book that summarized them.

There was no place for compulsory service in Haldane's plan, and Haldane's book met this issue head-on. The book was eventually published in 1910 and was called *Compulsory Service*.[4] Haldane persuaded Sir Ian Hamilton to write it. Not only was Hamilton a talented and experienced writer but he was, at the time, Adjutant General, a key member of the Army Council. He was also a prominent member of the Roberts 'Ring', and it was a source of embarrassment for him to publish views that were contrary to those of his old chief.

Hamilton's first argument was that the defence of Britain was traditionally in the hands of the Royal Navy. If any substantial enemy force managed to land, this would be mopped up by the newly reorganized Territorial Force, which comprised fourteen infantry divisions and fourteen cavalry brigades (even though these were under-strength and a number of the members had not fulfilled their annual training commitment). The second argument was that the regular army was well able to fulfill its role of garrisoning the British Empire, with the linked battalions at home training the men for the overseas battalions. In addition, the regular army was able to form a fully equipped and trained field force, relying on regular reserves to bring it up to strength. The British Expeditionary Force (BEF) that went to France in 1914 was put together in this way. These arguments rejected the need for a huge reserve of partially trained men: the end product of Roberts's plan.

However, the Haldane reorganization, despite its merits, suffered from an astonishing weakness. In 1905, staff conversations had been secretly initiated between the British and French armies. It was increasingly likely that, if France and Germany were to go to war, the British would be drawn in to support the French. Since the proposed BEF was so small in size, the British would be very much the junior partner of the French, who would be putting eighty-three divisions into the field. The German army was likely to be even larger. A major war between France and Germany was not a certainty, but it was likely enough to demand a change in the way in which British military policy needed to be planned. The British army in northern Europe could find itself alongside the French, suffering serious casualties fighting a large German army, and badly in need of reinforcements. This is when Britain would urgently require Roberts's large reserve of men with basic military training.

This is what actually happened in 1914. The Secretary of State for War was Field Marshal Kitchener. This was a political appointment and not a military one, although Kitchener did not fully understand this. He was a master of grand strategy and was the only leading figure who believed that the war would last for at least three years. He was also a powerful enough personality to persuade the government to allow him to recruit a new army, the largest that Britain had ever raised up to that time. A partially trained reserve would have greatly simplified his task.

However, Kitchener had another force that could have formed the basis of his new army. This was Haldane's Territorials. Kitchener deliberately refused to use the Territorials so that he had to build his new army from scratch. (He added new battalions to existing infantry regiments, and he designated these Service battalions.) Kitchener followed this plan because the Territorials were not highly regarded in regular army circles. Prejudice dies hard. A few Territorial battalions were sent to France in 1914, but most were formed into divisions and sent to garrison the British Empire. They replaced regulars, who in turn formed divisions that were sent to Northern Europe to fight the Germans, and to the Middle East to fight the Turks. Most of the Territorial battalions were shipped to France in 1915 and 1916, and these soon suffered enormous casualties. They did, however, demonstrate their effectiveness as fighting soldiers.

Shortly after the publication of Hamilton's book, the National Service League also published a book of their own, a piece of advocacy arguing the opposite case.[5] Their book was entitled *Fallacies and Facts. An Answer to 'Compulsory Service'*. Roberts's name was on the title page, although he contributed only the first of the three sections of the book, entitled 'A Nation's Peril'. The second section was written by Leo Amery, the historian and politician who had already established a reputation and was to have a long career in politics. The third section was the work of a Scottish professor of history, John Adam Cramb.

Amery went to the heart of the issue when he referred specifically to the menace of a militant Germany:

'But Germany is not only our greatest rival at sea. She is the most formidable military power in the world. She can put 1,700,000 men in the field, keeping over 2,000,000 more for local defence, for lines of communications, and for drafts.'[6]

There is no doubt, in hindsight, that the logic and vision of Roberts and Amery and the National Service League put them on the side of the angels. Some younger officers—notably Henry Rawlinson and Henry Wilson, men who would build important careers during the First World War—supported compulsory service. They can be seen in Plate 15. The published reviews generally thought that the war of words had ended in Roberts's favour.

Nevertheless, this did not affect the outcome. Although many people in Britain visualized the possibility of a European war in which Britain would be involved, no one—not even the politicians and military leaders—saw it as a matter of urgency. Compulsory service was politically and financially impossible, and the government that enacted it would probably have been thrown out of office. Compulsory service was not introduced until early in 1916, when Britain had already been at war for a year and a half and had suffered horrendous casualties. Men had to serve for the duration of the war; with the armistice, it stopped. Compulsory service was revived just before the beginning of the Second World War, and the generation of young men who came of age afterwards was also conscripted, with the last conscripts only completing their service in 1962.

As a result of royal favour, Roberts was dispatched in 1910 to visit the Royal Courts of Europe, to announce formally that King George V had come to the throne on the death of his father, King Edward VII. Roberts was accompanied by a number of officers, including a general with the courtly title of general-in-waiting. The job went to Sir Ian Hamilton, a confirmation that he and Roberts were still friends.

Britain entered the First World War on 4 August 1914. The BEF went to France, and Kitchener's call for volunteers generated a flood of recruits. The original BEF was badly mauled during the early battles: Mons, Le Cateau, the Marne, the Aisne, and the First Battle of Ypres.

Reinforcements were desperately needed, and two infantry divisions and two cavalry divisions were sent from India. They held the line, although the Indian troops found the climate in Northern Europe particularly hard. They were eventually transferred to the Middle East.

The arrival of the Indians triggered an immediate response from Roberts, who determined to visit them. He crossed the Channel and happened to be on the same boat as Sir William Robertson, who had a senior staff appointment at BEF headquarters and was returning. The two were old friends, and they had a long conversation about the war and Britain's neglect to prepare for it (which meant the inability or unwillingness of the government to introduce compulsory service). Roberts arrived at St. Omer on 11 November. The winter climate was alas too much for him, and he caught pneumonia. He died at 8:00 PM on 14 November. He was eighty-two. Arrangements were immediately made to repatriate his body and bury him in St. Paul's Cathedral, near the tomb of Lord Wolseley, Queen Victoria's other paladin. Before his body was moved to England, a simple service was held at the town hall of St. Omer. Contingents of British, Indian, and French troops attended, together with many foreign officers. Robertson was a pallbearer:

> 'As the body left the Mairie on its homeward journey, the day being gloomy and dispiriting, the sun burst forth and threw a brilliant rainbow over the town.'[7]

Wellington and Montgomery (and A. J. P. Taylor)

Garnet Wolseley and Frederick Roberts were contemporaries, and they can be compared. Although Wolseley served in the British army and Roberts in the Indian army, the similarities were greater than the differences between these small but highly professional forces, of which Queen Victoria was the supreme head.

In chapter 1, the Oxford historian A. J. P. Taylor was quoted as saying that Montgomery was the only great general produced by the British army since Wellington. He obviously did not consider the two generals

I have named Queen Victoria's paladins worthy of consideration. They both learned their professional skills with the military technology of the mid-nineteenth century. Horses dominated the battlefield because they provided both transportation and shock cavalry, with its important tactical role; small-arms fire was limited by muzzle loading; and field artillery had relatively small calibre and was also muzzle loaded. This technology was similar to what it had been in Wellington's day. How then did Wolseley and Roberts compare with Wellington? (Although a large increase in firepower had occurred in the 1860s and 1870s, the change in military technology was so great during the twentieth century that it makes no sense to compare Queen Victoria's paladins with Montgomery.) But to make some sort of comparison between Queen Victoria's paladins and the Iron Duke, I have chosen a single day (18 June 1815, when Wellington was forty-six) and a place (the rolling farmlands fifteen miles south of Brussels, near the village of Waterloo).[8]

Napoleon had been defeated in 1814 by a coalition of the largest European nations. The diplomats of the victorious powers then began an unhurried process of conferences in Vienna to reshape the frontiers of Europe. Meanwhile, the defeated French emperor was (it was thought) safely exiled to Elba, a small island off the coast of Italy. However, he had different ideas. He regarded his defeat in 1814 as a temporary affair, and in February 1815, after only ten months in Elba, he escaped to France with the clear intention of becoming again the master of Europe. Because of his continued popularity with the French people, he saw no difficulty in dislodging the Bourbon monarch who had been put on the French throne in 1814. As Napoleon rapidly marched north up the Valley of the Rhône, his old soldiers flocked to join him. But this period of euphoria lasted only a hundred days.

The victorious allies responded to Napoleon's escape with equal speed. Their armies had not been totally disbanded, and in Northern Europe, they prepared to meet the buoyant and confident French army. The Duke of Wellington began to assemble a large, mostly British, army. His comrade Prinz von Blücher, in the south-east, concentrated his Prussians. The two armies would join together, in the nick of time, on the battlefield of Waterloo.

On 16 June, in the path of Napoleon's march north, he encountered the British at Quatre Bras and the Prussians at Ligny, and fought brief engagements that slowed down but did not impede his progress. His army totalled 124,000 men and 370 guns. The men were all veterans, who were organized in five infantry corps and five cavalry corps, plus the Imperial Guard of infantry and cavalry. All these formations were commanded by experienced leaders who could operate independently if the situation called for it. (A French corps was only about the size of an allied division.) Napoleon commanded a confident and cohesive force that had, in earlier years, conquered Europe. Wellington commanded 93,000 men and 204 guns. He fielded twelve mixed infantry and cavalry divisions of British, Hanoverian, Dutch, and Belgian troops. The Prussian army totalled 117,000 men and 312 guns, organized in four large corps of infantry, cavalry, and artillery. Since Wellington's army was smaller than Napoleon's, it is easy to appreciate how Blücher's arrival managed to turn an indecisive fight into a total victory.[9]

At the end of the morning of 18 June, Wellington deployed his men behind a ridge, in a line stretching for three miles from west to east. There was defence in depth, and a number of strong points were reinforced—in particular, the farm at Hougoumont. Attacks and counter-attacks occupied the day, and these were marked by brutality and heroism. There were no surrenders. During the whole time, Wellington imposed his 'grip' on his command. Accompanied by a small staff, he rode behind the battle line and, on many occasions, gave tactical instructions to infantry battalions and cavalry regiments. He was unscathed, although some senior officers were less fortunate. Much blood flowed on the battlefield of Waterloo. Forty-five thousand men were killed or wounded: half were French and half were from Wellington's and Blücher's armies.

Late in the day, the Imperial Guard made a last gallant rally; but in the end, the French were routed. Napoleon rode away from the battlefield, and when, three days later, he reached Paris, he abdicated. He sailed away from Europe on a British warship to the lonely island of St. Helena, off the Atlantic coast of Africa. He did not escape and died there in 1821. Nineteen years later, his body was repatriated to Paris, where it lies today under the dome of Les Invalides. In the twenty-first century, he is still considered the greatest French soldier of all.

The British army that fought at Waterloo was the best in Europe, although it was not the largest. An important reason for its pre-eminence was that the infantry was exceptionally well trained, a legacy of Sir John Moore. In 1803, with Napoleon's *Grande Armée* on the Channel coast of France and a direct threat to the British Isles, Moore commanded the sector of the Kent coast that was most vulnerable. With flair, Moore trained a number of battalions camped around Shorncliffe, and he put together a larger force that grew into the Light Division—a formation that became a *corps d'élite*:

> 'By being taught to move quickly, men learned to think quickly. In the same way the art of fire was taught, not as an automatic contribution to blind mechanical volleys, but as a highly individualized application of the qualities of observation, vision, judgment, and skill.'[10]

Moore was loved by his men, and when he lost his life at Corunna in 1809, they all felt a genuine loss. As the Peninsular War continued, the skills of the Light Division transferred, as if by osmosis, to other divisions of the British army; and they also had the benefit of Britain's unique regimental tradition. Wellington led the army to a string of victories in Portugal and Spain that demonstrated the superiority of the British over the French. Many of Wellington's men at Waterloo were old soldiers from the Peninsula.

The British army was at its zenith at Waterloo. However, the impetus of improvement was not maintained after 1815, and there were also no developments in military technology. During the years after Waterloo, the British army changed its shape and function and became a force to garrison a widespread empire. But it contained no single large fighting force, as there had been in Wellington's day.

Wolseley was born eighteen years after Waterloo, and during his early years as a regimental officer and then as a general during the second half of the nineteenth century, his main job was active service in small overseas campaigns. Roberts's career was confined to India until the end of his long service. But Wolseley and Roberts—although they had progressive and generally successful military careers—never fought a battle that was remotely comparable with Waterloo.

Two Parallel Careers

Wolseley and Roberts reached the top of their profession. On the way, they were promoted regularly and received honours and decorations. Episodes in their careers—Wolseley's victory at Tel-el-Kebir and Roberts's tough march from Kabul to Kandahar—made them well known to the general public. It is appropriate to call them Queen Victoria's paladins, although the Queen had more affection for Roberts than for Wolseley. This book has followed their careers but has stopped short of making comparisons, e.g. how did they compare with their contemporaries? How did they compare with Wellington, unquestionably the last great British general? Finally, how did Wolseley and Roberts compare with each other? To weigh the two men in the balance, it is useful to summarize briefly their achievements.

Wolseley, born in 1833, had neither wealth nor influential friends, and he realized that progress in the army depended on his own efforts. As a young regimental officer, he fought in Burma and the Crimea, then in the Indian Mutiny and in China. He learned to understand infantry tactics, and he always used his initiative. His services were recognized by his superiors, and this gave him a flying start to his career. He became a brevet major in 1858, before he had reached the age of twenty-five. He returned to Britain after the campaign in China, and at the end of 1861, he became a staff officer and crossed the Atlantic to serve in Canada. During the following years, Wolseley held various brief overseas commands, and his successful record burnished his reputation with the public. At the end of each overseas assignment, he returned to the War Office, where he held staff appointments of increasing importance.

His first command abroad was the Canadian Red River Expedition of 1870; then he headed the Ashanti Expedition in West Africa in

1873–1874. Between 1875 and 1880, he was governor of various colonial provinces. In 1882, he commanded a force sent to Egypt, where he won the Battle of Tel-el-Kebir, his most outstanding military achievement. But he was less successful when he led the expedition up the Nile in 1884–1885 to rescue Gordon in Khartoum. This enterprise failed because of the formidable distances and the agonizing time it took to transport soldiers in boats and on camels. All these commands (except the Gordon Relief Expedition) enhanced Wolseley's reputation as a strategist and forceful leader; his writings (notably his *Soldier's Pocket-Book*) added to his fame. Wolseley's contributions were officially recognized. In 1873, when he was forty, he received a knighthood and the substantive rank of major general. When he embarked for Egypt in 1884, he was a peer with a seat in the House of Lords. Nevertheless, the scale of Wolseley's fighting commands was extremely limited. Only in Egypt, in 1882, did he command a force stronger than a division. His other three fighting commands were a good deal smaller; even the expedition to rescue Gordon was only two brigades. Wolseley's commands were all in striking contrast to the size of Wellington's army at Waterloo.

During Wolseley's spells of duty in the War Office, he was enthusiastically devoted to army reform, notably abolishing the purchase of commissions; creating a regular reserve by introducing short service; the linked battalion system; and the introduction of breech-loading rifles with bolt action. Important as these reforms were, they were administrative in the sense that they dealt with manpower and weapons. They were not aimed at improving the fighting efficiency and morale of the soldiers in the ranks. Wolseley at the War Office did not do the same job as Moore at Shorncliffe.

When Wolseley was in his fifties, three factors began to cloud his personality and his popularity in the army. The first problem was the feeling he developed that people in high places were conspiring against him and impeding his career. He was probably isolated: estranged from senior political and military figures who were outside his own close-knit Wolseley 'Ring'. Perhaps he also resented those officers who had been promoted because they were rich and had strong patrons. Wolseley's second problem was that he developed a strongly authoritative attitude that influenced his approach to his job. This made him increasingly unpopular with many people, including the Queen. Other strong commanders, before and after, had human warmth that made them popular: Wellington, Roberts, Montgomery, and Churchill (who, in the Second World War, was Minister of Defence and political head of the armed services). They got on well with their subordinates, but their orders had to be followed to the letter. Churchill's memoranda were printed with the words ACTION THIS DAY. He expected the many people who worked directly for him to be on top of their jobs.

Wolseley's journal during the Gordon Relief Expedition showed him to be increasingly introspective and pessimistic. He had emphasized, in *The Soldier's Pocket-Book*, that officers and men had a common interest and victory was equally important to both. However, as Wolseley became more dominating, he began to be more distant from the men in the ranks. This was his third problem. It was noticed by the ever-perceptive Ian Hamilton, who compared two popular generals, Roberts and Buller, with two less popular ones, Wolseley and Kitchener:

> 'Wolseley was too detached . . . the most impersonal commander I have ever met except possibly Kitchener.'[11]

Roberts was always close to his men, both Indian and British. Hamilton described his relationship with his Indian soldiers:

> '. . . these simple souls felt that their commander was their personal friend—which indeed he was—their *bhaiband*, their brother-in-arms.'[12]

When Wolseley eventually became commander-in-chief at the age of sixty-two, he was seriously ill for a number of months, and it was also clear that he no longer had the powerful drive he once possessed. Although he became a field marshal in 1894, he did not get on with Lansdowne, Secretary of State for War, who had trimmed the scope of Wolseley's responsibilities. As a result, he did not manage to boost the size of the army, let alone create a general staff in the War Office, both of which were on Wolseley's agenda. When the British went to war with the Boers in 1899, the army did badly in the field for a number of months. Wolseley, perhaps unfairly, was blamed for the problems. While Wolseley seemed to have less commitment to his duties towards the end of his career, this problem did not affect Roberts, who continued to fire on all cylinders until he retired, and even in the years that followed. When Roberts and Kitchener arrived in Cape Town in early 1900, their 'grip' was immediately apparent. The battlefield strategy they developed and implemented changed the fortunes of the British army and set it on the path to victory.

Roberts was born in India in 1832, and he returned to make his career there after an excellent professional education in England. He served in an artillery battery and as the junior staff officer until the Indian Mutiny erupted in 1857. In addition to his duties on the staff, he had opportunities for hand-to-hand combat, for which he won the Victoria Cross. At the age of twenty-five, he had made his reputation as an intrepid young officer. He then began to build a career on the staff, although he (like Wolseley) had never received any formal staff training. He received a number of promotions, but he had to wait until he was forty-five before he was given a command in the field. This was during the invasion of Afghanistan.

Roberts's role in this Second Afghan War of 1878–1880 made him a national hero. The Battle of Peiwar Kotal was a dramatic victory as a result of Roberts's strategy. His subsequent punishing march from Kabul to relieve Kandahar caught the public imagination. Roberts was knighted in 1879, and when he was raised to the peerage in 1892, he adopted the title of Baron Roberts of Kandahar. However, in comparison with some earlier battles and many later ones in the history of the British army, Roberts's Afghan victories were small-scale affairs. He commanded a brigade at Peiwar Kotal and a small division on the march to Kandahar.

Roberts's next step was two large peacetime commands in India. The first was in Madras, and the second in Calcutta, where he became commander-in-chief of the Indian army. He was a striking success, especially in Calcutta. The Indian army was strengthened by the recruitment of large numbers of men from the martial races of the north. Just as importantly, the tactical training of the army was improved. In achieving this, he relied on Ian Hamilton, who enthusiastically and imaginatively improved the soldiers' skill at arms. This did not mean target-shooting on the open range. The troops were encouraged instead to use their small arms effectively in simulated battle conditions. After Roberts's eight years in Calcutta, he bade farewell to India and was made a field marshal in 1895. At the age of sixty-two, Roberts accepted the tranquil position of commander-in-chief in Ireland.

However, in 1899, the tocsin sounded. Things had not gone well for the British army in South Africa. Lord Lansdowne had no hesitation in selecting Roberts, in preference to Wolseley, as the man for the job of vanquishing the Boers. He reached Cape Town in early 1900 with a greatly reinforced army. Roberts—with Kitchener, his powerful chief of staff—developed a battlefield strategy that succeeded in less than a year in defeating the Boer armies in the field. The guerrilla phase of the war continued for another eighteen months, but Roberts and Kitchener again worked out an appropriate battlefield strategy in the knowledge that achieving victory would be a slow process.

Roberts returned to England and succeeded Wolseley at the end of 1900 as commander-in-chief. However, as mentioned, he only had the job for three years because the structure of the War Office was changed and the position of commander-in-chief was abolished. When he was seventy-two, Roberts finally joined the half-pay list. But he did not have a peaceful retirement. He became head of the National Service League and started campaigning vigorously for compulsory service. This was, frankly, a hopeless cause, because the government would never accept the cost, and Haldane, the Secretary of State for War, had an alternative scheme: he wished to develop the Territorial Force. But Roberts was undeterred. He demonstrated his grasp of grand strategy since he was convinced that there would be a European war and Britain would be involved. A substantial reserve of partially trained troops would have prepared Britain for the conflict to come and would have made a big difference in 1914–1915. In the event, Kitchener had to build a large new army from the ground up.

As leaders in the field, Wolseley and Roberts demonstrated their tactical and strategic ability. But were they 'big' figures with strong personalities who were able to make things happen? This was more true of Roberts than of Wolseley. Roberts went from strength to strength when he was in his fifties and sixties. In contrast, Wolseley's energy seemed to flag when he was in his mid-fifties, after the failure of the Gordon Relief Expedition. This difference was perhaps noticed in higher circles, when Wolseley became a viscount and Roberts became an earl.

Ian Hamilton served under Roberts for many years and also knew Wolseley. Hamilton discussed them both and also their contemporaries: Kitchener, Napier, Buller, White, Brackenbury, Wood, Lockhart, Baker Russell, Donald Stewart, Graham, Herbert Stewart, and Pomeroy-Colley. Hamilton concluded that these men were not in the same class as the two paladins. But he also made the interesting point that Wolseley did not deserve to be put in first place:

> 'Of the two, Roberts was "our only general" and Wolseley "our only other general."'[13]

It is difficult to argue that Wolseley and Roberts can be compared with Wellington. Neither of the paladins commanded a large army in battle, facing a first-class enemy, i.e. a large well-trained European force. Wellington's achievement was, at the age of forty-six, to defeat the most powerful and aggressive European state whose army was led by one of history's greatest generals. Wellington restored the European balance of power. This was an achievement of historical importance. In my opinion, Wellington was in a league of his own—at least until the arrival of Montgomery. Montgomery was a young officer during the First World War, and it was immediately obvious in 1914 that this conflict was bringing unexpected tactical problems. Montgomery learned from the mistakes of his superiors. Unfortunately, the British commanders in the First World War were no better than pedestrian, although the French and Germans were no better.

French and Haig were the successors of Wolseley and Roberts and had had similar experiences of colonial wars. It does not seem likely that Wolseley and Roberts would have done any better than French and Haig in the First World War. They would have been as out of their depth in the densely crowded battlefields dominated by continuous artillery and small-arms fire. Breaking the deadlock of the trenches demanded technological changes, which meant scientific and engineering innovation rather than skilled generalship.

During the second half of the nineteenth century, Wolseley and Roberts helped to build the British Empire. Although it did not appear so at the time, the Empire was an organization that had little future. Three countries—Canada, Australia, and New Zealand—were settled by British immigrants who developed these countries economically and politically and transformed them into self-governing dominions.

But this did not happen with countries that had large indigenous populations and were governed by British proconsuls. India was the largest. However, when the Raj came to an end in 1947, there was a shock to the imperial system. Before long, the 'winds of change' liberated the other British colonies, most of whom became independent within twenty years. In these countries, the British left a positive legacy, but this was replaced by a new identity when India became three countries (India, Pakistan, and Bangladesh), when Malaya and two nearby territories became Malaysia, when Burma became Myanmar, and when Southern Rhodesia became Zimbabwe.

Wolseley and Roberts devoted their lives to the British Empire. As memories of the empire gradually faded, so did memories of the colourful careers and ultimate achievements of Queen Victoria's paladins. A. J. P. Taylor may have been intolerant, but his judgment was correct.

Endnotes

1. Kochanski, Halik, *Sir Garnet Wolseley. Victorian Hero* (London: The Hambledon Press, 1999), 247–267.

2. Jackson, General Sir William, and Bramall, Field Marshal Lord, *The Chiefs. The Story of the United Kingdom Chiefs of Staff* (London: Brassey's, 1992), 31–33.

3. Jones, John Philip, *Johnny. The Legend and Tragedy of General Sir Ian Hamilton* (Barnsley, South Yorkshire: Pen & Sword, 2012), 129–133.

4. Hamilton, General Sir Ian, *Compulsory Service. A Study of the Question in the Light of Experience* (London: John Murray, 1910).

5. Roberts, Field Marshal Earl, *Fallacies and Facts. An Answer to 'Compulsory Service'* (London: John Murray, 1911).

6. Ibid., 116.

7. Robertson, Field Marshal Sir William, *From Private to Field Marshal* (London: Constable, 1921), 217.

8. Snow, Peter and Snow, Dan, *The Battle of Waterloo* (London: The National Army Museum/André Deutsch, 2017).

9. Uffindell, Andrew and Corum, Michael, *On the Fields of Glory. The Battlefields of the 1815 Campaign* (London: Greenhill Books, 1996), 337–348.

10. Bryant, Arthur, *Jackets of Green. A Study of the History, Philosophy, and Character of the Rifle Brigade* (London: History Book Club, 1972), 32–33.

11. Hamilton, General Sir Ian, *Listening For the Drums* (London: Faber & Faber, 1944), 170.

12. Ibid.

13. Ibid., 184.

INDEX

This Index covers the complete written text of the book and the plates. It does not cover the maps or the endnotes that appear at the end of each chapter. (These provide full details of all the references in the text.) The names of individuals are presented simply, with the surname followed by the first name (and sometimes initials). Titles are not given except in special cases where the individual is known more widely by his title than by his name. Similarly military and naval ranks appear only sparingly: when the sources used in this book identify the individual's rank but not his first name, or when two men with the same name have to be distinguished from one another.

Guderian, Heinz 15

H

Haig, Douglas xxix, 17, 94, 245, 277, 280, 309-310
Haldane, Lord 141, 193, 296-297, 308
Halifax, Nova Scotia 122
Hamilton, Ian 13, 106, 151, 181, 183-184, 217, 222, 226-228, 239, 251, 261, 269, 279-285, 287, 295, 297, 306, 309
Hannibal 6
Hanover 213
Hanoverian troops 302
Hardy, Gathorne 193
Harper's Ferry 126
Hartington, Lord (War Minister) 234-235, 237, 245, 250, 253-254
Havelock, Henry 70-73, 82, 88, 92
Heilbron, South Africa 282
Heliograph signaling 182, 270
Himalayas 94, 109, 220
Hindenburg, Paul von 106
Hitler, Adolf 12, 47, 285
Holland 265
Hong Kong 85, 98
Hougoumont, Waterloo 302
Howard Russell, William 139
Hudson Bay Company 132
Hunter, Archibald 280
Huyshe, George 162
Hythe, School of Musketry 219

I

India 3-5, 28, 32, 39-40, 46, 62, 65, 88, 171-172, 182, 198, 207, 214, 254. 256, 259, 261, 275, 310
India, East India Company 33, 53-54, 57-58, 83, 132

Indian army 18, 32-35, 54, 87, 100, 111, 174-175, 198, 208, 215
Bengal Presidency, Calcutta: 111-116, 213-214, 223, 292
Bombay Presidency 214
Commissions 57
General Staff 106-107, 253
Madras Presidency 34, 83, 141, 213-221
Martial races 44, 216, 222, 226
Regiments:
  Bengalis 43, 57, 69, 71, 83, 87, 113, 222
  Gurkhas 54, 71, 179, 182, 188
  Punjabis 71, 75
  Rajputs 69
  Sikhs 43, 71, 174-175, 188
Reorganization after the Indian Mutiny 83, 193, 215-216
Size and structure 34, 58, 67, 71, 215-216, 223
Indian Civil Service 33, 53-54, 66, 107
Indian Mutiny xxviii, 34-35, 58, 63, 65-84, 87, 121, 146
Indian Mutiny: British casualties 72, 77, 79, 87
Indian Mutiny: British marching columns 72
Indian native religions and languages 32, 60, 67, 69
Indian Ocean 195
Infantry fire/musketry xxvii, 6-7, 30, 219-221, 227-228, 263, 276, 279
Infantry fire: breech-loading xxvii-xxviii, 30, 87, 140, 192, 219, 252, 263
Infantry fire: muzzle-loading xxvii-xxviii, 87, 174
Inkerman, Battle of 47
Les Invalides, Paris 303
Iraq 7

ABOUT THE AUTHOR

John Philip Jones is an American academic, born and educated in Britain. He graduated from Cambridge University with the Economics Tripos: BA with Honours, MA.

He had a twenty-seven-year career in international business, mainly with the J. Walter Thompson advertising agency in Britain, the Netherlands, and Scandinavia. This was followed by twenty-seven years of teaching and research at the Newhouse School of Public Communications, Syracuse University, New York. He was a full professor with academic tenure and was awarded the University Chancellor's Citation for Exceptional Academic Achievement. He became an emeritus professor in 2007. Concurrently with his appointment at Syracuse, he was, for many years, a visiting professor at universities in Australia and Denmark.

He is the author of seventeen books on marketing and economics (translated into ten languages), plus more than seventy articles in professional and academic journals. His main specialty was the measurement of marketing effects. Most of his books can be found on Amazon. He is a lifelong student of warfare and is a long-time member of the Honourable Artillery Company, London. He has walked over all the major battlefields of Europe (including Gallipoli), North America, and South Africa. Since retiring, he has written works of military history. Four published titles are listed below.

OTHER BOOKS BY THE AUTHOR:

The Successes and Sacrifices of the British Army in 1914. Soldiers Marching, All to Die. (2009).

Johnny. The Legend and Tragedy of General Sir Ian Hamilton. (2012). One of six books shortlisted by the Royal United Services Institute for the best military study published anywhere in the world in 2012/2013.

Battles of a Gunner Officer. Tunisia, Sicily, Normandy, and the Long Road to Germany. (2014).

Burning Tanks and an Empty Desert. Based on the unpublished journal of Major John Sylvanus MacGill, MB, ChB, MD, Royal Army Medical Corps. (2015).